NUCLEAR STRATEGY
AND THE
CODE OF THE WARRIOR

                    rages
                    strain
           Dog of Tartarus
           Guards of Tartarus
           Finks of the Bosses. War Makers

                  Not Enyalion. Enyalion
has lost his Hand, Enyalion
is beautiful, Enyalion
has shown himself, the High King
a War Chief, he has Equites
to do that

           Enyalion
is possibility, all men
are the glories of Hera by possibility, Enyalion
goes to war differently
than his equites, different
than they do, he goes to war with a picture. . . . . .

. . . . . in his mind
that the shining of his body

           and of the chariot
           and of his horses
           and of his own equites
       everyone in the nation of which he is the High King

he turns back

into the battle

                    —**excerpt** from Charles Olson's "Enyalion"

NUCLEAR STRATEGY
AND THE
CODE OF THE WARRIOR

Faces of Mars and Shiva in the Crisis of Human Survival

edited by
Richard Grossinger
and Lindy Hough

Io #33

North Atlantic Books
Berkeley, California

Nuclear Strategy and the Code of the Warrior:
Faces of Mars and Shiva in the Crisis of Human Survival

Copyright © 1984 by Richard Grossinger and Lindy Hough

Copyrights of individual pieces to their respective authors.

ISBN 0-938190-49-0 (paperback)
ISBN 0-938190-50-4 (cloth)

Publisher's Address:
North Atlantic Books
2320 Blake Street
Berkeley, California 94704

Cover and book design by Paula Morrison
Typeset in California by Birthe Rasumussen and Stan Shoptaugh

This is issue #33 in the *Io* series.

This project is partially supported by grants from the National Endowment for
the Arts, a Federal agency, and the California Arts Council, an agency of the
State of California

Nuclear Strategy and the Code of the Warrior is sponsored by the Society for
the Study of Native Arts and Sciences, a nonprofit educational corporation
whose goals are to develop an ecological and crosscultural perspective linking
various scientific, social, and artistic fields; to nurture a holistic view of arts,
sciences, humanities, and healing; and to publish and distribute literature on
the relationship of mind, body, and nature.

Library of Congress Cataloging in Publication Data

Nuclear Strategy and the Code of the Warrior.

    1. Nuclear warfare—Moral and ethical aspects—Miscellanea.
    2. Nuclear warfare—Psychological aspects—Miscellanea.
    I. Grossinger, Richard, 1944-   . II. Hough, Lindy, 1944-
U263.N76 1984   172'.42   84-18924
ISBN 0-938190-50-4
ISBN 0-938190-49-0 (pbk.)

CONTENTS

Grateful acknowledgement is made to the following for permission to reprint work:

CHARLENE SPRETNAK: "Naming the Cultural Forces that Push Us Toward War," from *Journal of Humanistic Psychology*, Vol. 23, No. 3, Summer 1983, pp. 104–114. ©1984 by Charlene Spretnak. Used by permission of the author.

ARCH OBOLER: Selection from *Night of the Auk*, originally published by Horizon Press, New York, 1958. Out of print. ©1956 by Arch Oboler, all rights reserved. Used by permission of the author.

JEAN GONICK: "Nuclear Anxiety: Past and Present," originally published in the *San Francisco Chronicle*, May 6, 1984. ©1984 by Jean Gonick. Used by permission of the author.

LINDY HOUGH: "Missilemen," from *Love and Power: The Transformation of the Shadow in the Nuclear Age*, unpublished work in progress. ©1984 by Lindy Hough.

HENRI GAUDIER-BRZESKA: "Vortex Gaudier-Brzeska (Written from the Trenches)," originally published in *Blast* No. 2, July, 1915, edited by Wyndham Lewis, London: John Lane, The Bodley Head. ©1915 by Wyndham Lewis, ©1981 by The Estate of Mrs. G. A. Wyndham Lewis by permission of the Wyndham Lewis Memorial Trust. Republished as *Blast: War Number* by Black Sparrow Press ($15), Santa Barbara, California, 1981. Used by permission of Black Sparrow Press.

FREEMAN DYSON: Specified excerpts from *Weapons and Hope*, a Cornelia and Michael Bessie Book, Harper & Row, Publishers, New York, 1984. ©1984 by Freeman J. Dyson. Reprinted by permission of Harper & Row, Publishers, Inc. and the author. Specified selection in "The Nabara," from *Selected Poems* by C. Day Lewis. ©1938 by C. Day Lewis. Reprinted by permission of Harper & Row, Publishers.

THOMAS POWERS: "What Is It About?," originally published in *The Atlantic*, Boston, January, 1984. ©Thomas Powers, 1984. Used by permission of the author.

RICHARD GROSSINGER: Selection from *The Night Sky*, Sierra Club Books, San Francisco, 1981. Selection from *Embryogenesis*, Avon Books, New York, 1985. Both selections used with the permission of the publisher and ©Richard Grossinger.

JAMES HILLMAN: "Mars, Rams, Arms, Wars," a talk delivered at the conference, "Facing Apocalypse," Salve Regina College, Newport, Rhode Island, June, 1983. To be published in revised and completed form in the collected papers of that conference by Spring Publications, Dallas. ©James Hillman, 1983. Used by permission of the author.

SRI CHINMOY: Selection from *Warriors of the Inner World*, Aum Publications, Jamaica, New York. ©Sri Chinmoy, 1976. Reprinted by permission of Aum Publications under the express condition that it be stated that the piece may not be reproduced without Sri Chinmoy's written permission.

DA FREE JOHN: "You Do Not Know What a Single Thing Is," from *Easy Death: Talks and Essays on the Inherent and Ultimate Transcendence of Death and Everything Else*, The Dawn Horse Press, Clearlake, California, 1983. ©The Johannine Daist Communion, 1983. Reprinted by permission of The Johannine Daist Communion.

Richard Grossinger

PREFACE

Nuclear war sits as a kind of zen riddle in the heart of modern civilization. There is no resolution, no relief, and no way of avoiding the consequences. We find ourselves staring not only at the end of consciousness but the end of history and the end of time. It is almost unbelievable that we could bring this on ourselves and our world; yet we stand at the brink without many ways of turning back. Our own individual deaths, grounded in biological mortality, are overwhelming enough, but to have a poisoned silence sweep the Earth moments after our own extinction, to have nothing living follow us, is unendurable. It represents the triumph of the deadliest gods and the demise of nature itself. In the shadow of this unimaginable event we go on day after day, continuing to engage the complexities of our existence. The threat that all this activity could be sheared off, eradicated and scorched into nothing in the space of hours, is the cosmological hallmark of the twentieth century. It is where we have come, out of the various decadent religions of the nineteenth century, into a rising (seemingly irresistible) tide of global materialism (and global nihilism), ruled by the rigorous but rigid forces of pure quantity — a quantity that has now swelled to its inevitable fruition in a bulbous malignant bomb, a bomb that could return all our dissatisfaction and torpor to the cosmic unconscious from which it came. We have become compulsively scientific, image-less — and now an anti-sun has arisen from our very minds. It is naive to think that this is only a political and strategic crisis; it is the physicalization of our crisis of faith, our loss of inner meaning and courage. The warhead is the collective recoil of our spiritual conscience; that is why we cannot wrench free of it or pull back from its compulsion. Only the process of engaging the riddle, of staring unflinchingly through its deadly ruses, is now productive — not as a solution (of course), but as a way of awakening ourselves to who we are and why this is happening to us.

I don't remember when I first became aware of the implications of nuclear weapons, but it was very close to my awakening to the culture itself, probably around third or fourth grade. I no longer remember a time when I did not fear a terrible blinding end. While still in grade school I turned on the radio in reaction to any unexplained and prolonged siren (and by now have done so at least a hundred times in my life, always to be reassured, strangely, by the ongoing inane chatter of America on the dial; ultimately, the chatter is disturbing in another sense, for it maintains the twenty-four-hour-a-day mindlessness and commerciality that beg the crucial questions of our lives — even when they pretend to address them, as in pseudo-serious talk shows). Yet turning on the radio assured me that America was still there. The worst time was June of 1961 when I was sixteen. I lived under a barely subdued terror for most of that month, sure that the end would come each hour. I started at every loud sound. I also saw *Night of the Auk* on t.v. at that time, and it shocked and depressed me in much the way people were more recently overwhelmed by *The Day After*. To this day I find *Night of the Auk* even more chilling — for the stark fragile beauty of its language, for the failure of learned men to avoid the "war" among themselves even after the Earth's incineration, and for its early dramatization of our fearful denial of the spiritual test we are undergoing. *The Day After* is, in a sense, part of the new tyranny of literalism, the reign of quantity; it is the prime-time marketing of our destructive capability. *Night of the Auk* was a prophetic statement of our imperiled humanity. And that is why I have brought it back into public attention here. Hopefully, the play itself will be revived, performed again, and even republished.

My worst attack of nuclear nightmare was adolescent, though hardly trivial for that reason. It subsided perhaps because I passed out of childhood into a world that was difficult in other incomprehensible ways and filled with all sorts of injustices and unbearable acts. I would not live forever anyway, nor would I get to the bottom of things. I don't know how that anxiety ended or changed into other things, though I recall precisely the elation I felt when I realized six years had passed from the time a camp counselor had promised: "No way we can make it through the next five years." I remembered and waited almost a third of my life then to prove him wrong. Anything else was a gift. But the nuclear fear was not just a symptom for teen-age anxieties nor (on the other hand) an actual literal threat; it was an aspect of the overall difficulty and sorrow of the world. I learned that it could be lived with as all the rest could — uncomfortably but as part of a desperate struggle for enlightenment before it was too late. And it didn't have to be honored moment to moment, for vigilance was also a destructive force.

In recent years I have had some trouble with people newly alert to the scope of the nuclear threat. Often they demand a rigid adherence to their strategies for removing nuclear weapons, strategies that usually share the unyielding literalism of the military. The longer one has lived with the lion the more humble they become in its teeth. Mindless anti-war activism is another form of bellicosity in the guise of denial of bellicosity. Nuclear weapons represent far more than stupid generals and unenlightened technicians. People and politicians have fought wars mostly from desperation and necessity, have built weapons in the confusion of mixed conscious and unconscious strategies, often with the goal of ending war. As a species, our ambivalences and nightmares stand out; even when we form implacable antlike armies and carry out atrocities, we are struggling with unconscious demons and on the verge of redemption. One might as well be anti-death or anti-disease as anti-war in the absolute sense. The warriors are inside us, to be embraced and understood, perhaps millennia from now to be ritualized into protectors of all life, all sentient beings. Even the nuclear bomb is inside us, and we must accept the wisdom of its message if we are to avoid its lethal retribution.

Paradoxically, we must depend on the members of the anti-war movement to raise our consciousness; their outrage and discomfort are an essential eruption of our dormant malignancy — most powerful and curative when they are least rigid: when they bear exotic death's heads and corpse dolls and put on underworld dances; least effective when they are reduced to bumper-stickers, regimented marches, and chanted slogans. These latter activities merely polarize people into ideological camps. Nuclear weapons must awaken us to an event outside political parties, even outside consciousness and outside history. They must incite a wild revival that no religiosity can claim.

We must awaken, we must make conscious some of what is unconscious, or we will blunder into Armageddon. The anti-war movement, though relatively powerless in superpower terms, is a faint but crucial beacon for consciousness at this time. Unless superior beings are guiding us or a magus in the soul of the planet is holding back holocaust, we must rely on ourselves to stay awake, even if we must do it dogmatically in an age of dogma. The magus may also abandon us if we do not affirm him in our waking minds.

So the images and symbols of nuclear activists are collectively healing, though in individual cases they may irritate people and alienate closet advocates by their righteousness and the unexamined lifestyles behind it. It is too late now to plan an elegant defense. We must make use of what arises spontaneously; we must use existing energy to create new energy, always billowing toward an unknown goal, an unforeseeable resolution. That is what the atom teaches us anyway: pure energy from mass, limitless power from the minute particles of creation. To that we might add the Buddhist precept: that all energy is (in the first place) mind too.

A great deal of anti-nuclear (to use the euphemism) writing is to wake us up, some of which is the writer waking him- (or her-) self up, reaching to the danger in an ever deeper part of the collective soul. We have included only a small amount of such writing because a collection of (even beautiful) peace poems does not touch the more subtle and paradoxical aspects of this dilemma. In making images of the end of time and the destruction of living beings and whole cities we startle ourselves, harangue ourselves, and even pity ourselves, but we also usually lead ourselves back simply to anger at the nuclear establishment for doing this to us. It is more important to find ways to empower ourselves and to take responsibility, even for acts which are not individually ours. In any case, the so-called "pro-nuclear" position is not that vulnerable. The majority of nuclear-weapons-advocates are equally disheartened by the present impasse and its implications; they argue that destruction may, in the end, be unavoidable and that, in any case, it is not avoidable by a retreat from nuclear weapons. The debate goes back and forth without resolution. The nuclear-advocates argue that the only way to avoid the use of such weapons is to deter war by a balanced arsenal. The corresponding anti-nuclear position is that deterrence is short-term only; if the weapons are built they must ultimately be used, either by error or misjudgement if not by arrogant calculation, and then the whole accumulated stockpile will go off, destroying all life on the planet. To this the advocates argue: well, even if that is to be so, it is our only hope because if we do not use the weapons to deter our enemies, they will be used anyway, either on us in our weakness or to blackmail us into surrender; then the world will be conquered by a ruthless dictatorship and there will be decades if not centuries of suffering. A humanist might then ask if even that were not better than destruction of life itself; after all, every dictatorship eventually crumbles from within. However, this is not a debate that we can reasonably expect creatures at our level of evolution and with our brief lifespans to resolve. No one is worrying about fifty years from now or even twenty years from now. They are trying to get through the next twenty-four hours, then the next month. Nuclear weapons are on the level of interest rates: metaphysical questions can be answered only through our living itself.

Anti-nuclear writings also express some of the new level of vigilance that has come since the ascension of Ronald Reagan. It took a gung-ho nuclear-arms-race advocate and an uncompromising militarist to awaken people to the fact that they were already half-awake to a world dangerously overarmed with nuclear bombs. A subtle almost inexpressible change has occurred, and even though it is difficult to trace or spell out, it has given rise to a mass movement. Nuclear vigilance and nuclear terror have been with us since Hiroshima, but people were lulled by the non-bellicose rhetoric of our leaders and the seeming mutual commitment of us and the Russians to detente. The mere fact that we have gone without a world war for a time longer than the time between World War I and World War II is reassuring to people: we have survived the Cuban Crisis and our fear of an imaginary "Red Chinese" foe.

But these reassurances are hollow in light of the actual danger: Ronald Reagan has done a service for nuclear consciousness, for he has brought the characters of *Dr. Strangelove* to life and shown that they were not mere fictive exaggerations (though they were also alive and among us before he took office). He has created the living image of a Hollywood president of uncertain emotional depth and wisdom who believes in the *Book of Revelations* as a literal deific prophecy. But he did not invent the dilemma; he is a symptom of our wish to deny the global crisis in all its aspects and simply to blame the Russians. But it is a terrible oversimplification to think that one person or nation could create a problem of this scale. Ronald Reagan is a specter of our somnolent sense of urgency, despite the fact that he may blunder into the dreaded nuclear war. He has made our situation worse, but he has also ended the latency period of nuclear consciousness, and in that sense he has helped to improve other aspects of the situation. Almost all of the writing in this book is post-Reagan and certainly would not have been done with the same urgency and depth of self-examination without his administration. Without him we might not actually *be* more safe; we might only *seem* more safe. *Dr. Strangelove or: How I Learned to Stop Worrying and Love the Bomb* could not have been written today. We can still laugh at it, but we cannot write it because we no longer feel the same irony or distance from the madness.

Historical political writing of the sort done by Freeman Dyson and Thomas Powers represents a new and earnest public dialogue that is more typical of the 1980s. Both authors present the very ordinary practical difficulties that contribute to an extraordinary crisis. In *Weapons and Hope* Dyson traces and documents the differing views of warfare between ourselves and the Soviets and shows how we will be unable to negotiate arms reductions as long as we live in two opposed interpretive frameworks and value systems. The American military accepts nuclear deterrence as a reality and purports to defend our populace behind its imaginarily concrete shield. The Russians, with their more recent direct experience of bloody wars and invasions on their own soil, view war as an uncontrollable and unpredictable pandemonium which, once unleashed, can take any wild course. They are not as involved in the fictive war-games reality that American planners honor. Of course neither side maintains an absolute position, but in terms of strategies of defense they worship incompatible gods.

According to Dyson, when the Russians say that they will survive a nuclear war, they are merely stating a centuries-old national credo — not just for war but for their ancient civilization. They conceive of themselves as the survivors of barbarian hordes from Asia, Napoleonic armies, and a Nazi war machine. They are too primitive, even with their mastery of the technology of the atom, to be bought off by our slick marketing of "deterrence." If *their* weakness is stubborn unexamined ideology, ours is our susceptibility to mercantile images. They have a rigid bureaucracy; we have a Madison Avenue government. In trying to sell the Russians deterrence as an assured and fully-tested product (and the mode of arms reduction that goes with it), our government is asking them to buy our definition of reality. They, on the other hand, continue to offer a reality so harsh and brutal that we see no safeguard in any compromise or world worth sharing with them.

As Thomas Powers points out, one of our ploys then is to bankrupt the Russians by trapping them in an arms race they cannot afford. As with a high-frontier star-wars defense, we try to impel them into our shiny modern high-credit reality. But in the process we may bankrupt ourselves and the world as well, bringing on a different global cataclysm. And, in any case, they will always steal our secrets (atom bombs, computer chips, satellites, etc.), whether they actually do or we imagine they do. We are part of the same superpower conspiracy to control the world by quantity, to bind the Third World to our image. On the level of espionage and counter-espionage, there are no longer enough patriotic loyalties to keep national secrets from either side. Once the international spy experiences the truth of the global corporate conspiracy, he is more interested in naming his price and getting his share of the pie than defending the rhetorical ideals of his homeland. Powers lists the mirrored atrocities (and accusations of atrocities) of both sides:

Q: *What about Poland, Hungary, Czechoslovakia?*
A: What about Guatemala, Cuba, Chile, Indonesia, Iran?
Q: *What about Afghanistan?*
A: What about Vietnam?
Q: *What about Hafizullah Amin?*
A: What about Ngo Dinh Diem?
Q: *What about Masaryk?*
A: What about Lumumba?
Q: *What about Sakharov?*
A: What about Martin Luther King?
Q: *What about the kulaks?*
A: What about the Negroes?
Q: *What about the purges, Gulag, Lubyanka, Siberia?*
A: What about Dresden, Hamburg, Hiroshima, free-fire
   zones, Agent Orange?
Q: *What about the SS-20?*
A: What about Pershing, GLCMs, SLCMs, ALCMs?
Q: *What about fifty thousand tanks in Eastern Europe?*
A: What about the neutron bomb?
Q: *What about world revolution and the triumph of
   Communism?*
A: What about "the last best hope of mankind"?
Q: *What about Khruschchev, "We will bury you"?*
A: What about Sen. Richard Russell, "If we have to
   start over again from Adam, I want to be sure he's
   an American"?*

" 'What do you think spies are,' asks John Le Carré's secret
agent: 'priests, saints and martyrs? They're a squalid procession
of vain fools, traitors too, yes; pansies, sadists and drunkards, people
who play cowboys and Indians to brighten their rotten lives. Do
you think they sit like monks in London, balancing the rights and
wrongs? . . . This is a war. It's graphic and unpleasant because
it's fought on a tiny scale, at close range; fought with a wastage
of innocent life sometimes, I admit. But it's nothing, nothing at
all beside other wars — the last or the next.' "†

It would seem that we are left with little choice now: either

* *Thinking About the Next War*, New American Library, New York, 1983
† *The Spy Who Came in from the Cold*, Avenel Books, New York, 1983

a grueling daily war of thievery and deceit that robs us of our national resources and identities, or the end of civilization itself. It is no wonder that ideological purists build shelters and await the end of the present civilization and the beginning of the next with anticipation and hope. Of course, the scientific establishment has now decreed a "nuclear winter," which will destroy all life on Earth after the exchange of bombs. Their scenario may be accurate, but it is still another attempt at deterrence, and to the peasant reality of both the Soviets and the Third World it must still look like an American public-relations scheme. Once again, our self-importance betrays us, betrays even our humanitarian and philanthropic intentions. We must not forget that the majority of people in the world do not have a life that many in the West would be willing or able to lead, and their numbers in Mexico, India, China, Africa, etc., are increasing dramatically. We likewise must not forget, and be willing to look within ourselves to see, that our own pious horror at the destruction of the Earth is at least partially linked to the share of the Earth that we hold. How much less might be our moral outrage and terror if we each held our appropriate fractional amount of the planet's resources. But then no nation would have the capacity or the need to assemble nuclear arsenals. So self-examination should be part of the raising of our consciousness — on this issue alone if no other. The Third World has always suspected Western liberalism, and that is why poor nations often ignore our messages of peace and seem to support Soviet stands, even against their own self-interest. It is their way of protesting not our monopoly or our greed (as they are often just as avid for the same goods); it is their way of protesting our arrogant pieties. They do not begrudge us the sword but they find laughable the notion that we expect still to control the world's wealth by our superior culture without the sword. Their whole lives have taught them the sorry relationship between power and justice. They don't want apocalypse either, but sometimes they must feel that any disruption of the present order would be an opportunity.

Our own credo of deterrence does have one advantage over the Russians' stubborn decree that they will somehow survive: we

recognize, if in the wrong way and for the wrong reasons, that
we are in a new world-age and the old rules don't pertain anymore.
Ideological rigidities no longer have the same power. But a spiritual
transformation is needed, not just a computerized war-game. We
intuit, dimly and in the distance, that unrestrained World War
must become archaic or played out hypothetically in symbolic
replicas. We do not see that our ideological rigidities, cruelly masked as democracy and freedom, must also be transformed in a way
that takes into account the present state of sentient life on our
planet. One deterrent means nothing without the other; the
atomic weapon is just a technological rigidity to support an
ideological one. But we have taken the first unconscious step into
a new ritual and a new millennium. There *is* a lesson in not yet
having fought with nuclear weapons — if only we can grasp its
true meaning in time.

Dyson and Powers emphasize a simple but key point: nuclear
weapons do not actually increase military capability. They freeze
nations into positions of not being able to fight any war, even of
self-defense; and they invite nuclear arming by an enemy. They
are, in a sense, the end of the military profession, its replacement
by computers and hypothetical wars, with greatly increased danger
and risk at no increase in security. The early atomic scientists also
thought of the nuclear bomb as the end to war as we knew it, but
unless the military fully accepts this, we can rely only on fortune
and rationality to prevent the absurdity of the use of strategically
meaningless weapons.

The notion that nuclear weapons are useless and that the vast
sums of money necessary for their manufacture and upkeep could
be better spent is probably one of the most workable practical solutions to nuclear war, though the idea of the same money going
for different weapons would hardly be attractive to pacifists. If
we take the position that war will always be hell and that warring nations will fight with what weapons they have (and we are
very far from a peaceful planet), then at least we might hope to
buy some time by tailoring our arsenals to fightable wars. As Dyson
shows, we can keep our hi-tech defense and move into new areas
of miniaturized weapons, but we don't have to destroy all life on

the planet. This is his ordinary solution to an extraordinary problem. It represents Gary Snyder's hope (expressed in the opening discussion) that nuclear weapons become tabooed, deeply tabooed — in Dyson's sense, not because they are immoral but because they are impractical.

The latter part of this anthology explores our cosmic and archetypal identity in the nuclear crisis. We must face the fact that nuclear weapons are not the only epidemic on this planet or the only perilous fact of our condition. We are born against all odds onto a pagan sorrowful world that has seemingly arisen from conflict, murder, and strife among living entities. We are in competition with other life-forms for the resources of this planet, and we are embattled within our own species. Nuclear war is a symptom of this dilemma, but it is not the malignancy itself. Our inability to undo its grip is also our inability to solve the other problems in our situation. If we somehow magically eliminated nuclear weapons, some other biological, cosmic, or psychological threat would replace them as the most advanced symptom — until we reached the disease itself. Even without the bomb our situation is desperate.

At the turn of the century we thought of war as an interlude in civilization — a madness, a distortion of ordinary life. But Freud pointed graphically to what we already suspected: a hidden and unfathomable unconscious realm from which our hostilities arise — irrationally and unpredictably, not even as pure instincts but as the distortions of instincts (archetypes, Jung later said, after the Nazis, powerful entities we shun and fear at grave risk of being possessed by them), and Toynbee pointed to a series of cataclysmic wars that did not seem to be sated by either the first or second global outbreak. It will take a great deal more than skillful diplomacy and good intentions to avoid destroying our civilization. We exist to a large degree at the mercy of unconscious forces, and we must bring some crucial aspect of them to expression in our lifetime. Those forces are ultimate, and real, and bigger than we are. They are not in a position to show compassion to us; only we have that power from our human-ness. So we must face them as they are, face ourselves as we are, not as we would like to be. The answer to nuclear weapons is not just abnegation of violence, hatred of hate, destruction of the destroyers; it is a new order of culture, a new ceremony, which will return these gods to a less menacing position.

The metaphysical question posed by nuclear war is like the question of creation itself: will everything really come to an end? Will all life-forms be destroyed, or will some survive and evolve in new directions? Will people survive in small numbers and fight (or not) Einstein's Fourth World War with bows and arrows? If the Earth is destroyed, is this then the destruction of everything? These questions have been asked by other generations for other reasons. We cannot know what spirit realms might succeed this reality, but we must face the real spiritual consequences instead of some science-fiction apocalypse.

If we engage in nuclear war and wipe out this world, and there is no other aspect of our creation, then we will have either fulfilled our pathology or given in to the pathological aspect of our nature. There will be a silence like that that preceded us. But even if the spirit worlds go on from here into other realms, and we wipe out this world, we will not enter some heaven or hereafter of the saved, scot-free. We will have to remake this world elsewhere through what is left of our spirit, and it will be all the harder and will take all the longer (in cosmic time), and we will have to do the hard yoga we did not do here. The Christian fundamentalists are simply wrong in expecting they can play Armageddon and then ride happily beside God into the Kingdom of Heaven. Nothing in nature works this way. There was work to do before the bomb, there is work to do to prevent the bomb, and there will be work to do after the bomb, whether we fire it or bury it.

THE PROBLEM

Gary Snyder, Richard Grossinger, Lindy Hough, Bira Almeida, Richard Heckler, Karin Epperlein, Martin Inn

The Warrior and the Militarist: A Discussion
March 31st, 1984

When this anthology was planned in 1983, Lindy Hough wrote a brief descriptive paragraph and sent it to prospective contributors. The "request for work" emphasized the archetypal aspects of war and the role of the shadow in human conduct, but Hough added notes to each person contacted, emphasizing the aspect she thought they could best cover or on which they might already have work. The note to Gary Snyder asked him if he would be willing to expand on his public statements about the unprofessional behavior of the Western military and the failure of our society to produce true warriors. Snyder was interested in the topic but wary of contributing to "yet another" nuclear anthology that might add to the level of misunderstanding about the relationship between pacifism and atomic weapons. He indicated that he was not opposed to war *per se* and did not want to join an anthology which had an unexamined anti-war premise. Hough suggested that these issues might best be explored in an open forum with internal martial artists, Snyder accepted the invitation, and an after-dinner discussion was held the last day of March, 1984, at 2320 Blake Street in Berkeley, the offices of North Atlantic Books.

The participants:

Bira Almeida — better known as Mestre Acordeon — is one of the few officially and truly recognized masters of *capoeira*. He graduated in *capoeira* from the "Centro de Cultura Fisica Regional" of Brazil in 1959. This center was the famous school of Mestre Bimba (1889–1974), the patron of *capoeira* and its most respected master. Almeida is the founder of the World Capoeira Association (1979) and the author of the book *Capoeira: A Brazilian Art Form* (North Atlantic Books, 1982). He is also the founder of the "Grupo Folclorico da Bahia" (1966) which won three international folkloric festivals. Additionally, Almeida is a folklore researcher, a playwright, a song writer, a musician, and a film actor specializing in Afro-Brazilian themes. He is a native of Brazil.

Richard Strozzi-Heckler has a Ph.D. in psychology and a third-degree black belt in *aikido*. He is a co-founder of the Lomi School in Mill Valley, California (1970). The Lomi School conducts workshops in mind/body awareness and trains therapists, educators, and health professionals through a blend of traditional eastern disciplines and modern psychological methods (including yoga, *aikido*, bodywork, gestalt, meditation, conscious movement, breath work, and communication skills). Heckler continues to teach at the Lomi School and is also in private practice. He is author of *The Anatomy of Change* (Shambhala Publications, 1984) and editor of a forthcoming *aikido* anthology from North Atlantic Books.

Karin Epperlein is a professional dancer, choreographer, actress, and teacher of *t'ai chi ch'uan*. A native of Munich, Germany, she has toured Europe, Israel, the United States, and South America in a number of productions. Recently, she has appeared in San Francisco in three productions of the International Theater Festival and two SOON 3 productions at the Magic Theater. She is now working on video films and teaching *t'ai chi ch'uan* in Berkeley and San Francisco.

Martin Inn is the founder and director of the Inner Research Institute School of T'ai Chi Ch'uan, which moved from Maui to San Francisco in 1972. He is a native of Hawaii who began studying the martial arts at the age of 14. After graduating from college he continued his studies in Seattle and Hawaii, then travelled to Taiwan where he worked with several well-known *t'ai chi ch'uan* practitioners. Upon his return he founded the Inner Research Institute in order to teach the short form of the Yang Style of *t'ai chi ch'uan*. Since then he has taught throughout the United States, in Australia, and the Republic of China. With Benjamin Pang Jeng Lo, Robert Amacker, and Susan Foe, he is the co-translator and editor of *The Essence of T'ai Chi Ch'uan: The Literary Tradition*

(North Atlantic Books, 1979) and, with Benjamin Pang Jeng Lo, the co-translator and editor of the forthcoming *Thirteen Chapters on Push-Hands* by Cheng Man-Ch'ing (North Atlantic Books, 1985).

Gary Snyder is a poet, linguist, lay ecologist, and practitioner of Rinzai Zen Buddhism, currently living in Nevada City, California. Some of his books of prose are: *Earth House Hold* (New Directions, 1969), *The Old Ways* (City Lights Books, 1977), and *The Real Work* (New Directions, 1980). A recent book of poetry, *Axe Handles*, was published by North Point Press in 1983.

Lindy Hough, co-editor of this anthology and co-publisher of North Atlantic Books, is an editor, writer, and poet. Her books include *The Sun in Cancer* (North Atlantic Books, 1975), *Outlands and Inlands* (Truck Press, 1978), and a book of essays in progress, *Love and Power: The Transformation of the Shadow in the Nuclear Age.*

Richard Grossinger, also co-editor of this anthology and co-publisher of North Atlantic Books, is an anthropologist and the author of a number of prose books, most recently *Planet Medicine: From Stone-Age Shamanism to Post-Industrial Healing* (Doubleday, 1980; Shambhala Publications, 1982); *The Night Sky: The Science and Anthropology of the Stars and Planets* (Sierra Club Books, 1981); and *Embryogenesis* (Avon Books, forthcoming, 1985).

Snyder: I've been working in the peace movement in the last couple of years. I've been in touch with people in the FOR and War Resister's League, and have a number of friends who still remember the pacifist years of World War II. A certain kind of pacifist language and mentality strongly influenced by Gandhi and the Quakers was already going around the time of the Korean War, but that got kind of washed away after Cuba. When Castro took over, the left began to flirt with violence; violence began to look attractive because Cuba was doing so well. It was romantic. We all know the history of the Civil Rights Movement and how it rapidly slipped away from a kind of Gandhian nonviolent stance into more and more sort of hit and kick back, and then a frankly pro-violence left began to emerge in the United States. And that all goes downhill in the end, to the t.v. spectacle of the Symbionese Liberation Army being totally obliterated. The foolish bravado and moral poverty of a "terrorist left" in the U.S.A. has been thoroughly exposed. Now the revived Peace Movement — Freeze and after — begins to invoke Gandhi again, which is excellent. But I have been feeling some discomfort about the renewed moral absolutism that comes with it. Gandhi's stance was based on a profound personal inner experience. To talk, as some do, about "making a world without war" when we'd be lucky to have a world without nuclear weapons, is talking hearsay and utopian theory. We can't just talk peace, we have to *be* peace, or it's another kind of bravado. I'd like a world without war; but we'd all settle for a world without wars that kill everything. I would settle for a world in which it's not possible to conduct more than a very ordinary low-level war. The military scale we're living with now is not only unpleasant; it's unprofessional. It isn't what a good military man even in the twentieth century would want. To say we want a world without violence is even more problematical. There is an eminent Buddhist priest in the United States who teaches Americans —who said not long ago: "There's really no difference between a husband and a wife arguing and the United States and the Soviet Union threatening each other with a nuclear war. We must confront the violence in ourselves." That's a kind of *non sequitur.* It's dealing with questions like this that got me going on this topic. I was thinking, if somebody wants to have a world totally without violence, they can work towards it, but let's start with going back to muzzle-loading rifles.

Grossinger: Of course it's an impossible goal. It can't be reached, so the attempt to reach it has consequences independent of the goal, perhaps even conflicting with the stated goal. That's the effect of all unattainable goals. The only thing wrong with absolutism is that the world cannot be altered in absolutist ways. No ideology can be imposed indefinitely without causing an eruption of its shadow, its opposite force. So an obsession with peace becomes an irresistible urge toward war. The peace movements of the world have admirable qualities, but I think even some of their strongest adherents are beginning to see that they are addressing the wrong questions. The psychologist Edward Whitmont deals with some of this in his recent book *The Return of the Goddess.* Let me read you a bit from it:

> Our rejection of greed and violence is at best half-hearted and of but limited value in controlling their destructive power. In fact, we have been extremely skillful in devising innumerable righteous justifications for our own violence. . . . The unpleasant fact is that the ego's striving for permanence, and its rejection of the urge for violence, is opposed by the persistence of the Dark God (or demon, if you will) in the recesses of the psyche. Violence, the urge for the destruction of form and the inflicting of bodily harm and death, continue to exert a forceful, exciting, and invigorating attraction upon the ego. . . . To an increasing extent, violence nowadays is perpetrated indiscriminately and without cause against the young, the old, and in everyday ordinary situations. It seems to be unleashed neither in anger nor out of economic necessity, but purely for the intoxication of satisfying a sadistic power urge. . . . Aggression is indispensable for adequate ego functioning and for the capacity to love and to relate. Ares, the God of war and strife, and Eros, the God of love and desire, are twin brothers psychologically.

He goes on to say that because aggression cannot be cut out of the human psyche, we must create ritual outlets for it, celebrations of its gods, mystery rites for sublimating its forces. But in the modern world we simply pretend to be rational and good and in control of our emotions and fate, and the result is sterile obsessive violence and inexplicable brutality.

One would like to think that in infinite spiritual time the lion will lie down with the lamb, and we too, and war will, not so much be eliminated as fused into a new structure as something other, as another face of the same god, less overtly destructive. But this is not likely within any frame of time in which we can imagine existing ourselves or anything like us existing. And, of course, other people say that war is inevitable, not only as an expression of aggression and the unconscious drives and necessities of our species but as a continuation of the struggle for survival within nature, the struggle in which our species arose. Of course you can accept the struggle between the lion and lamb but see war as a human invention.

Snyder: But you haven't even defined war yet. You see, that's the first problem, right there. People talk about war as though a game of Trobriand cricket or some New Guinea spear-shooting, or a bunch of Comanche and Cheyenne going out and counting coup on each other and killing one out of every fifteen are/were just the same as a nuclear confrontation. We should have different words for these different scales of war. It would help clarify what we're talking about.

Heckler: Jonathan Schell actually brought that out. War connotes a winner and a loser. If you talk about nuclear war, there's a possibility there may not be a winner at all.

Snyder: Well, that's post-nineteenth-century. In prior times there were no total winners or losers either. *Total* war, waged for the purpose of bringing the opponent to their knees, unconditional surrender, was largely a World War II invention. In the eighteenth and nineteenth century wars, unconditional surrender was never what they called for. War was a way to drive people back to the bargaining table. It was, as Von Clausewitz said, an extension of diplomacy. In many European wars, there was never the intention of destroying the ideology or the territory or the population of the enemy.

Grossinger: And certainly in wars of primitive people there wasn't that intention, at least the ones we've observed ethnographically — although one wonders about the validity of our fantasies of Stone Age tribes being destroyed by other Stone Age tribes.

Snyder: What fantasies are those?

Grossinger: Robert Ardrey, *African Genesis*, and all that — to pick a rather blatant and much-maligned example.

Snyder: Oh, all that stuff is very suspect. Ardrey doesn't warrant more than a sentence in this conversation.

Hough: In North American Indian wars was there a sense of destroying the enemy totally?

Snyder: No. They were not genocidal.

Grossinger: Modern anthropology doesn't seem to have found genocidal wars among native peoples.

Snyder: Of course there have been some genocidal events within civilized times. One of the very first acts of the new-formed Roman Republic was to "clean up" the tribal people to the north of Rome to the extent of virtually destroying them. But genocidal wars when they occur are the invention of civilization. Pre-civilized people don't do that. They don't have the resources for it; nor do they have the need for it.

Grossinger: In a sense the Stone Age fantasy is simply a projection of twentieth-century myths back on an unknown situation.

Snyder: I'm not sure even what fantasy you're talking about — something like the model of Cro Magnon eliminating the Neanderthal?

Grossinger: That's Ardrey's image. I don't agree with it because I think they're both our ancestors, but a like event may have happened at another time in other circumstances, perhaps even regionally without affecting major evolutionary trends.

Snyder: I believe that everybody carries Neanderthal genes. It was an intermarriage process. The Neanderthals were never eliminated. They were just intermarried with, interbred with totally.

Grossinger: However, the fantasy reoccurs in sociobiology and other theories of society and human speciation based on the genetic selection of territoriality and destructiveness. It comes to its natural and absurd consequence in the ideology behind the nuclear confrontation — the justification for such massive stockpiles of weapons. We partially absolve our blame and guilt by claiming that we are responding to the natural bellicosity and dark motivations of our species from the beginning. The Soviets come to represent the primal horde, reincarnated through Communism. We look at ourselves and see the same primal horde. Many of the nuclear strategists in fact argue that a "world without war" has been created by these terrible weapons because they frustrate the species' natural inclination to fight to the death.

Snyder: That's all very ahistorical.

Grossinger: We can talk in terms of history, but we can also talk about existing myths which have their own history of consciousness. These myths are believed by large numbers of educated people.

Snyder: The existing mythology is a combination of the things you just described: such as the assumption that we're driven to the point that we're at right now by "human nature," which is a totally false assumption. Elements of human nature are in it, but we are not driven to it — any more than a twentieth-century Industrial White Civilization is the only logical outcome of history. It's always the habit of people in whatever time or culture they're in to think that they are the mainstream of historical evolution. The West's own particular myth is a combination of Social Darwinism and Christian millenarianism. One of the most dangerous things underlying this particular confrontation is an unconscious metaphysical will to have a final Armageddon happen because it's the Millennium. That would resolve the *Book of Revelations* and cause the Kingdom of God to come.

Grossinger: We've even elected leaders who are confused on that point. We have a president who arrogantly not only expects Armageddon in his lifetime but imagines himself to have a fated role in it. Some people even think the Russians are our only hope for avoiding a nuclear confrontation because they don't have to sell disarmament to a Bible Belt of people who are already making plans for the Kingdom of God. And furthermore, they must know they are staring across the guns at a country full of such fanatics, preaching love and spirituality in holocaust.

Snyder: Exactly. It's a real post-Renaissance theme in Western history: that there's going to be an ultimate confrontation and ultimate destruction. So we're acting out Judaeo-Christian metaphysics.

Grossinger: It appeared during the '60s as the omens of the destruction of the Earth by Kohoutek the comet and volcanoes preceding earthquakes.

Snyder: California's going to fall into the sea.

Grossinger: I don't know that there's anyone who is not at least a little bit superstitious.

Snyder: Well, there are linear superstitions and then there are cyclical superstitions. Those are linear superstitions. We happen to be in a culture that's living in a linear time frame, so it has an end to it, a highly apocalyptic end at that. In a linear frame, every time you get two drought years people will say: we must be going into permanent drought! Or every time we get a few cold winters people say the Ice Age is coming. Whereas we know for a fact that in every century there will be two cold winters. Every thousand years there will be ten extraordinarily cold winters. That's all within cycles.

Grossinger: And the other half of the people say that the greenhouse effect is taking over and the Earth is heating up dangerously.

Heckler: I just want to go back to this idea of what you were saying, Gary, this idea of the myth. Let's say this unconscious need for Apocalypse is what we're moving toward, but what kind of need is this coming out of? It's almost as though we're trying to fulfill this prophecy of a light and dark force. Then once everything is destroyed there will be this kind of heaven on Earth, a final supreme deity to grace the survivors. I ask myself: What's missing then? What are we responding to? What's the need for that? What is it we want and why don't we have it without that kind of apocalyptic vision?

Snyder: Well, it's from a very dualistic world-view. Christianity tried to kick out the Manichaean heresy long ago, but Manichaeanism is still deeply imbedded in our world-view. For people who accept that apocalyptic vision the world is flawed as it is, incomplete, or, more deeply, the presence of Satan and evil is pervasive. Christian fundamentalists are very sharp on this: Satan is in the world. And they don't want to live in a world that has Satan in it. The Millennium or the Apocalypse destroys the power of Satan, and then it becomes the Kingdom of God. But to destroy the power of Satan, there must be a great purging, great purification, much destruction. The *Book of Revelations* describes in detail the great wars and conflagrations and waves of death that will sweep humanity. And then the meek shall inherit the Earth. It becomes the Kingdom of God. So if people are in that world-view, this world as it is is not good enough for them. They don't want to live in it the way it is. It's not absolute reality; it has no divinity in it. Animals aren't sacred. People aren't sacred. Trees aren't sacred. The world is just dirt. Antonin Artaud, when he went crazy near the end, expressed this quintessentially; he said: It's shit, it's shit; this is all shit. Matter is shit. And that's a very strong element of one part of the Occidental world-view that helps fuel the unconscious acceptance of this apocalyptic confrontation and makes people kind of half inside their heart hope it will happen.

Grossinger: Is this what you mean when you say that the militarist is an unprofessional warrior?

Snyder: The nineteenth-century militarist is a professional working for his government. In terms of Von Clausewitz, his job is to extend diplomacy on the battlefield. His job is over when they say: that's enough. We've gotten what we wanted, or we've had to give up a certain amount, but it's over. He is concerned with doing a good job. He is not a warrior, but he's a professional working for the state. If you go back another step in time, moving further away from the state, you arrive closer to the warrior — who is in some cases a class or caste figure or an initiatory figure; either he has been initiated or born into or trained into a class or caste who not only handles violence effectively and with restraint for the sake of the state, but might handle violence compassionately and carefully from a spiritual standpoint. And that's where I think the term warrior begins to apply. And then if you move back farther in history to some other cultures you'll find that the way of the warrior is a way of spiritually maintaining and confronting violence and containing it within a sphere that doesn't become true evil, but remains something manageable. You know more about this than I do. I'm just speaking from a certain amount of travel, reading, and thinking.

Almeida: I am not so sure that I know more about this subject than you. However, we certainly have a different approach on the issue. I got lost in your discussion of historical perspectives on war and warriors. My perspective is just that of a *capoeirista*. First of all, the term "warrior" has never been applied to a *capoeira* person and to call *capoeira* a martial art is somewhat forced and makes me uncomfortable. Let me explain. The origins of *capoeira* are obscure, making it difficult to determine how this art developed its current shape, a mixture of fight, dance, music and a way of life. Easily we can imply that it was used by the African slaves as an expression of freedom. However, this does not mean that *capoeira* was only a weapon used in actual fights. I believe that this freedom also can be considered the journey into a special state of mind that the *capoeirista* reaches through the practice of *capoeira*. We are discussing war at this moment and I cannot think in terms of war. Because of my background as a *capoeirista*, I only can think in terms of fight. I see no more similarity between "fight" and "war" than between a "fighter" and a "warrior" in the context that this term is generally used. A fight in the *capoeira* context is an important process of self-understanding because when one confronts a serious opponent he is also confronting himself in a situation that uncovers his weaknesses and strengths. I believe that the fight in this context is a step toward self-discovery and consequently toward a personal growth. This is an individual process that cannot be extended to a level of millions of people fighting with contemporary war artifacts, or to a massive extermination of human beings in a nuclear confrontation of nations.

Snyder: I like the term "fighting." Let's just say that fighting is not necessarily war. Fighting is not war.

Hough: And nuclear armaments don't really seem to be fighting. They are very far away from individual human contact.

Almeida: That's true. They're annihilation and have nothing to do with the kind of fighting I was talking about.

Hough: In my book I continuously compare nuclear war and pornography in the sense that they're both tremendously abstract forms. They're far back from the real thing that spurs them. Pornography is about five steps away from a real relationship with a real person, and nuclear armaments are many steps from really contacting your enemy. They both seem developed in a time of abstracting yourself, the same kind of era that gives rise to the assembly line and massive bureaucracies.

Almeida: I think that a nuclear war is also a comfortable kind of war. The person who is pressing the buttons does not suffer the fear of actual fighting. Certainly, there is a fear of retaliation, but it's very different from the feelings that come during a personal confrontation. Think about the time when weapons were spears, swords, and clubs. You see your opponent running down a hill with a sword in hand. You can only rely on your own skill to defeat the blows, or on your legs to flee. One might think that because more lives are involved, this last situation is more fearful. From an ethical and moral point of view, it is more dramatic. However, it is not the same agony of a drowning person trying to swim in a turbulent sea of emotions, such as the emiment sense of danger, the frightful confrontation with pain, or the possibility of an amputation without anesthesia.

Snyder: It's a perfect development for a white middle-class war — for people who don't like to get sick and who don't like dirt.

Hough: A war for businessmen.

Inn: It's a kind of war that doesn't take any kind of self-cultivation.

Snyder: It does have a lot of training, however.

Hough: Yes, math and physics; the elite of the society are in ballistics, trajectory planning. It's very attractive, very high-paying.

Inn: It's all an external type of cultivation. It doesn't cultivate the spirit.

Snyder: There's a cultivation of a certain kind: going through the correct steps in the correct sequence. But it's also like having a baby born in the hospital. You have experts fight your wars for you.

Almeida: The people that fought conventional wars in the past were a distinct part of the population, the warriors. The whole of society didn't have to fight in them. There is no similarity with a nuclear war that makes no distinction between warriors and children. In spite of this great difference between nuclear and conventional war, both are organized fights the purpose of which goes beyond the personal growth of the fighter. Because of this, the validity of any kind of war is questionable. Bringing this point to a personal level of confrontation, I think that we also should question when Myamoto Musashi took up the sword and cut off the heads of fifty or sixty people in search of his own self-development.

Snyder: That was the code of that class that permitted that.

Almeida: I do not accept a code that allows killing for personal growth. How is it different from one that allows conventional war for economic reasons or a nuclear one to keep another country from becoming more powerful?

Snyder: I am trying to think about Musashi now. He started out as a very rough man and actually violated the official Bushido code by being too violent, and then gradually came to control himself.

Hough: So some violence is okay, just not too much violence.

Snyder: Theoretically at least, Bushido holds that you don't use violence unless you've exhausted other means — that you don't draw the sword unless you've tried to argue your way out of it. It's the last step. Theoretically at least, the Bushido code is a code of restraint. With the capacity for violence comes the responsibility for restraint. It's like the Sikhs of the Punjab: you can't draw your knife out unless it draws blood. So you don't draw your knife unless you're serious. But the practice of Bushido was often abused and corrupt. Samurai were often swaggering bullies, or later, subsidized social parasites.

Heckler: One of the words I keep hearing behind all this is 'dignity.' We talk about Bushido and the Japanese tradition, and we always say the word "do" which is a way. That means there's an internal process. So my experience of combat comes both from being in the martial arts, and military training for a war in which one had to use muscles and sweat. But there was no dignity in this war. I'm talking about Vietnam now. A classical warrior could have dignity. I don't even know if the warrior's "war" is right or his killing is right, but there's a sense that there is some way or *do* that could make the warrior more whole — the possibility of being connected to something larger than his individual ego or simply having a good technique or slaying somebody. There's a historical tradition or context of being a warrior which gave one a feeling of being connected to something larger than individual self. The Vietnam War put people in the dirt, in the sweat; it had to do that. But there was no sense of dignity to it. It seems as though in this whole nuclear thing, it's not only the dignity that's gone but there's not that use of muscle. Or like in *capoeira* when we come into the *roda*, and it's two men, or two women, or a man and a woman, and you're facing each other, and you don't know what's going to happen. And it's the same thing in *aikido*. Even though you are confronting another person you understand that it's really between you and you. And even if you lose externally, it's still you and you internally. And even if you win, it's still you and you. This refers to the words of Master Ueshiba, the founder of *aikido*, when he said, "The opponent is within you." Whereas in the modern war you just have the lieutenant say: go out and do this, and you would look and you would think: that guy's a jerk; I wouldn't follow him around the block. And then there is the situation in the missile silos when they get the message to shoot the missile off, they have to back each other up. If one guy balks, the other guy pulls out a gun on him. There's no sense of dignity or path in this. It seems so abstract and impersonal that one doesn't have the opportunity to develop psychologically or spiritually.

I just came back from India and there was martial law because of an escalating conflict in the Punjab. I'm going through the airport, and my Swiss army knife was in my hand-bag. So the officer said to me: you can't take this. I told them I didn't want to give it up, so I said: put it in a little box and give me a tab and I'll pick it up at the other end. But they wouldn't go for that. We argued for about twenty minutes and the plane's going to take off. Finally, a higher-level officer takes me to the side, pulls the knife out, looks at me and says: if I let you take this on the plane, do you promise not to open it? I looked at him and thought: he must be pulling my leg. But I looked him square in the eye and said yes. He looked at me for awhile and finally said I could go with the knife. But the point is that this was a level of simplicity and straightforwardness where somebody's word was okay. My word meant something. There was some kind of dignity between us. He could look at me and say: you promise not to do it. He looked me right in the eyes, I looked back, and I said: I promise. And this connection meant something. I was doing *aikido* and *capoeira* on an interpersonal level, and there was something from those traditions that was alive and working in that moment.

Grossinger: What about generals like Scowcroft, or defense officials like McNamara and Kissinger who see themselves essentially as warriors balancing the incredible destructive power of hydrogen weapons with deterrence. They believe that deterrence alone has prevented the recurrence of the cycle of twentieth-century global wars. They've developed their own code of honor, their military existentialism based on the philosophy of preventing war. They don't think of themselves as military bureaucrats; they feel like philosophers of war and survival in a technological age run amok. This, of course, is based on their overall low estimation of the human race and how it will behave if left alone. They see themselves as the avatars of civilization; they are saving us from exactly that threat: what if you were a terrorist? They can't take that chance. Everyone is potentially a terrorist on an unconscious level, so everyone is suspect, even the most honored. And, of course, everyone collectively is an even greater risk. The code of the warrior was based on consciousness and myth; the code of the existentialist military man is based on the demons of the Freudian unconscious and the neo-Darwinian territorial war. To them the fight for dignity is over, banned by the weapons themselves and their overwhelming and equalizing power. Their view of the salvation of the species lies in turning the fight over to the war and into the service of the computerized battle, a sterile but predictable form of intelligence.

Inn: Chemical warfare is not fair; biological warfare is not fair. Neither is nuclear warfare, but we've already used the bomb. We've gone beyond the point of fairness. What do we do now?

Snyder: Nuclear war is considered fair by the same people who are trying to call chemical and biological warfare unfair.

Grossinger: I think they're distressed by the fact that once you get to a certain point it's impossible to exclude anything. The horror of Hiroshima is still not fully understood, but we live in its shadow. Nobody likes to face the severity of the point we are now at.

Snyder: But they do, though. Like very simply, when asked: are you really developing the possibility of first-strike capacity, our military says: well, of course. You have to have all your options open. In modern warfare there is nothing that's excluded from the possibilities of your thinking.

Almeida: In the wars of the past too. The warriors used whatever

they had available, poisoned arrows, boiling water and sorcery.
Snyder: Sometimes.
Almeida: In the end, always. The boxer does not use his legs during a match only because the rules of the sport do not allow him to do that. In spite of treaties and international agreements, in war it is different. Legal or illegal, any effective action will be used in order to save your skin or preserve power. Any other thought about this matter will be a romantic interpretation for a situation of real danger. So, it comes to the point: is there any kind of acceptable war? I agree with Richard when he says that the soldier in the front line has no dignity when he is ordered to kill or be killed. Maybe an old-fashioned samurai had dignity because he had a sense of pride derived from a culture that highly valued warfare. In a contemporary war, the descendants of samurais probably would not have such dignity because they lack a similar sense of pride. If one gets involved in war it becomes a real question of survival. Then, he will use all the weapons that he can. So, for many reasons there is no dignity in nuclear war, including the fact that the ultimate weapon will fatally reach others that do not believe in that war and do not want to be involved in it. For the individual fight the issue assumes a different perspective. At the moment you are fighting, your opponent becomes yourself. You confront your fears, your strength and weakness, your life itself. You do this without involving anybody besides your opponent and you. I have been involved in thousands of fights in my life, so I know what it is to feel this kind of thing inside. You know you must win. But to win means to win with yourself. But when you fight in a war, you have no dignity; you will be a samurai dying in the dirt and not wanting to.
Snyder: I think that's right. War to my mind means organized battles, organized conflict between nations, between states. War is a function of civilization.
Heckler: That's an interesting point. So much cooperation must happen in a war. Perhaps we need to ask ourselves how to channel this urge for cooperation to strengthen ourselves and our communities instead of defeating an external enemy. *Aikido* training goes a long way in working with our attitudes of cooperation and

aggression.

Snyder: And the organization in warfare is ordered from the top. The guy out there who has to be sent out by a general, the only dignity that he has is maybe believing what he's doing is for a good cause, and he's not even sure of that. That's the little shred of dignity he clings to.

Almeida: A good cause could be lots of money and power. Most soldiers and even generals went into war just for the financial reward.

Snyder: The footsoldiers who were sent out, many of them never even believed in what they were going out for anyway. Whoever was sent out in Napoleon's armies had no stake in that struggle and didn't even think they did. They had to be kept there by force. People have to be forced to go to war.

Epperlein: War has changed because forms of communication between people have changed; it's much more indirect nowadays, with all the media.

Snyder: At a certain point on the battlefield soldiers who don't keep going forward and start coming back will get shot by their officers. That's the threat that finally keeps them out there.

Epperlein: War is more indirect communication; it is really a symptom of our society now.

Snyder: More and more abstract.

Epperlein: More abstract, less direct confrontation.

Grossinger: We do keep coming back to the distinction between fighting of necessity and organized ideological war.

Snyder: Maybe not a necessity.

Grossinger: Well, it arises from people's perception of a necessity. But what I'm coming to is that the notion of the war being the "fight enlarged" isn't really true from an experiential point of view. Bira has pointed out the fight is a totally different thing. So what is war? Is it an invention of technology? Does an historical change occur in society when the person defeated fairly in a fight goes and gets a gun and shoots the warrior? I think that the power of warriors (like samurai or *t'ai chi* masters) to be a force in society and to serve as a kind of hidden army maintaining justice by never fighting, or rarely fighting, was diminished when they could be overcome by someone of much less skill and character simply possessed of a forged weapon. It doesn't seem fair that technology should so tip the moral pendulum, but it has, and the hydrogen war is the consequence of that writ large. Where is the warrior now? It's no wonder that the military existentialists can think of themselves as warriors because they too fight with deterrents and withheld power.

Inn: The warriors of the past were given a high status in society. They were the guardians of society — the samurai in Japan, the *ksytria* in India. Today with the threat of nuclear war and with the high prospect of total annihilation of life as we know it, the warrior-soldier is held in low esteem as one who will carry out this threat. He is no longer a guardian of society but a threat to the society that he is protecting by inviting nuclear retaliation. In the past the martial artist/warrior was a man who merged his practice with certain spiritual disciplines to make himself a better fighter. He did this by trying to solve the spiritual questions of existence and death. It was the merging of his art with spiritual practices which gave him a wisdom which others respected. But I don't see that the war and the fight represent opposite spiritual universes. In both the *T'ai Chi Classics* and *The Book of Suntzu* the individual's technique and strategy could be enlarged to a grander scale with armies, and one can serve as a model for the other. They both go back to the more basic philosophy of Taoism.

Grossinger: There isn't complete separation, but of course there's never complete separation between things in the world. So I'm not sure where that leads. I'm just thinking aloud. What you're saying is the fight and the war must both follow Taoist laws of nature. The forces that work atomically also work the mind and body of individuals, in their emotions, on and in society. So you are saying that although the forces of modern war arise from ideology and come from applied technology and conscious military goals, they must also represent ancient and eternal forces of the universe. But then what ancient forces do they represent? Is it possible that they represent other ancient forces than those that generate the fight and that the warrior feels?

Snyder: Yes. They represent the institutionalization of greed. War is a function of the institutionalization of greed, and only tangentially an extension of the human (particularly male) delight in collision.

Grossinger: So maybe war is not the fight writ large but writ small. The fight is the experience of the largeness of things; the war is a diminishment of that.

Snyder: War is greed writ large, using fight. Or misusing fight.

Grossinger: And a different technology.

Snyder: See. You cannot ignore history. You cannot simply be psychological and existential in these projections. There is a watershed that takes place when the state is formed, when the nation-state comes into existence. The nation-state moves by its own dynamics, which is the interests of a few as against the interests of the many. And the interest of the few is essentially greed. War is *their* greed using the willingness of young men to fight.

Heckler: Where does that leave us?

Snyder: I don't know.

Heckler: I come from the martial-arts and the psychological perspective, and I know historically what you're saying is true, but I always return to my own experience and I know as a martial artist that once you start to cultivate yourself, there's a tendency to say: does it work? Would it work on the street? Could I really defend myself? Can I beat the other person? What it is that the individual's trying to look for in himself seems to be a key question. The historical perspective, although true, is just not my perspective. What I know is my own experience, and I feel we all need to look within at our own greed and violence and love. But as martial artists, are we always stuck presenting our techniques to the greedy few? Can the martial arts be used as a way to work with our aggression and not simply a way to develop our paranoia or defeat someone?

Snyder: You've got three choices: one is, you work for the ruling elite; one is, you stay clear of them; and the third is that you fight them.

Almeida: The fighter went to war in the past because he was forced to, or because he found himself more qualified for that job than for carpentry or whatever. It does not mean necessarily that he went to show off skills or to test techniques. By this perspective, a traditional kind of war can be considered as an extension of an individual fight. But I do not believe that the fighters really assumed the cause of the war they fought in.

Snyder: That's what I'm saying too. It's the objectives of the ruling class, using fighters.

Heckler: It's an exploitation of the fighter and the warrior.

Snyder: Like I used to know guys back at the time of the Korean War. I was going to court myself at that time. And there were some non-nonviolent anarchists refusing to go to the Korean War. The judge was giving everybody a good deal if they'd say "I'm non-violent. I wouldn't hurt a fly." Okay, well, you can be a conscientious objector. Then these guys come along and say: "No, I'm not theoretically nonviolent, but I'm not going to fight your war." What's this argument?, they say. And the guy says: "Look, I'm just not going to have the state tell me who to kill. If I ever must do such a deed, I'll decide for myself." That's another perspective. This is an argument: the state is an abstraction, and one wouldn't want to do something as serious as killing without thinking through one's own thoughts on it. I knew men like that. They got sent to prison.

Inn: Another perspective is: would there be wars as we know it if women ran everything instead of men? Would they bring about something very different than the male-oriented world? If you had mothers sitting in front of the buttons, would they push it?

Grossinger: What we don't know is whether that's been tested yet. We don't know if Margaret Thatcher is a test of that. Is she? I don't think she is. Not Indira Gandhi. Women who arise through male society take on the male persona.

Epperlein: They have become men in order to succeed.

Inn: That's a theoretical question, and my suspicion is: it would be quite different.

Snyder (to Almeida): I've been reading your book, and it's very wonderful. The history of *capoeira*, like the history of *kung fu*, shows cases in which the fighters arose from below. They rose from the underclass. And those were not fighters like samurai who worked for the ruling elite. They came out of an oppressed class, to keep their own dignity, their own manhood. *"Karate"* means "empty hand": they couldn't afford weapons. *"Kung Fu"* means empty hands, too. When the Japanese took over Okinawa many years ago, they literally forbade anybody to own any weapons, and at the same time the samurai police of the Okinawan Islands had freedom to cut anybody down with a sword who looked at them cross-eyed. So they developed *karate* in Okinawa as self-defense against drunk samurai with swords, when they didn't have any weapons themselves.

Almeida: I do not know for sure if the slaves used *capoeira* as a means of self-defense. We *capoeiristas* like the idea of *capoeira* being primarily a fight. In my book I presented one of the theories about the origins of *capoeira* — as an "empty hand" fight against the invaders of the Afro-American civilizations developed by runaway slaves in the backland of Brazil. These civilizations were called *Quilombos*, and one of them, the *Quilombo Dos Palmares*, lasted for one century with more than 40,000 inhabitants. Many people explain the fact that *capoeira* uses more feet than hands as a result of the slaves having their hands chained during their fights to escape. This idea seems unrealistic to me. It is practically impossible to rely on an empty hand technique against fire weapons. So, I believe that *capoeira*, as a fight, evolved from ritualistics and dance movements. Now, there occurs to me one question: Would the fighter exist if there was no war to fight in?

Snyder: Were the gang fights in Chicago or New York or Bahia wars between different groups?

Heckler: I think it's an interesting question, and my first response is: yes. I think that it's also the work of a fighter, maybe a more awakened fighter, to put the notion of the warrior without a war into a context. From what I understand, that's how break dancing started. There were these gang wars in New York, and many people were getting killed or seriously injured. All of a sudden friends were gone: dead, in jail, or burnt out on drugs. Then somebody has the sense to see that this war mentality wasn't working. So they transformed this competitive urge to confront another gang into dancing, which was probably influenced by *capoeira*. There is this aggression and competitiveness that we all need to look at in ourselves and in our society. We need new rituals to work sanely with aggression, see what it is, and transform it.

Grossinger: American kids don't necessarily understand *capoeira* or take it on in context, but from seeing or hearing about the ritual dance-fight, they intuit something at its heart, and even though most of them are unfamiliar with its moves, they reinvent them from remote images in their own street context, even as Afro-Brazilians reinvented their own African ceremonies in the New World to make *capoeira*. What's wonderful about break-dancing is how extreme it is. War looks middle-class and mediocre beside it, a drudgery without imagination. I realize I'm talking psychologically, but war represents repression of certain instincts and archetypes which come out in *capoeira* or break-dancing. The modern war is, as Bira says, comfortable because it suppresses the real ritual outpouring of people's guts. The national leaders of world powers and arms negotiators embrace and give each other these big hugs as though there's some intimacy, but they're revealing nothing and exchanging nothing. They have defined the world in such sterile terms, human contact in such limited terms, that they are not capable of coming to an agreement, a real agreement, even as much as the street gangs are. They cannot "break." Street dancing may express ritual enmity, but it is personal, it is revealing and imaginative, so in its radicalness it's really more intimate. It transforms and heals aspects of the enmity, and makes an alliance; it fuses groups in a place of meeting. I think insofar as war represents greed it doesn't even bear good honest antagonism, which will transform its participants if acted through in an authentic way. War can never transform through intimacy; it is this other thing, cold and sterile.

Heckler: I think: why do I do these things? Why do I do *capoeira*? Why do I do *aikido*? There's a ritual in them that is very rich for me.

Snyder: And joy.

Heckler: And challenging. I've seen people take an *aikido* test, lawyers and doctors, totally competent men and women. They take this simple test in front of their peers, and it's one of the biggest rituals they've had in their entire lives. They're nervous, they feel themselves deeply, and they go through changes. The same in *capoeira.* It's so rich and it's so big; and we don't have these kinds of rituals and forms in our lives and educational system.

Snyder: It's because we don't get them.

Heckler: We get "Charlie's Angels" and we get "The A Team."

Grossinger: And nuclear war is another t.v. program. Sterile. A projection.

Snyder: Bira said this earlier, about the comfortableness of our modern war — well, I think that we fall into that comfortableness partly as a function of not having done "fighting" as young people, and gotten over that fear. The fact that people haven't learned how to feel a certain level of confrontation and challenge and physical contact as young people means that when they get older they're fearful, so they have to make their wars more abstract. And shoot from a greater and greater distance. There would be something healthy in acting it out on a youthful level. It doesn't have to be fighting. When I was a young man, I was a mountain climber. I never fought people, but I went out and risked myself on ice climbs. I got to see myself grow — while scaring the wits out of myself.

Inn: There's a tremendous element of danger in the martial arts. You're defeated either by your own ego or the other person's ego, and that defeat represents the challenge and resolution — whether you have the first level conquered, your own ego, and then the second level, the competition with another ego. It can be a mountain or a person. It's the danger that attracts us, the fear, the conquering of fear.

Snyder: I think it's partly the fear of fear. You have to learn that it's not half as bad in experience as it is in imagination. And then you become free of it.

Inn: I think that Buddhist discipline and the very abstract spiritual cultivation in the martial arts is the elimination of the ego, which will defeat you in a confrontation. But a very interesting outcome is that once you have conquered your own fear and ego in a personal confrontation, winning builds up a kind of external ego, so you become better and better through defeating your own ego. It's a dual thing.

Snyder: In learning how to deal with your own ego you also learn how subtle it is. Winning is really a very minor part of it.

Heckler: Other than break dancing one of the original American forms of ritual are these games where people go out and shoot each other with these paint pellets. They have organized teams and tactical little wars with referees, and it supposedly simulates combat. They go through the war, and then they have a party afterwards. It makes me think about what you were saying: if you do that as a youth, then maybe you don't have to do it later.

For some people if they don't have a ritual they think, well how can I face this fear, and if they're not going to climb a mountain, they think well, maybe I'll be in a war with this gun and see who I am under pressure. But perhaps we can simulate this whole thing in such a way that we can reflect who we are or who we can possibly be, in a way that is not destructive.

Inn: What about sports. Don't many of the sports come out of warfare? And there's the American love of violence and football. If we're not personally involved in our own challenge with ourselves in the martial arts, we need some sort of hero to do it for us.

Grossinger: I am looking to piece some of these threads together. For instance, the problem with things on t.v. is that people don't actually experience them but see them mentally and project onto them. I suppose that abstract and romantic warfare is the same. People imagine themselves through wars, but they don't experience them in actuality. They experience a fantasy of glory, a fantasy of explosions, a fantasy of handling powerful weapons. And these fantasies can be coopted by greed and then institutionalized, as Gary said. Greed must arise from the failure to confront fear, to confront mortality. The ultimate goal of greed would be to get enough protection around one's self to feel unassailable. Because the protection is only external, it is also illusory. Any real fight, any real war, even any real meditation instantly exposes your vulnerability and your mortality. Greed plays off people's illusion that they might live forever in a material sphere. Unable to transform or internalize experiences, they have to acquire external power in ever greater amounts. And once you get addicted to it, it gets worse and worse. It reminds me of the parapsychologist Jule Eisenbud's theory that what nuclear armaments represent is the fear of our own power, our real internal and psychic power. If, as he suggests, we have the power to change things by our minds alone, to kill with our minds, then we are engaged in a massive denial of that power. The more deeply we bury its secret and pretend to separate ourselves from it, pretend we don't have it, the more we need superarmaments. This weaponry is an enormous distraction to polarize us away from the truth at its heart, which is that we don't need it because we can kill with our minds. The nuclear bomb is voodoo sublimated and collectivized through technology. Whether one wants to accept the paraphysics of that, it does express the myth of what we've been talking about — that the failure to develop internal power and internal feeling processes rebounds externally to the same degree and represents itself in some sort of external pathology or violence as a cover-up for the fear and also the loss of power that lies at its center.

Epperlein: Nuclear power comes from our minds, from the nuclear scientists; it is our invention.

Snyder: I think it's not quite right to say it comes from us, though. I'm always very careful not to automatically let myself be identified with everybody. It comes from certain people who made the choice to be employed by certain forces to put their intelligence to work for pay and then to sell those inventions and let them be used by certain people. I think it would be very healthy for us to be careful about taking these things on ourselves. I won't take it on myself that just because there's a nuclear confrontation between the Soviet Union and us that it's *my* human nature: it's not *my* human nature. There are historical and social forces that caused that, forces I stand against and always have.

Epperlein: Sometimes not employed by the state.

Snyder: The ones that invented the nuclear bomb? They were employed by the state. And from way back.

Epperlein: But the way that they did it was not for the state. It's because it's their profession; it's because they're interested in the atom.

Snyder: They had the choice of which project they would work on. You always have the choice to say who is going to pay you. Where does your money come from? Who pays your salary?

Grossinger: But there is a degree to which it's pure knowledge, and it would have been discovered anyway.

Snyder: In the history of the atom bomb that break goes way back. At the point where the pure knowledge of subatomic physics, the possiblility of nuclear explosions, began to move toward practical application, it was a conscious choice in every case.

Grossinger: But I think most of those people made the choice because they thought it would be discovered anyway, and possibly by the Germans or Japanese.

Snyder: They knew the consequences when they went to work on it.

Epperlein: I think not. I think they didn't know that. . . .

Snyder: Oh yes they did. You can read the history of it: see Robert Jungk's *Brighter Than A Thousand Suns.*

Epperlein: Yes, as an energy.

Snyder: It's one thing to know theoretically that such an energy is possible. It's another to take a job with somebody who is going to make it happen.

Grossinger: Don't you feel it's a case of: what if the next guy's a terrorist? They did it only because they didn't want to be beaten to it.

Snyder: The history of it is: that the refugee German scientists who fled Nazi Germany — this is in *Brighter Than A Thousand Suns* — and came to the United States, and this includes Einstein, were so appalled by what was happening to the Jews, and were suspicious that their colleagues left behind in Germany with the same knowledge that they had would be going to work trying to make an atomic weapon for Hitler, that they convinced Roosevelt that they should start a program in this country in that direction. Since many of those refugees were Jews, if the Nazis hadn't been doing a heavy number on the Jews, the atom bomb probably never would have been developed.

Grossinger: I find that hard to believe. It would have just waited for some other war, or cold war.

Snyder: You know things don't just happen automatically. It takes an historical combination of events, times, and places for things to happen. Einstein himself was extremely dubious about going ahead on this, but because of what was happening in Europe, he overcame his own fear of it and went to work on it. And then the intensified hatred and dislike of Nazism brought liberals like J. Robert Oppenheimer into working on the project. Oppenheimer would have never worked on it if he didn't think Nazism was so evil.

Grossinger: But what I can't believe is that the critical constellation of events wouldn't have occurred in a different way years later.

Snyder: I'd say not necessarily. It would be too deterministic to say that that's automatically going to happen. Also, it takes funding. It doesn't happen without funding, and because of the war, because of the reputation the Nazis had, the chemistry between Roosevelt, Einstein, and Oppenheimer — and Teller, they threw a lot of money into it not knowing at all that it was even going to work. You might not ever get the funding together for such a program if there wasn't a whole lot going to make it happen. At any rate, there's a real history behind it, and the history involves conscious choices made by many individuals, including a number of scientists who were equally qualified to work on it and refused to — names you don't know, because they never got famous, because they didn't work on it.

Epperlein: But I also think civilization in general is the cause of inventing nuclear power, nuclear weapons — getting power over the world with your mind.

Snyder: Whose civilization?

Epperlein: Our civilization.

Snyder: Look, there's all these countries in South America who never invented any atom bombs. They didn't even invent jet airplanes. But they're civilized.

Epperlein: I mean all the civilizations on this planet.

Snyder: It doesn't follow. No, it doesn't follow. The difference between Latin European culture and Northern European culture is striking in that regard. They are both civilizations, but Latin civilization does not involve technology on a mass scale. Northern European civilization does. It happens to be a peculiar quality of Northern European civilization. It's not a quality of Mediterranean civilization to develop an atom bomb.

Grossinger: I see the point, but it's hard for me to accept. I guess

I believe the opposite, that it was inevitable and that it represents the quintessential crisis of this creature on this planet. To me the development of nuclear technology is an outcome of the evolution of life. But I can see too that there might have been other technologies, other modes of civilization, ones unknown to us of course, that were never developed.

Snyder: My sense of history and events is never one of inevitability. I don't believe there's any one linear process that's inevitable. At every point the karma is open. We are making our fates constantly. We are not creatures of fate; we make our fate now. Oppenheimer made his fate and made our fate; Einstein made his fate and made our fate. But it's open; it *was* open.

Grossinger: I can accept that our present now is open, perhaps in the sense of the homoeopathic literature where it says that whatever disease the patient has, whatever the symptoms are, that's the beginning point of the cure. You cannot go back hypothetically to a less pathological state, even one that existed five minutes ago, but you could have changed the whole course of the disease by treating it then. You don't say: if only the person hadn't gotten this disease. . . . if only I had acted five minutes ago. . . . Where you begin, as long as the person is alive, is the particular dynamic of the present; and as long as the person is alive, the disease has a cure, though it may take a miraculous yoga to attain it. A month or a year later it might be a totally different disease with a different cure. I feel that way about the nuclear problem in our civilization.

Snyder: I agree, but I would also say: not only do we start right here, but part of our cure is realizing right away that it wasn't inevitable, that it wasn't human nature, and that it wasn't even the only thing our civilization could do. We are free of those inevitabilities.

Almeida: I agree with what you say, but I also think that there could have been a worse alternative.

Snyder: Could there be worse?

Almeida: I think so.

Grossinger: We could have had a nuclear war already.

Snyder: Oh, all sorts of things could have happened. Hitler could have won the war, taken over Germany and France. But you know when they went into Germany after the war, they had some OSS men running ahead of the troops even, that went right into the labs and the offices of the German nuclear scientists, to see how much they had done and how far they had gone, and those guys had stonewalled it and hadn't done a thing for Hitler. They were nowhere near the development of an atomic weapon in Germany. They weren't about to do it. They stonewalled it. They wouldn't cooperate. And so, in a sense, it was all unnecessary.

Heckler: Well, one thing is for sure now. The knowledge is out there. And that's really what we're dealing with. If we stop building them, somebody else will. It's a question of how we *now* deal with this knowledge.

Hough: And it's a major industry, selling the nuclear weapons to other countries.

Heckler: One place that I take my work is in education. I mean I'm thinking: that information about weaponry is out there, it's happening. How can we teach kids about conflict resolution? There's always going to be a .38; there's always going to be a knife; there's always going to be a fist. Likewise nuclear bombs. The militarist seems so far away, but I feel that it might be worth it to work with kids. Someday they're going to be holding the gun. Even if it's all melted down: we have it.

Snyder: We have to start making some things taboo.

Grossinger: How can you trust rational behavior that much?

Snyder: But it will become taboo. If we survive at all it will be because nuclear weapons will have become tabooed, deeply tabooed, so deeply tabooed that even though the knowledge is there nobody will go after it.

Heckler: Do you think it would override that greed?

Snyder: Granted some minor cultural changes, yes. Greed doesn't have to be institutionalized.

Heckler: But if it's an element in our history and it's remembered, then it's an element we need to work with.

Snyder: There are many things in our history that we have forgotten. Some very powerful knowledges in the past have been lost, partly because they were abused.

Hough: You mean like alchemy.

Snyder: Yes. Or like killing with your mind. They became taboo.

Grossinger: According to Eisenbud, the trouble with making them taboo is that we externalized them. As nuclear weapons.

Epperlein: In Europe the peace movement looks very different from the United States, and it's very strongly on a personal level for people. The peace movement means more working with yourself, with your neighbors, with your own state. That is something that has arisen very strongly from fear of a nuclear war. I'm from Germany, but the peace movement is now very strong in Holland, Denmark, in France, in Germany — in Italy, even there it's really strong. People get together and start to create a different lifestyle to counteract that real threat which is everyday there. Something has already changed with people. Governments are not interested in that of course because what it does is it brings people away from being able to fight for the state. The awareness is more on collectives of people and communicating with people, whoever and wherever they are.

Hough: When Mitterand was here and was asked about the Greens, he just flipped it off like a fly and said it was nothing, it wasn't strong.

Epperlein: The Greens are not necessarily the peace movement. What I am talking about as the peace movement is something which is actually happening in the people. It's not an institution. It's more an awareness of people who want to integrate that fear into their lives. Being bombed and being destroyed is not such an abstraction to people in Europe, so they want to make it part of their life and change something. It's interesting how fast the minds of the people change under that pressure. The threat of nuclear war has this positive effect of bringing people closer.

Heckler: I've often thought that. It's surfaced a certain fear and really made people come into contact with themselves in a new way.

Epperlein: They're much more gentle. They try to be not as aggressive.

Inn: Don't you feel that because America has not suffered a real war here, we don't feel it, it's very abstract?

Snyder: That's why we're so belligerent.

Hough: Also, grass-roots peace-movement people who just organize often aren't talking about real things. They can be mindless and belligerent too.

Snyder: Yes, I know.

Grossinger: I have trouble with such people, but I also have trouble with my attitude. It seems indulgent and arrogant on my part. I have no patience for someone who always shows up with another petition to sign or a poster for another march. I react negatively to that because it seems automatic and out of touch with the turbulent reality of our situation. It's reduction of consciousness, which leads away from the possibility of change. People softening and opening in themselves are cause for hope; people just identifying with something, even the "right" cause, don't give me much hope. You don't see real compassion for the human condition in them. It's more: this is my allegiance; this is what I'm for; and you better believe I'm on the right side. I'm not sure that reaches the opposition, or the part of all of us that's stuck. But you get political strength and change through numbers, so I don't challenge its value.

Heckler: You're talking about the aggression in it, right?

Grossinger: Yes, well, the passive aggression.

Heckler: Like: we're going to have peace damnit, or I'll wring your neck. When the Dutch were in Bali, the Balinese, at one point, started to commit suicide to defy their oppressors, and the Dutch couldn't stand that so they started shooting them.

Snyder: That's a government type of reaction. It's a decision made by an entity that's into having all the power and all the say and is frustrated by not having it. If the underclass finds a way not to respond, it infuriates them terribly.

Heckler: Well, Gary, you always have that historical response, but I feel there's something personally psychological. . . .

Snyder: The government is a psychology too.

Heckler: All I can say is that it's inside us, that's where the looking has to be done.

Grossinger: When we lived in Richmond, the alternative school that our daughter Miranda went to decided it was going to teach the peace movement to first through third graders, and the teachers put lots of letter-writing and peace marches onto the calendar. During the time that that happened, Miranda fell more than a year and a half behind grade level, and she was bombarded with a whole lot of boring rhetoric for which she had no context. She was denied basic tools of thought and evaluation and instead fed a party line. The teachers and parents felt they had to act to counter a terrible threat to the planet, but it was partly because many of them had failed to be aware of that threat most of their lives that they acted as though the weapons had just been put into place yesterday and were a pure and unique upsurge of right-wing evil. Their anger was righteous and self-aggrandizing and suggested guilt. It was almost hysterical. They were going to ram peace and love down everyone's throat. They were going to fill the kids with an ideology which could only confuse and harm them because it was so fixed and demonic itself. In people shouting peace I sometimes hear only a narcissistic masquerade of denial — pure denial of their own inner truth. When we objected in the parent's meetings we got screamed at by people who accused us directly of supporting nuclear war and of not realizing the direness of the threat.

Snyder: That sounds very Berkeley. You've got to believe Berkeley sounds real weird when you're up in the Sacramento Valley. You know these people who put these programs out on KPFA on the radio don't realize that guys driving giant tractors in the ricefields in the northern Sacramento Valley — these guys are driving back and forth in these huge tractors cultivating four thousand acres of rice — and they're laughing their heads off.

What I find about those people, about that mind-set, is that it has its own level of aggression in it of course, passive aggression, but it seems to me that it's shortcutting something that we've been talking about for their children in their health — which is: learning how to have conflict — that the solution doesn't abstractly lie in saying: we're going to eliminate conflict from ourselves and the world; it must lie in the direction of how, artfully and skillfully and compassionately, to engage in conflict.

Grossinger: Well, naturally a number of kids got confused and didn't know if they were for or against the bomb; the kids were just too young to comprehend the issue, so they were drawing these pictures of missiles falling on houses and great explosions.

Epperlein: Kids thought they were doing the right thing.

Grossinger: And the whole thing of peace marches and standing up together in hope has been ruined for Miranda because it's been imposed on her so authoritarianly. She thinks: "marches, yuk!" It's the worst possible school activity — boring, frightening, involving crowded cars and preoccupied adults. It doesn't make good "peace" kids; it probably makes some of them into Hell's Angels later on. And that doesn't mean you can't do it, but I think education has to be through internalization, not ideologization. A big California weakness is to be so ignorant of history as to think that each new radical thing that comes up is a turning-point in the universe. Californians tend to think that history moves at the speed of our lives.

Heckler: I know people, peace activists, who think once we all come to our senses we'll be able to settle down with our old lady on 40 acres of land and be peaceful from then on. Kind of like peace is a static thing.

Grossinger: And there won't be a resolution on that level. I think it's the realization that a "world without war" won't be created that way that makes one object to that kind of oversimplification. If people believe their own simplifications, then they might not be up to the real task that's at hand.

Snyder: A specifically American weakness is the ignorance of Marx. The rest of the educated world, whether it's far Eastern or European, is absolutely appalled by the failure of the American intelligentsia to read their Marx and to digest it, to understand what was being said there. I was in Sweden last year. Everyone is so astute historically and politically on such things. Even the best educated Americans have this big gap which is European history and is Marx. Not to become Marxists but to go beyond being Marxists.

*

Heckler: I was thinking about how when Bira first came to this area, a lot of the other martial arts were these combative types and Bira actually had to fight these guys. They were really good fighters. My experience in that area is that when you beat somebody, then you are over them. There's an unconscious automatic hierarchical system. So Bira encountered these people from East Oakland, Berkeley, and San Francisco; he basically beat everybody, and then showed them that he respected them. And it was so surprising to everybody because that's the thing that didn't happen. If you beat somebody you were the next rank up or had ten more dollars, or in Japan they have dojo-busters, they challenge you and defeat you and it's their dojo. But from Bira's character and temperament, there issued from a sense of: I respect you. In fact, maybe I respect you more because we've just gone through this fight. It kind of set a whole context for how I see *capoeira* in the Bay Area. Its like that term "constructive conflict." We all have conflict in us and by closing our eyes or going on marches its not going to go away. We need to interact with our conflict and construct something workable and creative with it.

Snyder: I did a lot of study on Plains Indian fighting. Those guys had such class. They threw their lives away a lot, you know. They really did throw their lives away just for style. It's really incredible, though. It had nothing to do with war. It had to do with style as much as anything. It had to do with name. It had to do with doing something that the other guys would say: wow, that was far out.

Grossinger: Very elaborate break-dancing.

Snyder: Like riding single-handedly into an enemy group, just taking off and riding straight into it, without anybody backing you, that was one of the things that they would do. Almost certain death. And it was all done real stylishly.

Almeida: Sometimes you don't have a second chance because you did a stupid thing. It's good to fight, though, I think.

Snyder: It's probably good to live too.

Almeida: I think it is important for a person to have the chance to fight in order to understand better one's self and the others. For me, the comtemporary war is meaningless and it is not the right way for the warrior because it is indiscriminate death. You cannot grow from death. But you certainly grow from the training for the fight or even the fight itself. I have a very down-to-earth perspective on that because life takes more guts than philosophy. It is like a great *"jogo de capoeira"*; not so much theorizing and speculations. There is lots of talk about internal and external power, how to kill with the mind and so on. Sometimes it seems to be a fantasy to get lost in. The real thing is to kneel under the *"berimbau"* and fight whatever kind of *"jogo de capoeira"* it commands. Talking about philosophy, I really like Marin classes because they make me think about things that I know almost instinctively without verbalizing them. One day I said in class that my master told me that *capoeira* is treachery. From that moment on Richard Heckler has been asking me what is the treachery of everyday life. It is a hell of a question.

Snyder: The first noble truth of Buddhism, *Sarjam dukha*, everything is impermanent and unsatisfactory, and always treacherous.

Grossinger: It's just too bad it had to lead to nuclear weapons.

Snyder: If people accepted that truth, they wouldn't even have to have nuclear weapons. As you said, it's fear that generates greed. You can be fearless in the world if you have made peace with impermanence and suffering.

Heckler: Do you think you need a practice in order to experience that?

Snyder: I think for most people, yes. Some people experience that principle existentially and directly. But it seems to be rare. It seems that our ego gives us little defenses and protections, even everyday garden variety ego. To learn not to rely on those crutches is what a practice is, is to keep them naked. And then finally to make you laugh. And then you begin to be fearless. You begin to be. Meditation is like fighting. Meditation is a kind of fighting. It's where you just simply sit down and confront yourself. And keep confronting yourself.

Almeida: We Brazilians do not meditate so much. Maybe that's the reason that the economy is so bad in Brazil right now. I feel a constant desire not to compromise what you are. That is what makes *capoeira* interesting to me. It is a challenge to improve techniques, to try to understand more and more about this art that reflects so much of you. *Capoeira* is like a mirror in which you look at yourself before you wash your face in the morning. You see yourself simply the way that you are and you are there by yourself and yourself alone. You have no one from whom you ask help.

Heckler: This may be a good meeting Gary, you can take a class from Bira and then show him some meditation.

Almeida: A good idea.

Grossinger: This taping gave us an excuse to have a meeting together that we might not have had otherwise. It wouldn't have worked if we had just had a party.

Snyder: You're right, a party is not quite the right form. And it's hard to get people to say, let's just sit down together and talk about something. Unless you have an ostensible reason to do it. So it's a good game. It's helped me clarify some of the things I'm trying to think through. I find it hard to work with this. I find certain conflicts in myself that I'm still working on because I'm still trying to understand, as I'm sure I always will be, the many levels of the meaning of the first Buddhist precept: not to be harmful, not to harm. This is the fundamental moral precept of Buddhism. The rest are in a sense just variations. Thich Nhat Hanh, the Vietnamese Buddhist priest said we mustn't be dualistic even about war and peace, or about warlikeness and peacefulness. Peace contains war, war contains peace. In any situation, in any place, in any condition, even in the battle right in the middle of the war, you must appreciate and be grateful for the little bit of nonviolence or a little bit of less harmfulness or intelligent nonharmfulness that might be practiced there. And we must be alert in a parallel way in the realm of peace to the kinds of aggression that take place.

Gordon Feller

SPIRITUAL DIMENSIONS OF WORLD ORDER

It is time to go beyond the usual parameters of the nuclear debate. It is time to begin asking ourselves how The Bomb has affected the human soul itself. By exploring The Bomb as symbol, we can penetrate more deeply into the amazing mirror nuclear weapons have created. Extraordinary changes in society, in attitude and in values have emerged world-wide since Hiroshima, changes that show us a thousand ways in which The Bomb has become the guiding metaphor of our time.

The world has been noticeably speeding up: economically, technologically, culturally, politically, militarily, scientifically, and intellectually. We often hear of an "information explosion," not infrequently in the same breath that we speak of the "population explosion." The explosive character of contemporary society is mirrored nowhere better than in atomic and hydrogen bombs.

Amidst explosion, "implosion" is simultaneously and just as radically transforming our lives. Although only a handful of scientists and their students used the word "implosion," it entered into real usage with the inauguration of the atomic age. Reflected in the subatomic process of implosion is a world experiencing shrinkage—in today's jargon, the "small world" of "spaceship Earth." At every level, bar none, things seem closer: ideas and discoveries, causes and effects, movements and events, people and places. They are each converging one upon another, imploding.

How does something implode and explode at the same time? One is tempted to refer the question to a nuclear physicist. Rather than look at it from an outer world perspective, shift gears for a moment and view it from the angle of inner consciousness.

Implosion and explosion are *not* simultaneous in the physics of the nuclear reaction; the first follows the second by fractions of a second. And so, too, in the macro-dimension of modern social reality. The Age of Exploration and physical expansion was an explosive event, paralleled by the Age of Enlightenment's intellectually and culturally introspective implosion. Global reach of this sort has today crystallized into multinational corporations, who, despite their often blatant wrong-doing, have brought us closer together, causing an implosion of humanity upon itself. Material well-being effected by the technoscientific explosion produced in its turn a population explosion that has brought humanity — finally — face to face with itself. Distance has shrunk: we can be places today we only dreamed of being before. Time has shrunk: we can be there today more quickly than at any other time in history. Post-industrial societies have come into direct contact — and confrontation — with prehistoric stone-age peoples. We imploded into one another, after exploding out from behind old rigid boundaries.

The atomic process which catapulted us into the nuclear age depends almost entirely upon the *liberation* of an enormous untapped potential. Out of the interaction of particles come energies which have heretofore existed only in latent form; this is a liberation process once again mirrored in the post-Hiroshima world where among others, colonies, women, minorities and children have been liberating themselves from outmoded patterns of domination and repression.

Since 1945, the political and military configuration of the globe has undergone a wrenching process of transformation. During the Cold War we bore witness to the world-wide liberation of the forces of militarization, repression, and authoritarianism. Stimulated by the destructive potential of the atom and the actions of the two superpowers, latent world-competitive tendencies have emerged, manifesting an enormous material expansion and distortion in scientific and technological spheres of life. Although we sometimes tend to view it in a generally negative light, the widespread positive effect of this trend has been to liberate vast subtle *human* energies and resources of which the West's "human potential" and "voluntary simplicity" movements have been but two of dozens of expressions.

For better or for worse fusion nuclear energy seems to be "coming of age" in the early 1980's. It differs from fission in that the energy reaction is produced not by the division and separation of atomic structure but rather by the union of separated parts into new and more integrated wholes.

Fission is an expansive process that multiplies forms and regenerates atomic energies. It mirrors the expansionary tendencies of human consciousness and awareness characteristic of our entire century. Fusion, on the other hand, is an integrative and unifying symbolic presence which mirrors the shrinkage and coming together of once disparate and separated worlds.

The creation of a critical mass of energy-bundles within the nuclear core is essential to having either a successful fusion or fission reaction. Only when that critical minimum of actualized energy mass has gathered together can an explosive release of energy occur. In the societal counterpart, we today are being told by both futurist and mystic alike that only when a critical mass of awakened and activated human beings come together in either consciousness or form will we have the non-violent chain reaction of global transformation needed to assure human survival and dignity.

A critical mass of dedicated persons *can* make the difference, perhaps even enough difference to move the world back from the nuclear threshold and forward into planetary civilization.

In almost every conceivable manner, the release of the energy of the atom has revolutionized human and natural life on this planet. Every aspect has been affected, and the result has been a broadening and deepening of the world crisis. The passing of the old civilization and the birthing of a new, more humane global culture has been sped up by the energy of the atom to a degree that few of us are aware. The struggle to free humanity from the death grip of the nuclear menace promises — if we succeed in preventing a major catastrophe — to transform life as we have come to know it.

At the densest, physical level, the surface of the earth is spotted with thousands upon thousands of reactors, missiles, waste storage sites and laboratories using nuclear materials. A truism which gets asserted quite often these days is that "never before in human history has the survival of the planet and the human species upon it been so seriously threatened." At the same time, however, the potential for spiritual growth and fulfillment is expanding under the weight of the arms race, a fact which often gets neglected in increasingly popular apocalyptic writings. To unravel this paradox we have created by and for ourselves is also to suggest one path by which we may make a conscious choice and collectively opt for awakening, rather than destruction.

Since World War II this planet has been undergoing transformations whose pace and quality are unprecedented in recorded history. The release of the energy of the atom has been discussed and written about to a greater extent than any other single event in history. Yet, despite the millions upon millions of pages and the billions upon billions of words spoken on the subject, I believe there is an important — no, a fundamental — dimension and dynamic which has been consistently overlooked.

The release of atomic energy symbolized, ironically, the birth of the spiritual heart in humanity. How, one asks, could the death of 150,000 human beings and the destruction of two large Japanese cities, constituting probably one of the most heinous crimes of history, be a spiritual event, let alone a high point? Who would dare entertain such an absurd suggestion?

As always, the answer comes in digging more deeply. A clear and careful distinction exists between the devastating effects of the atomic blasts and the symbolic meaning of the discovery of the energy of the atom. Symbolism has a psychic meaning which penetrates to the depths of both culture and civilization. A symbol, like a word, is the outer signal of an inner event taking place at levels of being and thought not immediately accessible to the normally physically-conscious mind. Therefore, the symbolic is in fact no less real than the event from which it draws its symbolism, and to which it refers for its basis in earthly reality.

The political struggle to abolish nuclear weapons and halt the spread of nuclear reactors has raised important questions about the social impact of the presence of nuclear materials on our planet. (By "social," I mean broad shifts in the distribution of political and economic power, modes of social organization, and the like.) Stated in its simplest terms, the nuclearization of physical power and militarization of security have revolutionized the whole of the human social order. Concomitantly, the denuclearization and demilitarization of the globe will have an even greater revolutionary impact on the state of the world.

Choices made in society about the energy and resource base are value decisions, born of certain very basic attitudes toward the earth and humanity's relationship to it. On the plane of human-nature relations, those who advocate and adopt the nuclear option hold what economist and peace researcher Kenneth Boulding called the "open cowboy" paradigm of the planet, a vision of an endless and enduring capacity for the planet to handle despoilation of its body. From the beginning of the nuclear fuel cycle in uranium mining operations through the end when nuclear wastes destined to radiate millions of years are buried in the sea or under our homes and farms, the cycle goes on. The "open cowboy" view is insensitive to Earth's needs for cleanliness and respect. Only in this more refined and sacredly held state can she provide us in turn with the physical sustenance on which we depend for daily survival. To lack awe in the face of the wonder of life, or to lack a sense of honor for this planet on which the miracle of life has occurred, is to invite exploitation and rape. These become almost *expected* actions, since with this paradigm human beings should feel free, like the cowboy of an era gone by, to grab and destroy without regard for other life.

The "open cowboy" paradigm on the vertical plane of relation between human beings and the natural world on which we depend and with whom we share life is an inherently dangerous one. It fails to be cognizant of the physical limits of our biosphere; it is an embodiment of one of the darkest sides of ourselves, a side which we have come to know all too well over the millennia. The massive material resources required for endless rounds of nuclear arms competition and for expensive and dangerous nuclear power plants have begun to sap that once idyllic dream of unlimited supplies and limitlessly fulfilled demand. As the manifestation of a highly centralist and authoritarian paradigm upon which some multinational corporations and almost all governments seem to base their decisions, it is especially threatening. As a species we stand at the edge of a precipice.

Nuclear transformation itself is a symbol. Einstein's famous equation $E = MC^2$ tells us — in the most simple of interpretations — that all matter, when sped up to the speed of light multiplied by itself, is equal to the energy found in pure states in the universe. At the core of every atom of matter is a Life-energy; its release can bring forth untold quantities of power. At the core of every particle of life, at the core of every living thing, including you and I, this reality also holds true. Each atom of our being has this power, and as collectively we are made up of countless such atoms, the potential power of every human being can be called "divine" in its potential and magnitude.

Symbolically, the energy of the atom foretells the release of unimaginable creative potential from within every human being — if we can make it beyond the nuclear threshold itself. It is the story of human beings on a journey, our beginning or awakening of that nuclear center within every atom of our being, to the life energy from whence matter comes and to which all matter returns.

The materialist's world-view of the life energy is indefensible in the face of this revelation of power and strength. The interchangeability of pure energy and seemingly inert matter means *all things are Life* and all objects are parts of the One Life in which we live and move and have our being.

Charlene Spretnak

NAMING THE CULTURAL FORCES
THAT PUSH US TOWARD WAR

In the current wave of peace activism, speakers are sometimes heard to say that the movement is attempting something new in the history of humankind: peace. That view is inaccurate. The "killer ape" theory of early human society has been displaced in anthropology by evidence that cooperation was the key to survival. In Neolithic Old Europe, according to archaeologists, no evidence of fortifications and warfare has been found prior to the invasions of the patriarchal, nomadic, Indo-European barbarians from the Eurasian steppes, beginning around 4500 B.C. (Gimbutas, 1974, 1981). The matrifocal Old European societies thrived peacefully for thousands of years, leaving behind sophisticated goddess-oriented art and egalitarian graves. In a survey of 156 more recent tribal societies studied by anthropologists, Sanday (1981) has presented numerous cultural patterns ranging from habitually violent to habitually peaceful. Clearly, making war is not a genetic imperative for the human race.

Women and men can live together and can relate to other societies in any number of cultural configurations, but ignorance of the configurations themselves locks a populace into blind adherence to the status quo. In the nuclear age, such unexamined acceptance may be fatal as certain cultural assumptions in our own society are pushing us closer and closer to war. Since a major war now could easily bring on massive annihilation of almost unthinkable proportions, why are discussions in our national forums addressing the madness of the nuclear arms race limited to matters of hardware and statistics? A more comprehensive analysis is badly needed—unless, as the doomsayers claim, we collectively harbor a death wish and do not *really* want to look closely at the dynamics propelling us steadily toward the brink of extinction.

The cause of nuclear arms proliferation is militarism. What is the cause of militarism? The traditional materialist explanation is that the "masters of war" in the military-industrial complex profit enormously from defense contracts and other war preparations. A capitalist economy periodically requires the economic boon that large-scale government spending, capital investment, and worker sacrifice produce during a crisis of war. In addition, American armed forces, whether nuclear or conventional, are stationed worldwide to protect the status quo, which involves vast and interlocking American corporate interests.

Such an economic analysis alone is inadequate, as are the recent responses to the nuclear arms race that ignore the cultural orientation of the nations involved: They are patriarchies. Militarism and warfare are continual features of a patriarchal society because they reflect and instill patriarchal values and fulfill essential needs of such a system. Acknowledging the context of patriarchal conceptualizations that feed militarism is a first step toward reducing their impact and preserving life on Earth.

(1) First, patriarchy—at the level of individuals, groups, or nations—operates on the model of dominance or submission. Respect is thought to be gained only through superiority and control. Every situation is perceived as hierarchical; occupying any position other than the pinnacle of the imagined hierarchy creates great anxiety. A clearly visible element in the escalating tensions among militarized nations is the macho posturing and the patriarchal ideal of *dominance*, not parity, which motivates defense ministers and government leaders to "strut their stuff" as we watch with increasing horror. The Reaganite/New Right/Christian Right forces are determined to "make America a man again." They are baffled when the European peace movement views their John Wayneisms as warmongering rather than awesome virility.

A dominance mode requires dehumanizing "the other"— women, people of color, or foreign nations—and idealizing oneself. A common refrain in America during the Cold War of the 1950s was "Nobody wants war—except the Russians." Our government and military leaders convinced themselves that the Japanese are so monstrously base as to justify our being the first nation to build an atomic bomb and explode it among civilians. The American decision to drop the first atomic bomb into the centers of Hiroshima and Nagasaki, instead of rural areas, was not made hastily; rather, our leaders considered those civilians so "other" that our military designated those cities as "virgin targets," never to be subjected to conventional bombing, on which we would eventually test our new weapon. The obsession with dominance led to our initiating still higher levels of potential destruction with the hydrogen bomb and multiple warheads, and to our refusal to renounce the principle of first use. The cult of dominance and toughness also deeply influenced our policies during the war in Vietnam (Fasteau, 1975). In March 1983, we witnessed the continuation of this patriarchal *leitmotif* in President Reagan's call for American military control of space, using "killer lasers," particle-beam weapons, and microwave devices.

A dominance mode requires the brandishing of symbols of force and power. During the Carter administration, according to William Perry, then undersecretary of defense, military lobbyists flooded the decision makers in the legislative and executive branches with a kit produced by Boeing that provided upright models of Soviet and American missiles. Theirs, alas, were much larger than ours and although this initially stemmed from their lagging technology (the new Soviet SS-20s are much smaller), the message was that we "suffered an inferiority" (Stern, 1982). Senator Gary Hart (D-CO), a member of the Senate Armed Forces Committee, recalls that the central image during that period of successful lobbying was a "size race," which became "sort of a macho issue" (Stern, 1982). More bluntly, political analyst William Greider (1982) has recently noted, "The glossy ads from defense manufacturers nearly always feature a phallus of destruction." Maintaining that men are no less susceptible to hidden sexual appeals than are women, he posits a correlation between such public lobbying and the fact that opinion polls show a much higher proportion of men than women supporting President Reagan's "bloated defense budget."

But symbolism alone does not breed satisfaction: The only circumstance in which the military can *prove* its superiority and dominance is the state of war. Conveniently, the military believes war, even if "limited," to be inevitable and it is not alone in our patriarchal society. Eugene Rostow, former director of the U.S. Arms Control and Disarmament Agency, has been widely quoted regarding his insistence that we are now living in "a pre-war world and not a post-war world" (Scheer, 1982). Many military personnel have been conditioned to consider the question of war as "when" rather than "if." Recent interviews with National Guardsmen, who are now being equipped with new, sophisticated weaponry in a program to make them "partners" with the Army, reveal an alarming eagerness to prove dominance: "We're ready to go over there and beat those guys!" (National Public Radio, 1982).

(2) Warfare is held by many people to be the ultimate initiation into true adulthood and full citizenship. This deeply rooted belief surfaced as an unexpected element in the struggle to pass the Equal Rights Amendment, for instance. Feminist lobbyists in state legislatures throughout the 1970s were repeatedly informed, "When you ladies are ready to fight in a *war*, we'll be ready to discuss equal rights." These same legislators vociferously oppose the admission of women to military academies and careers. War is *their* game, a private father-son ritual of sadism. The winners can take their place in the patriarchal hierarchy; the losers are buried or made to beg for crumbs from the slashed budget of the Veterans Administration.

Certainly the pressures to go to Vietnam without examining very deeply the rationale for the war were great. The boys (the average American soldier there was a working-class 19-year-old) knew something about war, they thought, from Hollywood renditions of it, and finally they too could proudly swap war stories "like Dad." Most of all, their families and society simply expected them to "do the manly thing." So they went. Among those assigned to European bases, discontent and depression were common if they could not get sent to Vietnam to "prove their manhood" on a battlefield. The young soldiers who did go to Vietnam found the actual experience of guerrilla warfare to be cruelly ironic: It was so hellish that anyone with any sense was very scared every single day of his year-long tour of duty, causing him to wonder whether he had failed the grand initiation. This is one reason so many of those veterans remain conflicted about their combat experience and refuse to discuss it, even with their families. Their brutal Prussian-style training had radically altered their psyches in order to prepare them for situations that they found did not exist (Eisenhart, 1977). There have been as many suicides among Vietnam veterans since the war as there were combat fatalities (Capps, 1982).

Is there any evidence to indicate that the new generations of sons are suddenly being raised without the age-old macho glorifications of doing "a man's duty" in a war? Or are those pressures still nurtured among our citizenry on a vast scale even though a major war in the nuclear age would very likely mean the poisoning of the planet and the extinction of all life? Although the people who protested against the war in Vietnam—and they were primarily middle class—are probably raising their sons to resist cultural glamorization of the soldier's role, many Vietnam veterans have expressed the unshaken opinion that most of the protesters were simply afraid to "be a man" and to go to war (CBS Special Report; see "What Vietnam Did to Us," 1981). Presumably, this belief is being passed on to their sons. Several veterans at the dedication of the Vietnam veterans' monument in Washington, D.C., in November 1982 shouted, "Give us a war, and we'll win it!" *(New York Times)*. Other veterans are bitterly disillusioned. As one man told a reporter at the dedication, "We all have children now, and we don't want them to march off like tin soldiers without thinking again" (AP release). This father's views are probably in the national minority if the recent boom in the sales of war toys is any indication.

(3) The experience of basic training traditionally implants patriarchal values by reviling women as a foul and lowly class (Eisenhart, 1977; Bliss, 1981; Gerzon, 1982). Recruits and soldiers who fail to perform are scornfully called by derogatory terms for female genitalia. They are continually addressed as "faggot" or "girl" by a screaming drill instructor. The ultimate patriarchal

insult of being woman-like has often been imposed throughout history by castrating the vanquished, literally or figuratively. Lyndon Johnson buoyantly told a reporter the day after ordering the bombing of North Vietnamese PT-boat bases and oil depots, the first act of war against North Vietnam: "I didn't just screw Ho Chi Minh. I cut his pecker off" (Fasteau, 1975).

In basic training, harshness and insensitivity are praised; raw aggression and dominance are equated with masculinity. After serving his (patriarchal) country in this fashion, a young man returns to society with certain deeply etched beliefs. In addition to identifying security with hierarchy and well-defined chain of command (a concept the 30 million veterans in this country often apply to business and political situations; Bliss, 1981), the men have learned that "feminine" sensitivity and women, in the world beyond Mom, are not respected and that women are certainly not viewed as equals.

In more extreme cases, which were legion after the Vietnam war, many young veterans were horrified if they happened to feel sensitivity or empathy or other responses valued by women. They feared they might be slipping down into the denigrated class, where such weakness would render them vulnerable. A very common behavior pattern reported among both disturbed and relatively well-adjusted Vietnam veterans is simply their refusal to "open up" to women. Many of the wives at the reunion of "Charlie Company" in 1981 spoke of this loss of psychological intimacy. "I wouldn't say the Army made my husband a man; it made him a different man," said one woman sadly. Several other wives nodded in agreement (CBS Special Report; see "What Vietnam Did to Us," 1981). A wide range of this response has been documented by pscyhologists and therapists working with veterans (Lifton, 1972; Meredith, 1982).

(4) The ritual of the archetypal father slaying his son is as old as patriarchy itself. In classical Greece, young warriors were raised with myths of fathers and sons being treacherous, deadly rivals: Uranus, the Sky Father (mate of Gaia, the Earth Mother, whose mythology long pre-dates his) hurled his rebellious sons,

the Cyclopes, into the underworld. Cronus, another son of Uranus, castrated his father as he slept. Laius attempted the murder of his son Oedipus, yet was himself murdered later by that son. In the Judeo-Christian tradition, the Holy Bible sanctified stories of the Great Father ordering Abraham to murder his only son Isaac, ordering all men among the faithful similarly: "The firstborn of thy sons thou shalt give unto me" (Exodus 22:28). Such demands culminated in the Great Father's sacrificing his own son, Jesus. The son's last words were a poignant cry to his father, echoed millions of times in the minds of dying young soldiers: Why has thou forsaken me?

Psychoanalysts recognize that many fathers (in patriar-chal/hierarchical cultures, where men must constantly compete with one another) are wrenched by a horrible jealousy toward their sons, so compelling that they *must* murder them, symbolically if not actually. The sons are rivals who will grow up to compete with and perhaps surpass them. These dynamics of the patriarchal family are currently being championed by the Christian Right, who oppose all statutes establishing children's rights—and, of course, women's rights—on the grounds that such legislation disrupts "God's line of authority in the home." The late Brother Roloff, who was director of the Lighthouse home for errant children in Texas, advised national radio audiences on fundamentalist Christian fatherhood: "A child needs enough punishment to break his stubborn will and let him throw up the white flag and say, 'Daddy, you win; I surrender.'" One can observe numerous individual exceptions to the model of father-son antagonism and there is obviously great richness and spiritual sustenance in the Judeo-Christian teachings, but the desire of the fathers to break the sons is a constant in patriarchal culture.

(5) Patriarchal culture alienates men from the life-giving processes, so their concern becomes the other half of the cycle: death. To be present at and assist in a birth, to cuddle and soothe a baby, to be involved intrinsically in a child's slowly flowering maturation over the years—all of this is denigrated as "women's work." Quite apart from such endeavors, (patriarchal) men focus their

attention on the eventual but imminent arrival of death, dwelling on it as an obsessive theme in much of their art and literature. In patriarchal tribal cultures, men display their kills, whether an animal, a human head, or a scalp, with the same pride that women show in holding up the newborn (Sanday, 1981). Birth imagery for the most horrifying death machine ever devised was used frequently in the Manhattan Project; finally, the men were able to cable President Truman: BABY IS BORN (Gerzon, 1982).

Otto Rank observed that the death-fear of the ego is lessened by the killing of another; that is, acting in the dominant role of giver of death distances one from the role of receiving it. Such action would be particularly appealing to people who are culturally forced into an obsession with death, for example, men under patriarchy. The only situation wherein large-scale killing is not merely allowed but enthusiastically encouraged is war.

(6) The bloody "red badge of courage" that warriors wear signifies honorable access to flowing blood in patriarchal cultures. During the June 12 peace marches in New York, San Francisco, and other cities in 1982, many of the demonstrators wore T-shirts or political buttons with the message *War Is Menstruation Envy*. Surely that is going too far! What does it mean? It refers to the extremely ancient association of blood with honor, sanctity, and power—which occurs in patriarchal culture only in a male context wrenched from women's procreative power. The blood mysteries of woman—her bleeding in rhythm with the moon, her growing *people* from her very flesh while she withheld the sacred blood and grew round as the full moon, her transforming her own blood into milk for the newborn—were the sacred foundation of humankind's first and longest lasting religion, dating from c. 25,000 B.C. When the invading waves of patriarchal, nomadic horsemen, the Indo-Europeans, migrated from the Eurasian steppes into peaceful, matrifocal Old Europe (c. 4500 B.C.), they introduced a religion centered on the warrior's glorious death in battle, bathed in his flowing blood.

Like other proponents of the new Indo-European religions, the Judaic fathers determined to invert and coopt the power of sacred blood. They announced that woman was actually a "foul sink," while the truly sacred blood was to be found in men's new imitative ritual of drawing blood from the male genital in circumcision. The invention of Christian mythology also played upon humankind's 25,000-year-old tradition of revering the sacred blood: Christ displayed his bleeding wounds, and the faithful drink it as their transubstantiated wine. The flowing blood of the soldier is celebrated on nearly every flag of our patriarchal nations. "Blood and Honor" was the motto of the Hitler Youth Movement, inscribed on a phallic implement of destruction, a dagger, and presented to each boy when he completed the initiation. Wartime spectacles of "blood'n'guts'n'glory" are the High Mass of patriarchy. *"You say that a good cause will even sanctify war; but I tell you, it is the good war that sanctifies every cause"* (Nietzsche).

*

The pressures of patriarchal values and assumptions entangle men in a closed system of possiblilities. Most men are uncomfortable with the six "necessary" conditions named here, but their very identity is so intermingled with patriarchal ideology that they cannot effectively critique the system that has pushed us so close to annihilation. After I had spent more than a year delineating the cultural forces of modern patriarchy that continue to feed militarism, I came across Professor Sanday's (1981) anthropological work, which identifies many of the same dynamics in those tribal cultures that are patriarchal and violent:

> Male dominance in myth and everyday life is associated with fear, conflict, and strife. . . . In these societies [described in *Female Power and Male Dominance*], males believe that there is an uncontrollable force that may strike at any time and against which men must be prepared to defend their integrity. The nature of the force and its source are not well defined, but often they are associated with female sexuality and reproductive functions. Men believe it is their duty to harness this force, with its power over life and death, to prevent chaos and to maintain equilibrium. They go to extraordinary lengths to acquire some of the power for themselves so that they will

not be impotent when [not *if*] it is time to fight. Men attempt
to neutralize the power they think is inherent in women by
stealing it, nullifying it, or banishing it to invisibility.

Most men in our patriarchal culture are still acting out old
patterns that are radically inappropriate for the nuclear age. To
prove dominance and control, to distance one's character from that
of women, to survive the toughest violent initiation, to shed the
sacred blood of the hero, to collaborate with death in order to hold
it at bay—all of these patriarchal pressures on men have traditionally reached resolution in ritual fashion on the battlefield. But
there is no longer any battlefield. Does anyone seriously believe
that if a nuclear power were losing a crucial, large-scale conventional war it would refrain from using its multiple-warhead nuclear
missiles because of some diplomatic agreement? The military
theater of a nuclear exchange today would extend, instantly or
eventually, to all living things, all the air, all the soil, all the water.

If we believe that war is a "necessary evil," that patriarchical
assumptions are simply "human nature," then we are locked into
a lie, paralyzed. The ultimate result of unchecked terminal patriarchy will be nuclear holocaust.

We have choices. The question is whether we have enough
time to achieve a major shift in thinking before any of the 50,000
nuclear warheads around us are exploded. The debates and discussions on the proposed nuclear freeze have revealed and strengthened
a vast and complex nationwide network of citizens concerned with
the probability of nuclear war. Those grassroots forums on current
political and economic influences on war should be broadened to
include such topics as: Do the boys and young men in our community, including our National Guardsmen, associate manhood
with going to war? Shall we oppose films and advertising that portray war and warheads as sexy and glamorous? Are our children
playing with war toys and our teenagers with videogames such
as "Missile Command," on which they practice dispatching and
destroying multiple-warhead missiles as if they were as benign as
model trains? Do we consider qualities of sensitivity and emotional/
psychological intimacy so unmanly that boys should serve a certain
amount of time in the military in order to have such "feminine"

tendencies squelched? If we refuse to play our-missiles-are-bigger-than-yours anymore, are we willing to devote attention to sane alternatives for structuring human relations, from local to international levels? Do we consider the Russian people "other" than fully human, hence deserving of the most destructive devices we can invent? Is the patriarchal ideal of dominance a self-destructive posture that terrorizes opponents into retaliation? Can we honor heroes who do not shed blood? Shall we honor our peacemakers as much as our famous generals?

*

The causes of recurrent warfare are not biological. Neither are they solely economic. They are also a result of patriarchal ways of thinking, which historically have generated considerable pressure for standing armies to be used. The inclusion of this fundamental dimension in our efforts to contain militarism and build a secure peace is not going to be initiated by the White House or the Congress; it is a "trickle up" raising of consciousness that has already begun. We can only hope it isn't too late—for the prenuclear, patriarchal assumptions that still guide our society are part of the deadly time lag Albert Einstein warned us about nearly thirty years ago: "The unleashed power of the atom has changed everything save our modes of thinking and we thus drift toward unparalleled catastrophes."

FACING HOLOCAUST

FACING A FEW OF THE FACTS

Something Big is going to happen! Something Big is going to happen! We have to prepare!

What is it? What's going to happen?

I don't know!

Then how can we prepare? How can we prepare for it if we don't know what it is?

I don't know! I don't know! Just prepare, that's all! Prepare!

*

The guru tells you about the Great Truth that remains the same throughout all eternity while everything else just comes and goes.

The prophet tells you you're in big trouble and it's going to get much worse if you don't clean up your act, and maybe it's too late anyway.

The commissar tells you what you're going to do for your own good whether you want to or not.

The revolutionary tells you your hour has come and nothing can stop you now.

The shrinks and their cousins tell you whatever you pay them to tell you.

The leaders, the newspapers and the TV tell you lies, lies, lies.

Where will you turn, baby, *where will you turn?*

*

The headlines are not reassuring. You laugh at them, shaking your head with gentle disbelief, and then forget them. Who really gives a shit anymore? Who can be seriously concerned about a situation so utterly hopeless? Only the well-intentioned fools, filled with outrage or alarm, who never seem to realize that all they're really doing with their efforts to save the world is throwing their own little twig into the conflagration, adding their little squeak to the roar.

Fools. Are they really fools? Or are they the salt of the earth, the models, the heroes and heroines who point the way for the rest of us?

Who can say what they are? Or what anyone is. The bottom's dropped out of the world.

*

What are you going to do? I mean *really*: what are you going to do? Do you actually believe anything is going to stop the drift toward disaster? The drift of an entire planet? Do you actually believe we're going to be saved? Everything is heading straight to hell, the whole thing is falling apart, the whole world is going insane. Do you really believe all this can be halted or reversed? *It's too late. It's all over. Just dig in.* Everything was always headed this way, building up to this — we can see that now — and we're the ones privileged to watch it happen. We're the generation privileged to know the whole story, the whole great drama, from the beginning to the end. We're going to see the curtain come down. Our understanding of humanity is the most profound. What difference does it make if it ends now or in a million years?

*

The whole past, every bit of it, everything that ever happened, is entirely vanished, gone completely. Whatever fragments survive exist only in our memories, and then only when we're actually remembering them, only in the living moment in which they are actually being remembered. The future, of course, also doesn't exist. No past, no future. Nothing exists but this living moment, right now, and even this moment, like memories of the past or anticipation of the future, is only held there by our minds.

So what is lost, and who loses anything, if the world comes to an end?

*

Many decent responsible people seem to have decided to face

the end enjoying music and screwing. If there's nothing we can do about it, what's wrong with celebrating life right up to the end, along with the rest of nature? Other decent responsible people shuffle around with downcast eyes and troubled expressions; they hope they'll be able to confront certain death with the dignity appropriate to a noble being in its hour of tragedy. Like the captain and the crew singing hymns on the deck of a sinking ship. Still others, also decent, also responsible, are determined to go down fighting, defiant to the last.

It'll be business as usual, however. Business as usual. Our ordinary nervous daily lives, nothing quite settled and nothing quite appropriate, exploded into sheer screaming terror. Don't you think so? Sure. And it's OK. Who are you to be critical?

*

Now you could say that we have to save the world for the sake of future generations, so humanity can continue to evolve toward its divine destiny, or that we have to save the world to keep the faith with past generations, so that their labor will not have been in vain. In either case, it's humanity itself we're supposed to be concerned about, "Humanity" with a capital H. Something bigger than you and me, in other words.

But you could also say fuck that way of thinking. Unless we choose to make them an issue, the dead and the unborn are out of the picture completely. They have nothing to lose, they can't suffer, and we don't owe them anything. There's nobody but us; we are what's at stake. We're the ones, we and our children, who have to figure out how to face this incredible nightmare. All by ourselves, and *for* ourselves.

*

Just think of it: the dead are going to kill the living! We're not doing this to ourselves. It's the momentum of the history they made, and the damage they did, that's going to kill us. We're not committing suicide, we're being murdered. By the dead! Talk about bad karma!

*

In the whole history of humanity, there have only been two human situations. The one that ended about fifty years ago, and ours.

True, there were other times when people thought the world was going to come to an end, although of course they were wrong. But it was always for a good reason, always as part of the scheme of things. Divine retribution, the end of a cosmic cycle, the arrival of the Kingdom of Heaven — there was always a meaning, so it was always acceptable.

But our situation is different.

Or at least it appears to be.

*

It's really just a question of style; there's no right and wrong in a terminal situation. Different people will face the end in different ways, that's all. There's nothing unworthy or debased in refusing to think about a calamity so immense, so beyond our comprehension; it's not more "elevated" to look it in the face than to ignore it. We're not morally required to try to save the world. To eat, drink and be merry is not shameful any more than to join organizations is exemplary. Everyone has a right to their way, and every way is just as human as every other way: they're all human — fully, completely, totally human. Make your choice, play your role, respect everyone.

*

Existence is clearly a gift. We have done nothing to earn or deserve it, so we have no right to complain if it is withdrawn. For awhile, we existed. For awhile, there was something rather than nothing, and that something was clearly a miracle glorious beyond glory, and we, whatever "we" are, woven somehow into that miracle, are a "place" where it becomes aware of itself. More could be said about all this, but it would just be glory heaped upon glory. The proper response in the recipient of a gift is gratitude.

*

You keep thinking that maybe somehow everybody's going

to pull it together at the last minute and save the world. A rally in the eleventh hour. The whole human race suddenly realizes it's now or never, and in one stupendous spiritual and physical exertion actually rises to meet the occasion. But at the same time you know this is a fantasy. You know what people are like, and you know what we're up against.

We became four billion interchangeable parts in one giant death machine and anything we do on the scale of the death machine's power is just more machinery. That's cold reality, feet on the ground. The ways we came to think and live and work, the end we created for ourselves by thinking and living and working in those ways, and the various ways in which we then confront that end *all add up to one life style*: it's all one reality, in other words, one circular dynamic. Preparing our end and confronting our end are the same process. To oppose our actual way of facing it with some fantasy about how we might save ourselves is nonsense: the situation and the response are a single reality, they cannot be separated. It could even be argued that this is the only way it could have happened, that all along, from the very beginning, this was our only destiny. Who knows? But look around you: you don't see what *should* be and you don't see what *shouldn't* be: you see what *followed*.

*

"What will we tell the children?"

A silly question. The children already know. Knowledge of the end is in the air we breathe, in every moment of our lives, every glance and tone of voice, every institution, artifact and encounter. We grow into it as naturally and inevitably as we grow into physical maturity. Knowledge of the end is everything, this whole reality. You don't have to worry about "telling the children." You can stop whining. We've already told them. With matchless eloquence.

*

You look at the pavement and imagine weeds, the same weeds we see now, sprouting through acres of rubble and up-ended slabs, gradually covering the lower levels of evidence. Except at the "epicenter" — one of our new words — the skeletons of buildings will still stand, maybe tipped a bit from the vertical. And of course there'll be automobile wreckage everywhere — chassis, engines, bumpers, seat springs: probably strips of fused rubber baked into the cement. And bones. There'll be bones. Bombed-out cities. Silent streets.

The urban environment is beginning to appear temporary. We know that soon the Earth will be moving in again, so beautiful and calm. It'll cover up all this shit. New things will be born.

You look up at the sky. It's going to split open and explode from horizon to horizon. We all glance speculatively up at the sky now, from time to time: not in actual fear, but because *that's where it will come from.*

*

You love so many things about life, there's so much to love. Is that why the end seems so terrible? Because all those things will be no more? Singing, laughing, swimming, loving, the sight and taste of Earth's numberless marvels, the never-ending shower of miracles: *everything*: the whole soaring mind-blowing ecstasy of just *being* here, in a *universe*, *digging it*. All those wonderful beautiful things, gone forever. Or is it the suffering? The moaning mutilated survivors, begging for water, the terrible radiation sicknesses, the agony of children? Or is it simply the personal fear of pain and death? Or is it just the great colossal tragedy of it, the waste, the senseless destruction?

Or are you one of those pugnacious types, completely disillusioned with human beings, who really doesn't care? Too full of a kind of sullen battle-hardened self-respect to waste your time talking a lot of crap about all these things no one is going to do anything about anyway. You're part of the picture also. Tough as nails. You've been around. You look people straight in the eye, you know the bastards are lying and you don't back off an inch. Belligerent: you stick your chin out. And just like any of the rest of us you might die while you're "on hold," listening to muzak or a recording, impatiently tapping on an ashtray with your ball-point pen. Lots of people will die "on hold," fuming with vexation, enraged that they might have been forgotten, trying to keep from slamming the phone down and losing their place in line and having to start all over again. What a way to die!

*

If this is the end, we ought to exit in style: we ought to flaunt an undaunted spirit before the eyes of the universe. We should leave in processions, dressed in costumes, strutting and shaking tambourines, drinking beer and tossing roses, with flags and floats, brass bands, jazz bands and cheer leaders setting the rhythm, like a Mardi Gras parade. All the cultures of the world represented, all our magnificent achievements. A festival of humanity. The gods are skeptical about us, you know; they scratch their chins and exchange glances. We ought to leave them something to remember us by. We screwed up, no doubt about it. But when we were great we were the greatest: no one could hold a candle to us. We've got class, pride, guts and soul. We've got *verve*. We're not going to look like losers. Right? Let's show them how the *humans* bow out. In style!

*

You don't want to fight on either side. A plague on both their houses! You just want to be left alone. When history comes rapping on the door you want to sneak out the window and slip away into the hills till it's all over. Live on the Earth where nothing ever happens: no history, no progress, no nothing: just the four seasons, the sun, the soil and the sky.

You don't need the slogans and the programs. You don't need the parties, movements, alliances, coalitions and committees, the meetings, conferences and conventions, the leaflets and pamphlets, the angry or jubilant fanatics screaming from the podium. There's a vicious unconscious menace lurking behind all political passion: you can see it in the way they size you up. Violence, verbal or real: that's all it is. Power: the struggle for power and the continuous identification of enemies. No matter how solemnly they may abjure it, no matter how loudly they may deplore it, political people have secretly reconciled themselves to carnage: that was the real decision they made: all the rest is excuses.

So avoid history. Stay out of it, keep a low profile, duck and hide. Be committed to life. History is just one long tormented agonized march to hell. Can't they see it? Can't they see they're all part of the same death trip, no matter which side they're on? History is madness, suffering and madness: we're either conscripted into it or our allegiance is seduced and then betrayed. Stay out of it. Have the guts to say no to a noble cause. Be a history-dodger. Everybody else is going to die.

You just want to be left alone, that's all. But you know there's no escape. There are no hills to hide in. There are no hills anymore. It's just a matter of time. You pound the table now and then in wild-eyed defiance, but inwardly you crumpled long ago. You shuffle through one week after another. At twilight, seated by the window, you raise a haggard glare toward the fading light and pray.

*

Right up to the very end people will still be going through the motions. That's what so incredible about it. Everything we do is unreal, everything is bullshit, madness and hell, yet nothing can break the spell that keeps it going. We're all like mechanical dolls, busily puttering and scurrying around, completely absorbed in our own little worlds — and if we ever glance over our shoulders, hastily, vaguely startled, at the giant shadow of death looming bigger and darker on the horizon every day, we only return to those little private worlds, those dreamy feverish pursuits, with a resolution even more urgent, an energetic absorption even more desperate, as if the only response to a horrible reality is an even more single-minded devotion to fantasy. You could also say that people become so totally overwhelmed by the pressure of survival, as the pace speeds up and conditions deteriorate, that they simply lose the ability to stand back and get an overview, they can't break the grip of the details, they can't stop running — not that it would make any difference anyway. At any rate, there's no way to stop the pretense because there's no way to stop the machine.

And all this, it should be quite clear, is no one's fault. There's no guilt and no responsibility. Everyone's doing their level best. This is the way things happen at the end, that's all. If people could do something about it, if we could act, it wouldn't be the end!

*

Every now and then you think of someone you know as a person who is also, just like you, living at the time of the end, and you realize, as you must and with humble irony, that sharing this fate is now your deepest bond with other people, the new and final foundation of our common humanity. Take anyone you know, look at them from this point of view, and you see them as they really are.

Take a very simple example. Someone's seated in a restaurant absorbed in the menu, trying to decide what he wants to eat for dinner that night. So many things look delicious! How to choose? He laughs helplessly and a bit self-consciously at his dilemma, aware of the disparity between the intentness of his approach and the triviality of the occasion, and, offering absurd suggestions and beginning to feel impatient, everyone jokes about his gluttony, his indecisiveness of character, his well-known history of vacillation and ambivalence. Finally he throws up his hands and plunges into a selection, the waiter wearily smiles, rolling his eyes, and the subject of discussion changes instantly. Everyone is animated.

Innocence. While all this was going on you suddenly thought of the end and the word that came to mind was innocence. He finally decided on spaghetti and meatballs, his original enthusiasm before all the other dishes caught his eye, and he looked sad and preoccupied when everyone filed out.

Innocent. Therefore condemned. We eat, we drink, we screw, we sleep. We're simple. We can only handle a small scene. A handful of people is all we'll ever remember, a handful of people is all we'll have time enough to love. A circle of friends, a family. One face, just one face, can overwhelm us! History, the immensity of history . . . it's beyond us. It baffles us. Confused, suspicious, vaguely insulted, we refuse to budge, we just hold our own: with dignity. Everyone likes to eat out now and then.

But the thought goes further. In this smallness our strength resides. It's our native ground. Our stronghold — for whatever that's worth.

*

You go on trying to do things the right way even though there doesn't seem to be any point in it anymore. Maybe it's the instinct of good workmanship. Or maybe it's because you know how terrible the alternative is: character rot; your personality disintegrates and you become some kind of bum or degenerate. One of those people who smile confidently but plead with their eyes at the same time; you can't tell whether they're begging for help or hoping you won't see through the facade: it's probably both. A tremendous variety of human types flower at the end, all sorts of people, all sorts of improbable combinations. The end is a great stimulus to individuality.

But you have to go on trying, you have to keep the faith. Even when everything seems futile. The end is a great challenge. We have to struggle to speak, to explain things, articulate ideas when the whole world to which the words refer is about to be destroyed; we have to exhaust ourselves in endless haggling about right and wrong, in endless disputes which always become insane as the night wears on because the world in which the dispute takes place is itself insane; we have to throw ourselves into all sorts of endeavors haunted by the bitter sinking certainty that there'll be something flawed or false in them every step of the way, something empty no matter how sincere our effort, because the substance has dropped out of life, because nothing is ever what it seems to be anymore. The end is a *great* challenge! It brings out the best in us!

*

Listening to music now is no small thing. If there are any survivors interested in reminiscing about how it happened, they'll certainly spend some time talking about the role of music at the end.

Think of it this way:

We can hear the same piece of music as many times as we want to, and each time it's the same: each time is the *same* time. Each time we hear it we escape from linear one-way time and enter into the eternal present of cosmic time, an eternal continually repeatable *now*: we enter another world, a world outside of time, the timeless world of the music. Music, in other words, *defies the end*. Listening to music we escape from history, which is precisely what we long to do every minute of our lives.

No wonder we turn to music almost religiously! It's a refuge and a consolation, beautiful, invulnerable and untranslatable, within and without at once, at once nowhere and everywhere, as faithful to us as we are to it. Music is instantly aware of every secret huddling fretful and desolate in our souls; it speaks to our every mood and weather, even those of which we aren't conscious; it offers itself fully and indiscriminately to everyone who approaches it with a pure heart, regardless of their past deeds. It calms our troubled devotion, uplifts our battered spirits, pacifies our bewildered weariness and renews our will to live. It allows us to forget. We love it, we love those who write and perform it for us, we can't imagine life without it. We stumble home from work, exhausted and tense, and head straight for the stereo. First things first.

And what does all this remind us of? You guessed it! Music is just like God! They must have something to do with Each Other!

*

You try to be aware of the subtle changes, the insidious gradual transformations that go on unnoticed till all of a sudden one day you pause, look around yourself stunned, and realize you've been living in a dream — as if some huge vicious animal had been creeping up soundlessly behind you all along, inch by inch, waiting till it was close enough to pounce. You try, but life is very tricky; it's hard to stay on top of things.

There's nothing inside holding it all together. That's the problem. Anything can happen. Anybody can do anything. No matter how crazy or far out it is, there's always an argument to defend it. Always an excuse, a point of view, a new interpretation.

You try to stay on top of things, you try to protect your life. But there are snipers smirking in every tree, training their sights on you. Ambushes and imposters. Treachery. Who knows what your kids will drop on your lap tomorrow? Who knows what's happening right this minute that'll make you mutter a year from now, ruefully, "I wish I'd seen it coming"? You hunger for something sacred. Some changeless truth avowed by everyone, something clean and pure and shining and untouchable, everlasting, that isn't even in the same world as all this shit. Another world completely. Something absolutely the opposite of this.

There's nothing you can rely on here. That's the trouble. There's no foundation, nothing you can rely on.

*

Graduation ceremonies always make you think of the end. The irony of the word "commencement"! It's too much. The feeling is most poignant, of course, if it's an elementary school. All the bright shining faces, the girls flouncing around in their party dresses and the boys trying to sit still on the stage, everyone chatting, darting, breathless with secrets. No problem more urgent than stifling laughter. What obscene madness can have possessed us? What devil from hell? You fight back tears. All these little people, so bursting with life.

Life, life, life. A whole planet teeming with life. How did it ever happen? What's it all for? From the individual point of view the aim is a completed life span: just live out the allotted span of life. But there's a larger picture, we are told, a larger truth. What can that be? There's just no way to know.

*

When you think about it now, with the so-called struggles of the sixties a full decade behind you, when you really try to envision what might save us or emerge victorious from the wreckage, one thing, at least, is clear: it won't be anything organized and goal-oriented. Forget that. It won't be an organization or a party or a movement or any of that kind of crap. It won't have a plan or a purpose or a program and it won't think about means and ends. It won't think at all, as a matter of fact. It won't be future-oriented. All that stuff is where we die: it's history. You can see that now. No regrets, but you can see that.

You've decided, instead, that the world will be saved by people who aren't trying to save it. You've watched them in action. Now you smile when you're alone, confident, detached, serene — although you never really feel alone anymore. You don't hope, you don't fear, you no longer worry about survival. You've seen something. There's no way to describe it. Either you see it or you don't. It's everywhere, it's everything, it's invisible to the eye, and the thing that acts most like it is grass. Just plain old grass.

*

So what if we become mutants after a holocaust? What's a mutant, anyway? Maybe we're mutants right now. Whatever adapts belongs there, that's the way it works. If it's alive and kicking, Good Luck to it. Good luck, you funny-looking thing! Hang in there! Life is beautiful!

*

How do the politicians become insane? How do they become the enemies of the human race? It's really incredible when you think about it. Why doesn't just *one* of them ever go insane in public, crack up under the pressure or actually plan it in advance, and start screaming the truth at a press conference, just *one* of them? Why hasn't it ever happened? Are they *really* androids, plastic robots? Have they been drugged? By whom? Are they pre-selected and trained by some secret organization? How do they learn to smile and talk that way? It's truly a miracle: a testimony to our limitless potentials. And that's just the politicians. If you try to imagine where the "military leaders" come from you could *really* go out of your mind! Those guys are *not like us!*

*

People come up with some pretty far-fetched ideas at the end.

We are urged, for example, in response to the emptiness that invades our souls, to share our real feelings and express our emotions freely. Then we won't feel lonely. We're also urged to have fun — just do anything that makes you feel good, it doesn't make any difference what it is. Be happy. Some people, on the other hand, prescribe hard work to reclaim our errant spirits from self-indulgence. Everyone has an answer. There's no shortage of answers.

You smile: faintly, contemptuously, wearily, remotely. Answers. Emptiness. Childishness. You'll just live your life out, that's all. There are things that must be done regardless of circumstances. These are the things you'll do.

*

Everything that happens now is a portent. Economic trends, protests, "scientific breakthroughs," murders, election returns, nuclear and chemical developments, teenage styles, musical styles, the latest statistics, the latest bizarre stories, the academy awards, official announcements . . . everything points toward some kind of breakdown. Toward chaos. Every new piece of information jibes with all the others, every detail confirms the thesis, every event is new evidence. We nod with grim satisfaction. The universal premonition is validated without fail.

Strange to live in such times. Actually eerie. You wonder what it was like to live before all this happened, before it fell apart, when the world made sense and there was a scheme of things and everything had its proper place. Tragedies could befall us, and certainly did, there was evil, but nothing could threaten the foundation: that was impregnable. No matter what happened, people must have felt basically secure: the ground beneath their feet remained firm. They had confidence. That was probably the fundamental feeling. Confidence. Faith. Confidence in what, though? You can't even imagine what they had confidence in! Order? Justice? God? Probably God.

*

If there's a nuclear holocaust, what will be remembered? Who will be doing the remembering? In what kind of setting? Filthy men and women wrapped in scorched blankets, huddled over fires kindled from the debris of incomprehensible ruins, whispering, in desperate awe, the fearful explanations of their wild-eyed sages? Mutants, only approximately human, lisping the conjectures of approximately human brains? Who knows? Maybe the damage will be much more restricted. But if the self-consciousness of world civilization is annihilated with its technology, or drastically degraded, which seems likely, humanity, or its descendants, will probably only remember that there was once a terrible fiery calamity of some kind, a great Judgment or Day of Reckoning given as punishment for some cosmic transgression. It'll become a myth. A myth about pride, a lesson in humility. Which is what it really is, of course. A lesson in humility. On the other hand, it might be remembered as the consequence of a sneak attack, long foreseen and feared, launched by the Russians — or the Americans or the Chinese, the communists or the bourgeoisie. That would be too bad. Wouldn't it?

*

Maybe the cities *ought* to be destroyed. Did you ever think of that? Maybe they no longer advance the cause of life, if they ever did, and it's time for them to be recalled. Removed, like tumors, from the face of the Earth they disfigure. Maybe some great surgeon in the sky, a close friend of Mother Nature, is pulling on his rubber gloves right now and selecting the scalpel. It's been argued that these things take care of themselves, you know: that the world strives for balance and harmony and that in the long run equilibrium is always restored. "Whatever goes against the Tao will not last long."

Crazy talk. But with a ring of truth. Think of it: the cities are where history is made. And it's history that's coming to an end. History, cities, death. Death of all kinds. What do you go to the country for? What are you trying to get away from?

*

Sometimes you speculate that key people may rebel at the

last minute, just flat out disobey orders, refuse to push the buttons that fire the missiles. You wonder about it. A spontaneous mutiny in the name of sanity: they just won't be able to go through with it. Maybe; but don't count on it. These people have been very carefully trained. "Programmed" would be more precise: they're not really "people" as we ordinarily use the word. Anyway, you can be quite sure that this contingency has been foreseen and the appropriate safeguards incorporated into the system. They're thorough, our friends in the "command centers." They know about "the human factor." They've studied it from every angle, with great sympathy. Even with compassion. Genuine compassion.

*

What you imagine when you think of the end is the wild flight from the cities. Millions of people scrambling to their cars in a frenzy of terror, hurling children and food into the back seats and leaping behind the wheel, millions of cars smashing into each other at intersections in the mad race for the freeways, fist fights at every telephone, knives and bullets at every gas station, the air filled with smoke, sirens, gunshots and screams. The missiles are on their way.

This picture is printed on everyone's mind. It doesn't take very much imagination. And as for the aftermath, maybe you saw the films taken by Japanese cameramen in Hiroshima and Nagasaki. No words can describe it. No philosophy, no spiritual posture, no human resource whatever, is equal to it. When the lights go on everyone is silent, in tears.

You inhabit this reality. If you could think your way around it or above it or through it or out of it, you would — but you can't. The mind stops dead right here, at the end. It makes perfect sense not to think about it.

*

You see it this way, you see it that way, you see it any way you want to see it, you don't see it all. It's the end of the world.

I'm a good person, I'm a humanitarian person, I love the planet, I love people, I want everybody to be happy. I want peace.

But this thing has gotten out of hand. . . . There's just no way to fit it into my schedule. . . . Sure, sometimes I lie awake at night wondering what's going to happen to the good old human race. I worry about it. So what? I fall asleep, I wake up in the morning, I go back to work. What else am I supposed to do? . . . I love it all. I love the whole thing, the whole planet and everything on it, especially the oceans, I love water, but I love it all really and if this is the end, well, it's just the end. Right? Everything comes to an end. . . . I just can't get into it. I mean I just can't get all that worked up about it. . . . I think about the children. Why should they have to die? They're innocent. No future for them. It's not fair. I don't care so much about myself, I've lived a little, I've seen life, you know? But the kids should have a chance. I have kids. . . . Yeah, I know the world's coming to an end. Who doesn't? I just don't have time to worry about that right now. I have my own problems to deal with. . . . It's like Rome. It's the fall of the Roman Empire all over again. History repeats itself. You never step into the same river twice. It's a cycle. Over and over again. The same things. Here today, gone tomorrow. . . . Well, I think our President's doing the best he can. We have to be strong to defend ourselves, and they have to know it. That's the only way to preserve peace. I know it's a terrible way, but it's all we can do right now. . . . I'm just going to live my life out, that's all. I'm going to hope for the best. It's bigger than I am. . . . I just can't bear to think about it. It's too terrible, just too terrible. I cry when I think about it. I just cry. I lie in bed at night and cry. Sometimes even during the day, when I'm alone. . . . Well, I don't know. I don't know that there's any point in getting so excited about it. Letting it interfere with your life. I mean, why? What are you going to do about it? . . . It's a judgment, that's all. It's a judgment. You break the rules, you pay for it. You sow and you reap. It's a law. . . . Sometimes I wish the bombs would fall already, just to get it all over with. . . . I never talk about it because it's too emotional, you know? But sometimes I think maybe we should all talk about it. Maybe we could do something then. I don't know. . . . I feel terrible. But what can I do? What can I do? Little me! . . . Sometimes I think, why did

I have to live in this time? Why was I born in this time? I'm not meant to be here. . . . Sure, but what's it got to do with me? What's it got to do with me? What do you want from me? I'm nobody. Mister Nobody. . . . If it ever happens, you know, the missiles, the warheads, whatever they are, the holocaust and all that, I'm sure I'll be totally terrified, just freak out completely. I'll probably die of fear. But in a way it all seems so unreal. It just seems unreal. It's hard to take it seriously. . . . I've heard about it, I know about it, now just leave me alone. What do you expect me to say? . . . I don't think I can die. I know it sounds crazy, but I just know I won't die completely. Some part of me will go on living. Nothing ever dies. My friends say I'm a mystic. . . . It makes me love everything even more. Isn't that the way it should be? I mean I just love everything now, I love life, I love people. I love the city. If it's going to be the end of the world we should love it while we have the chance. . . . I know everybody thinks about it. I just know, even though we never talk about it. It's our shared secret. I can tell. I have insight. . . . I think we should go in there first. First strike. We can do it. They're just holding back because of the communists in government. Nobody wants to admit it, but it's true. They can't hide it anymore. People are beginning to open their eyes. . . . Once I asked my father if he ever thought about it. He looked away and mumbled something. I couldn't catch it. I think he said sometimes. I never asked him again. My mother told me not to talk about it. . . . We don't need those pesticides. We don't need all those chemicals. Cancer, hydrogen bombs. Pollution. It's sick. The whole world is sick. I don't know how it happened. It's money, really. Money's behind it all. The almighty dollar. . . . I just hope it happens after I'm gone. I know that sounds terribly selfish, but I really feel that way. I don't want to see it. I want to die with hope. . . . Oh I don't know. When you gotta go, you gotta go. Right? I live with it. It doesn't stop me from enjoying life. I enjoy life right up to the hilt. And then some! . . . It was science. Too much science. Not enough humanity. . . . I think about my future. I plan for it. I don't just give up and not work for anything because the world may come to an end. Nothing is without risk. I don't throw in the towel. The world is beyond my control. I'm not. That's my philosophy. . . . Oh we deserve it. People are so stupid. If they're going to do all these terrible things, they deserve what they get. . . . Well what do you expect me to do about it? Walk right into Russia and tell them to throw all those bombs away? They'd shoot me on the spot! . . . You just look at it. Overpopulation, the military situation, all this violence, the hot spots, the economy, the build-up. Nuclear power. The hawks. Where else can it go? Right? You can see it coming. It's inevitable. . . . I used to dream about a good life. A good clean life, decent, you know what I mean? Neighbors, friends, everybody helping everybody else, a good environment for the kids. Forget it. . . . It's greed. Everybody wants it all for themselves. Instead of sharing, working things out, they try to get it all. Me first, number one. So there's tension. Everybody's afraid. A cold war. Bigger bombs. Then one day, Bang! It's all over. Just like the cave men. . . . Think of all this suicide. There's much more of that than you think. Why? Because they have no hope. They see no future. They see no reason to go on living. . . . The pollution is slow, the nuclear war is fast. That's the only difference. It's all going the same way. . . . It makes me appreciate everything more. I see how precious everything is. Every moment. I wouldn't have realized. I don't take anything for granted now. I'm more open. . . . I'm ready for it. If it's going to happen I'm going to be ready for it. That's the way I live my life. Take it as it comes. . . . It's just disgusting. It's tragic. Sometimes I think it'a all a bad dream. I just refuse to admit it into my life. . . . Well, it's one of those things that everybody knows about but we just can't do anything about it. . . . Once I really looked it in the face. I can't explain it. But I know there isn't any end. It just isn't the end. It's something else. It's just the way things are, that's all. . . . It won't be so bad. A lot of this is exaggerated. Everybody won't die. We'll rebuild. Like they did overseas after World War Two. Now you go over there, you wouldn't even know there was a war. . . . This was all predicted. It's in the Bible. All you have to do is read the Bible. . . . I hate them. I hate the people who are doing this to us and to our children. To the environment. I don't see why they're allowed to live. They have no right to live. . . . I used to care but now I don't. What's the use? . . . How do you know who to believe? Everybody tells you something different. Everybody's got their line. Interest groups, special interests. The war machine, the ecology people. The oil companies. Even the doctors lie. . . . If it happens it's God's Will. We don't have to understand it. It's beyond us. . . . I still have hope. I'm one of the crazy idealists who still have hope. We'll pull out of it. We always have. We still have free will. . . . We've abused the Earth. We've abused Creation. Our societies have been irresponsible. We've lived by false values. Now it's all coming back at us. . . . It's a pretty messed-up world. I think about it a lot. I don't have any easy answers. . . . Yeah, it's my life! My one and only life! I want to live! . . . Once someone whispered to me in a bus that the world was coming to an end. I was embarrassed. I didn't know what to say. But I never forgot her. I remember her face.

NIGHT OF THE AUK (excerpt)

ACT III

SCENE I

THE TIME: *A short while later.*

RUSSELL *(still straining his eyes through the binoculars)*
The bastards!
The maniacs!
Which is their continent?
Which is ours?

(he calls to Mac)

What do you hear?

MAC
Nothing! Nothing!

RUSSELL *(turning away, Dr. Bruner takes his place at the lenses.)*
Smashed them! I always said
We should have smashed them,
Exterminated them
A dozen years ago!
I've got to get down there, quickly, quickly!

(he has moved restlessly over to where Mac sits listening)

Well? Well?

MAC
Nothing!

RUSSELL *(roughly, shoving him aside)*
Let me!

(he sits at the Communications Center and begins to tune the

*frequency dial and listen to the headphones. Mac moves over
to where the doctor still stands looking out.)*

MAC *(he simply stands there; he makes no attempt to use the
binoculars)*
Is it . . . really happening?

BRUNER
The color—unmistakable—fission of the elements!
God help them!

MAC
Are they bombing us . . .
Or we them?

BRUNER
I stood in a graveyard, in college days,
And yelled, "Hey, bones! Hey, bones!
Who's right, who's wrong?
Hey, bones! Hey, bones!"

RUSSELL *(calling)*
Lieutenant! Get to your station!

(moving toward the computer)

I'll get the figures of arrival.

*(MAC goes back to the Communications Center as RUSSELL
goes back to the central computer. DR. BRUNER stands looking
out into space a moment longer, as ROHNEN slowly moves over
to him)*

ROHNEN
Is it . . . truly war?

BRUNER
It is war . . .
I say the word—it has no meaning.
How can they *truly* be at war?
I remember when we first turned the key of formula
And mocked the Sun,

Some of the architects of fission
Built a clock,
And set it ticking
And said for all to hear:
"We have moved the clock of science a hundred years ahead
    of time.
That ticking is a time bomb of extinction
Unless you quickly move equal years ahead
Within your own hearts."

(he turns away)

Within *my* own heart! . . .

ROHNEN
What will become
Of my golden voyage now?

MAC
Satellite One!
I got them!
They're sending on C.W. now!

(as RUSSELL *begins to talk, he waves him quiet)*

I can hardly—

(decoding)

"It—began—when—"

(he strains to hear)

I cannot hear!
No, there it is again!
"Living hell—
Retaliation missiles—"

RUSSELL
I knew it!
They!

BRUNER

They! They!
Does agony have a nationality!

RUSSELL

I'm a soldier!
They are my enemy!
What the hell are *you?*

MAC *(straining to hear)*

The words . . . I just can't understand. . . .

ROHNEN

Send them a message!
Ask them have they forgotten I am returning!

RUSSELL

He is returning!
Jesu!

ROHNEN

Listen only to me,
and send—

MAC

Wait, wait!

(he lifts a puzzled face)

The words—he's sending now—
I don't understand them—

(slowly, as he decodes)

"you—triggered—off—."

RUSSELL

What the hell is that!

ROHNEN

It doesn't matter!
Tell them—

MAC *(straining to hear)*
Nothing more!
Faded into nothing!

ROHNEN
Will you listen to me?
Send them a message—
Tell them I am a non-combatant—

RUSSELL *(interrupting)*
"You—triggered—off"!

> *(he slams fist into hand as he turns toward* ROHNEN*)*

Yes! Of course! You!

> *(as the others look at him in amazement)*

You and your strutting oratory,
They heard you!
In collective fear they listened to you take clear title to the
    Moon,
A launching platform for a million warheads!
And so they lifted collective fists,
And smashed out in collective fright!
Now tell me this:
Are we winning,
Are we losing,
And, damn you,
Where's *my* place down there
To make a stand?

ROHNEN *(dazedly to* BRUNER*)*
Why didn't they wait! . . .

RUSSELL *(explosively)*
Wait!

> *(he turns to the porthole again, intent on what he sees through
> the binoculars)*

ROHNEN

Yes, wait!

The completion of this great flight was my own
fulfillment!

And theirs!

The sky could be release for them!

The sky could be escape for them!

The sky could be their own salvation, too!

(he turns to BRUNER*)*

Why didn't they wait!

BRUNER

That was my own naive hope—

Not violence,

But in the slow growth

Of man's own maturity. . . .

Yet what waits, Lewis . . . what stays?

Everything on Earth

And in the skies,

Transmuting unseen, second by millisecond,

Nothing static, nothing certain,

The firmest mold of state

With glittering cupola of high resolve,

The frailest night fly balleting in summer arc-light,

The basalt mountain,

The clod of dirt,

The child, the old,

You, I,

This hand, this breath,

All is changing . . .

Only change itself is everlasting. . . .

RUSSELL *(suddenly; he has been looking through binoculars again)*

Satellite One!

I see it!

There!

(DR. BRUNER and MAC *move up to him*)

To the right
At two o'clock!

BRUNER
I see— I see—
Bright reflection—

ROHNEN
Where? Where?

MAC (*ears intent to the receiver*)
It's the Satellite!
Space one!

> (RUSSELL *moves over quickly to the computer and punches the keys*)

ROHNEN (*eyes to glasses*)
It'll be all right now!
It'll be all right!

RUSSELL
Two hours, thirty minutes, twenty seconds more
And we'll have ourselves a grandstand seat!
Then you'll see what crop
Those bastards reap
For their aggression!
You'll see—

> (*they all cry out as a blinding flare of light, through the porthole, momentarily lights up the interior of the Space Ship. They crowd around the glass and stare out.*)

MAC (*tensely*)
Satellite One!

ROHNEN
I— I can't see—

BRUNER (*in awe*)
One sheet of flame. . . .

RUSSELL
They blasted it out of the sky!

ROHNEN
Where will we land now?

(he screams the words)

Where will we land?

THE CURTAIN FALLS SWIFTLY

ACT III

SCENE II

THE TIME: *Two hours later*

> AT CURTAIN RISE: ROHNEN *and* MAC *are at the Communications Center;* RUSSELL *is at the instrument panel; the doctor is looking out of the Earthward observation glass.*

ROHNEN
Keep on trying, keep on trying!
Send the signals endlessly!
Tell them I am neither combatant nor enemy.
I lead a Scientific Expedition—International—
My only purpose one of common good, of universal knowledge!
If we are lost, they lose all that I bring to them from Outer
   Space within this sacred vessel!
Yes, send them that! They lose! They lose!
Tell them to send a ship
Into space to bring us back to Earth!
Tell them I will reward them—any sum—they've but to ask it!
Keep on sending! Make them hear you!

> (MAC, *face tense, continues to work the telegraph key.* RUSSELL *moves slowly over to where the doctor stands by the porthole)*

BRUNER
The stockpiles of fission
Are afire with spendthrifts. . . .

RUSSELL *(wearily)*
Is it night there? . . .
Did the missiles sneak in darkness? . . .
Are we on knees or they? . . .

(DR. BRUNER shakes his head hopelessly)

RUSSELL
I wouldn't want the answer. . . .

(at the doctor's look)

The enemy's without face,
The victory's without voice,
And I'm permanently detached from duty!
Yes, by a rendezvous—

(he looks at his wristwatch)

At 0-600
With a crematorium! . . .

BRUNER *(softly)*
0-600. . . .

RUSSELL
I checked it out on the computer . . .
Very definite, that damned transistorized impersonality! . . .
Will it bother you the waiting, doctor!

BRUNER
Every man waits,
How long, how long? . . .
We know. . . .

*(the two men stand for a moment in a silence broken only
by the sound of the radio telegraph key)*

RUSSELL *(deliberating throwing himself out of the thought of
death)*
Have you heard the size of the golden carrots
He's been dangling in front of Mac's nose
To send those urgent nothings into nothing?

And Mac, in the green optimism of his years,
Functions in the palpitating hope
That somehow the rescuing cavalry
Will gallop up the Milky Way
With neon banners flying!
I don't imagine you've got any fresh green optimism, doctor?

BRUNER *(his eyes beyond the porthole)*
The flashes—when will there be an end to them?

RUSSELL *(looking out the porthole again)*
I'll say this much for him—
Our Leader used one small piece of foresight
In choosing you and me!
At least we have no blood-ties down in that hell-fire
For whom to wet this place with bitter lamentations!

BRUNER
Yes . . .
We are the Fortunate Two. . . .

RUSSELL
Doctor,
I'm sorry about before—
Hitting you over the head with the flag!

BRUNER *(his eyes still looking out the Earth-side bubble)*
It is all right . . . I have loved my country. . . .

RUSSELL
Sure, sure!

BRUNER
I have always been loyal to the dream,
The ever-improving dream. . . .

RUSSELL
Yeah, sure!
But if they've been throwing half as much as we at them,
Or the reverse,
Then the only loyalties left

Are to the deepest bomb shelters,
And the lead shielding,
And the pumps
Sucking that filthy fissioned air
Through filters!

BRUNER *(softly)*
What have they done
To the beautiful Earth. . . .

RUSSELL
Who gives a damn?
That's not my problem now!

> *(in the silence we hear, again,* ROHNEN's *voice as he dictates to the radio man)*

RUSSELL *(he looks quickly over toward* ROHNEN)
"You triggered off the war!"
Did I really deify the bastard with powers of war?

BRUNER
I thought you spoke an echo of the truth. . . .

RUSSELL
Jesu, you yourself spoke the facts when you said that nothing
    waits!
And Military Chiefs have human bellies,
Human nerve-ends, human backsides,
And that push-button war could well have started
From a belly-ache, a nervous tremor,
Too much Vodka, or a short-circuit in a San Francisco standby—

BRUNER *(the binoculars at his eyes)*
Ended!

RUSSELL
Huh!

> *(he quickly looks through the binoculars)*

Jesu! Black as blindness!

(he looks at his watch)

Not quite sixty minutes!
The One-Hour War!
They missed it by one whole hour,
The General Staff!
Yeah, they'd figured throw it or return it massive, and inside
of two hours—knockout!

(his face grows somber)

Or defeat!
The hell with that!

*(he turns sharply away and goes back to his desk where he
sits and begins to write in the log.*
MAC *moves over to where the doctor still stands by the
porthole)*

MAC *(kneading his tired fingers as he indicates* ROHNEN *who is now
talking with quiet intensity into the hand microphone)*
Did you hear him?
He's offering a million bucks for anyone who'll come upstairs
and get us out of here!

(at the doctor's silence)

Is it still going on?

BRUNER
We think it's ended . . .

*(*MAC *sits at the binoculars and looks out. After a few seconds,
he slowly turns away)*

MAC
What's the matter with me, doc?
It's black,
And yet I see it clear as if it's lit up on a screen:
The dead, the burning dead, my mother, Dorothy! . . .
And yet I sit here . . . cold . . .
Are you . . . cold? . . .

BRUNER

I am an old glacier. . . .
I stand ice-covered. . . .

MAC

But why? What's wrong with us?
Why don't I cry? For them! At least for me!

BRUNER

Perhaps each of us has lived with evil for too long. . . .

MAC

But murderers have wept!

BRUNER

Yes, in another, younger time.
Then men did wrong but always under the censoring eye of
    God!
The eyes of God were burned out long before—

(*he indicates beyond the porthole*)

That flaming Hour;
In the racial gas chambers,
In the test-tube crematoriums under toadstool clouds!
We and our fathers have lived through too much horror and
    deceit!
The scar tissues have thickened over pity and compassion!

MAC (*slowly, as he hangs up the binoculars*)
Do you know how much time we have?

BRUNER

Yes.

MAC

I do not think I want to know. . . .
Did we really trigger it off?
Is there a chance of another space ship relaying us on to a safe
    landing?
How will it end—
Will we hit the air

And flare out like a match tip?
Or will we curve off into space
And be like them,
Frozen in a wandering tomb? . . .

(he shakes his head in wonder)

My questions runneth over!

BRUNER *(wearily)*
I have no more answers. . . .

MAC
When I was a kid,
At breakfast table my father would always start his newspaper
    reading the obituaries.
He'd say to mother
"Hey, do you know who died?"
And I'd sit there shivering, thinking:
"Someday, somewhere, somebody'll say:
'Hey, do you know who died?'
And it'll be *me!*"

BRUNER *(going up to him and putting his hand on his shoulder)*
Come, I'll give us both a sedative.

MAC *(shakes his head negatively and turns and stands looking out
    the porthole)*
So dark. . . .
Doctor, did you ever ride along the city streets at night,
And pass the houses,
At night the houses,
The row on row of lighted windows,
And think about the people living there?
I used to do that.
All those people,
And wondered of their laughing, and their loving,
All their arguments, and what they're eating, worrying,
    saying. . . .
All those lighted windows,

All those people,
I'll never know. . . .

BRUNER
Perhaps, in another life. . . .

MAC *(shaking his head)*
I don't believe that stuff! . . .
Or maybe just a little. . . .

> *(he turns back to the porthole and looks out into the darkness)*

That the elemental atoms, molecules, protons
Of our decay,
Return to space
And form something somewhere . . .

> *(he repeats the word softly)*

Somewhere. . . .

> *(the doctor looks at him, then moves over to where* RUSSELL
> *sits at the computer)*

RUSSELL *(glancing up at him; his finger traces the sheet before
him)*
The final graph!
Whatever chance we had was blown up
When we dodged their flying coffin!
Our margin burned up then.
The computer and my slide rule
Have finally reached that last miserable agreement! . . .
Do *I* believe it yet?
All my life I've lived with facts . . .
Metered . . . slide-ruled . . . univaced. . . .
What kind of fact is death?
Who has seen it?
Who has weighed it?
What graph is charted for the anti-neutrons, anti-life that
orbits in it?
All I know about it is that damned endless night!

If I could know that night, in death,
I'd be content to die!
Yes, if once in a thousand, thousand years
I could wake to know that me, me, I lie here in death!
But nothing . . . *nothing!*

(BRUNER *picks up a notebook that was lying on the desk*)

RUSSELL

That's Kephart's stuff.
I'm cleaning house.
An old conditioned Army reflex!
I'll guarantee you this:
We'll be a shipshape meteorite!

(*he fingers through the material on the table*)

At least I'm saved that:
The packaging of last effects for next of kin!
I'll give you odds
That specie's rare down there tonight!

(*the doctor has been concentrating on the notebook in his hand*)

BRUNER (*quietly*)
You're sure this belonged to Jan Kephart?

RUSSELL
In the bottom of his bag!

BRUNER
Have you read it?

(*the tone of the doctor's voice turns* RUSSELL'*s head. He puts out his hand, and the doctor puts the notebook in it*)

RUSSELL (*as he reads*)
Christ!

(ROHNEN *comes over*)

ROHNEN
> Mr. Russell, I want an exact fix on where we are!
> I must transmit it to my friends—

> *(as* RUSSELL, *deep in examination of the notebook, pays no attention to him)*

> Listen to me, Mister!
> I must know exactly where we are!
> I'm sending urgent messages—

> *(*RUSSELL *without warning, suddenly spins around and slaps* ROHNEN *across the face with the back of his hand, sending the man staggering.* BRUNER *stands watching in horror, as* MAC *stands frozen in place.* ROHNEN *tries to get away up the ladder to the Communications Platform, but* RUSSELL *drags him off and slaps him down.* ROHNEN *falls to his knees and cowers as* RUSSELL *slaps him again)*

MAC *(rushing up and trying to grip his flailing arm)*
> If you hit him again—General or not—

> *(*RUSSELL *throws him off;* ROHNEN *breaks onto the lower platform;* RUSSELL, *free of* MAC, *goes after him, and slugs him hard, and* ROHNEN *collapses.* DR. BRUNER *hurries down to kneel by the fallen man)*

MAC
> Why? Why?
> What did he do to you?

RUSSELL
> To me?
> What the hell do you mean to me?
> Can't you see the red of murder?
> Lt. Kephart was a precise man
> Who kept precise records!
> The time we slept,
> He did not sleep!
> Oh, our sainted Major Lormer!

How could I have been so damn blind
When this creep pulled him out of a hat of a thousand better
   qualified technicians!

MAC
But—but what—but what—

RUSSELL *(the notebook is still in his hand)*
It's here, *here!*
Lormer drunk, holding, adoring!
This bastard putting airsuit on him,
Opening the goddamn hatch for him!
Remember how he stood here?
"He was my friend! . . ."

   (he thrusts out the book at MAC*)*

Read it! Read it!
Murder! Screaming murder!

   (as ROHNEN *cries)*

It weeps!

BRUNER
Be still!

ROHNEN *(as he weeps)*
This Golden Voyage!

RUSSELL
Shove your goddam golden voyage!
Now's the time for facts!
Tell them how you really did it!
Tell them how you conned the man!
That the geiger counter lied?
That you'd tricked even the mechanism so he'd be the first to
   walk to immortality?
That you'd make us wait for him,
Turn back the clock of take-off automation?
What else? What else?

ROHNEN
You drank, you slept,
You didn't care that for me it was failure!
What did standing on other worlds mean to you who had your
own worlds?
I was going out myself, I, I,
And he stopped me!
He put his drunken arms around me,
Pleading, and then his lips—
I let him go!
I made him go!
He was pollution in this perfect place!

RUSSELL *(grabbing him again)*
All right! Does that justify shoving that poor fool to burning
death?
No, you're the pollution! You! You!
Crud, subhuman!

BRUNER *(shoving him away)*
Leave him alone!
If he's subhuman,
What are you?
Where's your humanity?
Where's one mortal word, one thought
You've had these hours for the tortured dead
To bind you to this human race you seek to champion against
this man's small misery?
The millions who looked at sky
And screamed in human agony!
The other millions who now crawl the ashened Earth,
Their flesh a ragged shroud around them,
Their blood a brewing poison!
Give me further evidence of *your* firm kinship to them, Tom
Russell!
That you suffer, too,
Your function ended, unfulfilled?
When have you last known pity beyond your own identity,

General Russell?
If he's subhuman,
Because the hormones in him speak another language,
What true humanity does *your* blood speak?

CURTAIN

ACT III

SCENE III

THE TIME: *An hour later.*

> AS CURTAIN RISES: ROHNEN *is seated at his desk, face buried in his arms.* RUSSELL *is walking toward the open hatch with the spare radar in his hand.* BRUNER *is seated on the rim of the Engineer's Platform.* MAC *is seated in the observation bubble.*

RUSSELL *(dropping the radar down the hatch)*
Well, that's the last we can do without! 580 pounds of the best
damn equipment!

> *(he lowers himself into the hatch and disappears.* BRUNER
> *moves over towards* ROHNEN)

BRUNER
Lewis . . . Lewis, we stripped the ship.
It's the only way we can gain time.
For every pound we throw out
We'll gain another second's thrust of jet.
Lewis, surely you hear me!

ROHNEN
Why do you speak to me here?
I am still there . . .
Weeping . . . crawling. . . .

BRUNER

You have done many things well.

ROHNEN

Give them name!

BRUNER

For the little that is left,
Give *yourself* a name!
Reach to heaven for it—in final understanding—in love!

ROHNEN

What love?
When have I loved?
Loved the dead lips of my mother?
Loved the paid lips of strangers?
Whom have I loved?

(*he turns away.* BRUNER *stands there a moment, then walks slowly away*)

MAC

Is he okay?

RUSSELL (*has just emerged from the hatch*)
Sure, let him rest!
His sobbing wearied him!

(*at* BRUNER'S *look*)

I know, I know,
I heard you well!
Maybe now's the time to file my own brief!
Pity's the sainted word, isn't it?
Pity, commiserate,
Understand the deeper motives and drip compassion!
Well, I hate and say so, Mister!
That's definitely out of fashion, isn't it?
Uncouth, unclean, and very immature
To say I hate!
So people go around with Judas smiles,

And tell themselves the dirty bastard's not to blame,
It's all his unconscious motivations,
They're at fault, his papa, mama,
Hormones, genes, but never him!
And all the time the dripping acid
Of their own intestinal fury
Etches ulcers, cancers, and the holes in head of nervous
  breakdowns!
Not for me, no, thank you!
When I hate, I hate and say it!
And I hate him, Mister!
He, for me, is all the creeping nothings with a bankroll,
A smart one with a predatory papa who got there first,
A tiny bit of guts, perhaps,
But no, it wasn't really guts, just the itching tensions in him,
Driving him to build this artificial ball
To prove that he's got two himself!

*(he crosses to the hatch with the computer discs and throws
them in)*

Let's dump this junk,
And buy a couple of extra minutes for me to shoot my mouth off!

*(he fastens the hatch lock and pulls the handle. We hear the
hiss of air, the alarm bell, and the distant clank of the air-
lock opening and closing. He sees* MAC *in the observation
bubble looking at him, and crosses over to him)*

You know, friend, I underestimated you!
I thought you'd still be straining for the sound of rescuing hoof
  beats!

MAC *(grimly)*
  Should I be?

RUSSELL
  You saw the blue prints:
  We're designed to home on Satellite two thousand miles in space!
  That's it!

MAC *(flatly)*
All right! That's it!

(they work in silence for a moment)

MAC *(as they work)*
You— you think *no one's* alive? . . .

RUSSELL
What the hell's the final difference?
Were that war fought with knives and clubs,
Mankind, as a form of life, already had been judged and
    damned!
No, no, I'm not climbing on the Holy Wagon at this late date!
I'm talking ice-cold fact!
Ignoring all those No Trespass signs on fields of checks and
    balance,
We went ahead to kill our personal microscopic predators of
    sickness, plague,
With germ and virus-enveloping vaccines and golden molds!
And like the rabbits of the prairie,
We've multiplied our thin-skinned selves,
Until our kind was burdening the Earth,
Year by year more millions beyond millions,
And would have kept on, in our blind fecundity,
Until every inch of Earth would swarm with us
Like starving locusts,
A writhing mass of black, white, yellow, brown and red,
A crawling, undulating sea of hunger,
Cast in our own damned stupid image,
Skeletons reaching to the empty heavens!

   (BRUNER *had moved over to where* ROHNEN *lies; now, without
   turning, he calls)*

BRUNER
Men, come here!

   (MAC, RUSSELL *following slowly, goes to where the doctor
   stands by* ROHNEN'S *bunk)*

RUSSELL
What's with him?
Has he got another "movement accidental" to display?

BRUNER
He's dead. . . .

(the men stare in disbelief)

RUSSELL
What—

MAC
Dead!

(as DR. BRUNER *reaches down and takes the poison vial from the inert hand, the body crashes to the platform)*

How long?

*(*RUSSELL *has turned away)*

BRUNER
Cyanide's a sharp, quick knife. . . .

MAC
But why?

BRUNER
Sometime there comes a weariness beyond the bear of bones,
To lose the weight of self-reproach
In sleep. . . .

*(*MAC *slowly turns away toward the observation bubble.* RUSSELL *crosses to the escape hatch, a piece of apparatus in hand)*

RUSSELL
Now's the time, I should imagine,
The pity turns on me.

(as DR. BRUNER *does not answer)*

Well, say it!

BRUNER

Strange, one's memory scanning under tension. . . .

(his look is distant)

I keep thinking of four students sitting in a squat-legged huddle
On a street called Yashimito,
Hiding the nakedness, in one small shadow,
Of their blackened skin.
The noonday Sun blazes yellow patterns through their lidded
eyes;
High overhead the single varicolored cloud mushrooms
malignant shelter.
"We were on our way to school," one says,
"We were talking many things,
Important things,
The length of crawfish in the river,
The holiday when we would leave our books and go in fields
To play with kites and many fancies.
A flash, a blaze . . .
Now we sit,
No room for laughter in our dying blood."

RUSSELL

What does that mean?

BRUNER

On the day we bombed four students on that street called
Yashimito,
I think you and I left the human race,
And lost ourselves forever in the bloody jungle
Of the leopard and the praying mantis.
Oh, we had sanctimonious phrases to offer up
For history's record:
The "Practical Considerations"
So dear to politicians eyeing history's judgment.
And so, with none of that outmoded chivalry of warning fairly
given,
We broke their back with one quick crunch,

And cheered a reddened flag of sudden victory.
But on their streets, and in their houses,
In the churches, schools, and hospitals,
In the dentist office, in the playground,
The flame of our treachery to humanity
Seared the flesh, the blood, the very genes
Of four ferocious students armed with all the terrible retribution
Of their abacus, textbooks, and lead pencils.
I ask you what had we done in all the intervening years,
We, high moralists, hope of Earth,
With that great treachery crouched upon our conscience?
What mass confessional has absolved us?
The new push-button transmission from Detroit?
The precise duplication of the color spectrum on our TV screens?
The frosted bowels of self-defrosting
Deep, deep freezers?
A dog died on the street and we wept.
The serum dripped from all their million wounds
And their sightless, scarred faces burrowed into ground,
And we turned our heads and asked
The latest batting average of A.T.&T., and who's on first!

RUSSELL

I've been wondering for some time why the hell you begged to
    come along!
Now I know! The nuclear scientist's unhappy conscience:
"Oh, woe is me, what have I done, I'll put on flying sack-cloth
    and ashes!"
But now, by God, you're not even contrite scientist!
"Change, change, all is change!"
I heard you well before:
"This turns into that and nothing's static!"
All right! What have *you* changed into?
I'll tell you, Mister!
A neutralist!
A goddam everybody's-wrong-and-right, do-nothing neutralist
Who'd let the whole damned world go down the drain
While he sits on his superior ass in static judgment!

I tried, by Jesu, I tried to do my job down there,
But what did you do before they started racing armaments?
Answer me that!
What in hell did you do?

BRUNER
   I?

RUSSELL
   Yes, you!
   What did *you* do?

BRUNER *(slowly)*
   I? . . .
   I—I wept a little at the bomb . . .
   Then I drank a great deal . . .
   Then—then I think I went into a classroom and closed the
      door. . . .

   *(he moves into the observation bubble and sits there staring
   out into the darkness beyond)*

RUSSELL
   All right! Then don't you try to lay off on me
   Your misery in retreat!
   I, for one, have lived my life with cold reality.
   I haven't found God on my slide-rule,
   But I have found order in the universe,
   A thing of force and counterforce!
   Call the motivating factor what you will,
   Deify it or give it mathematical equation,
   There is no pity in the Name or Sum.
   It pours, with calculated ruthlessness,
   The contents of the test tube down the drain when experiment
      has failed!
   Our species failed, somewhere along the line,
   And so today, perhaps, we joined
   The Dinosaur and Great Auk—

   *(he throws what is in his hand on the refuse pile. A new alarm
   begins to "Ping")*

RUSSELL
We're falling close to 0-600!
So why the hell do we stand here
Like politicians on a platform!
It's ended!
Today is gone, and tomorrow's blown up, burned out,
    extinct!

MAC *(softly, turning to* DR. BRUNER*)*
That isn't true, is it?
They are not all dead, are they?

BRUNER
I—I do not know . . .

MAC
You both know so much, know *that!*
Everything's a viewpoint for you!
Where's your viewpoint now?
He's this—you're that—
And between the two of you, you take the world and throw it
    farther than it is!
That's easy for you, old men,
Now you've finished with it!
You've had it, both of you,
The loving, eating, waking, sleeping!
But what of me?
Have you twin Gods decided I, too, have had enough?
I came along because I thought
That even if I died,
I'd move the world a little!
Now he says it's gone forever!
Well, is it? Is it?

BRUNER
Forever?
What forever?
Tomorrow's forever
Or ten, a hundred million years forever?
Four billion years that Earth moved in its orbit,

And billions more it will be there
Until the Sun destroys itself in supernova!
So which forever?
Who can look into such a womb of time?
Mac, only this I know:
As the sabred teeth tore at this throat,
The Neanderthal's thought screamed in his head:
"The end, the end!"
When the Conquistador's sword flashed high in Aztec sun,
The High Priest, in agony before the final agony, cried out:
    "Ended, all ended!"
At Waterloo all ended,
At Agincourt all ended,
At Calvary,
And Dachau,
Ended, ended,
A million times in agony man has ended!

RUSSELL *(he has been listening intently)*
Where is the parallel!
There the slaughter stopped with a club, a sword,
The arrow, bullet, gas chamber!
Now it's on the wind,
In every breath they die!

BRUNER
The seed will not die!
It will build its own immunity to the air-borne scourge,
And the children of that seed,
Remembering what we had done,
The pseudo-realist—the practical ones—
Old Scientists,
Old Generals,
Old Businessmen,
Old Politicians,
Old Revolutionists—

    (he hesitates)

And Ancient Neutralists—
Perhaps remembering us, those men of that tomorrow will give
  their youth
Idealism where we gave cynicism,
Ever-renewing hope where we gave disillusionment,
True compassion for all
Where we gave close-lidded prejudice and cash-register
  chicanery
Or double-tongued dogmas and dialectics,
And erected curtains of bamboo, iron, or chromium plate
That hid the face of man . . . from man. . . .
And if they fail again, in that tomorrow,
The Earth will be the home of lizards once again,
Or small mice,
Or wondrous insects,
Iridescent wings
Rising in great clouds,
Seeking only the warming sun,
At war only with the contrary winds. . . .

(MAC'S *face is bright with wonder*)

RUSSELL *(softly)*
You left out one for them to remember:
Old intellectuals—who maybe knew a way out—
But let the rest of us get lost . . .

(*he turns and moves slowly toward* ROHNEN'S *bunk*)

BRUNER *(intercepting him)*
No!

(*his shoulders slump as he faces the reality of the situation.
He steps aside.* RUSSELL *picks up the inert body of* ROHNEN *and
carries it to the hatch,* MAC *helping him. Together they lower
the body through the open hole into the hatch.* RUSSELL *sits
at the edge of the hatch, strikes a match, and lights a cigarette.
He inhales the smoke deeply and lets it out slowly*)

RUSSELL

You know, you talked of strange memory scannings . . .
I've had them, too,
These passing minutes . . .
Thinking of a story—a family story—
Told around our supper table
When I was a very little boy.
Real pioneering stuff, our family was supposed to be—
Coonskin caps, and Conestogas,
And breaking backs in Santa Fe mud! . . .
Well, this story's told of one of my great, great
     grandmothers—
Her name? Forgotten dust!
On a day when
The father went hunting in the hills,
And the watching Iroquois came riding.
The drum of horses,
One moment, one moment only
To push the kids into the fort-like house,
Slam the timbered door,
Throw the heavy bolt,
Grab up the musket and wait, wait,
Quite safe, inside the stone-sheathed house,
Until the Indians tired and would go . . .
And then a cry,
Thin as a little bird:
"Mother, let me in!"
A quick survey—Mary, Ellen, John, Jim—
David! The youngest boy! The dearest!
"Mother, let me in!"
Four huddled kids, wide-eyed—
And one out there . . .
Open the door?
The tiny fists were pounding,
The circling Indians silent, thin-grinned, waiting . . .
When the father of that long ago,
Came down from the hills,

A little wind-devil of dust moved in the distance,
And a red knife lay on the threshold.
And the door? Unopened . . .
I've often thought of that day, such a long, long day ago . . .
"Mother, let me in!"

(he inhales deeply on the cigarette. When he speaks, it is almost as if to himself)

I never had to think much . . .
Beyond my job, I never really had to think.
All my answers—I got them cheap . . . headlines . . . barside . . .
It's so much easier to hate
Than think. . . .

(he crushes out the cigarette, then turns down the hatch ladder)

I'll check it out.

(as he starts down again, he stops)

And you'd better check out the landing equation again.
I think there's a new variable.

(he suddenly reaches back and pulls the hatch cover down over him. For a second the other men stand there frozen, as the heavy metal clangs shut, then they rush forward and pull at the hatch cover)

BRUNER
Russell! Russell!

MAC
He's locked it from inside!
Russell!

BRUNER
Russell!

(the two men continue to cry out and pull futilely at the heavy hatch cover until there is a sudden clang of an alarm bell and the flare of a red light on the control panel indicating that

the outer door to space has been released. We hear the rush of air and the distant clang of the outer door. MAC *in the lead, the two men rush to the rear porthole and look out. What they see is reflected in the horror on their faces. After a moment,* DR. BRUNER *turns away.* MAC *is silently weeping. Wearily,* DR. BRUNER *walks to the switchboard, turns a control, and the light and the alarm bell stop)*

BRUNER
Who'll write this epitaph for all of us:
"They knew too much too soon . . .
"They knew too much too late . . ."?

MAC *(tightly as he holds out his hand)*
Doc! The cyanide!

(as the doctor looks at him)

I don't want to wait!
I don't want to burn!
The quick knife! You said it yourself!

BRUNER *(suddenly remembering)*
What did *he* say!

MAC
Huh?

BRUNER *(in growing excitement)*
What did Russell say?
The last thing he said!

MAC
I—I don't remember!
Something about 'Check the computer . . .'

*(*BRUNER *rushes to the computer, pounds keys, and the mechanism whirs)*

MAC
What—

BRUNER

The last equation was for *four* of us!

(he hands the tape to the young man)

Russell gave us a new variable . . . for *two!*

(as MAC *seizes the computer tape and studies it, a new-toned alarm begins to ping)*

BRUNER *(sharply, as* MAC *hesitates)*
We're falling into Earth!
We'll swing around and miser out the thrust of jets,
And if Death comes,
We'll ride Him down!
Strap in!

*(*MAC, *with an exultant yell, dives for the main platform seat and the two men strap in on each side of the main switch.* BRUNER *throws the main switch, the great roar of jets begins, quivering the air, and the men strain at their belts against the great deceleration as the red light rises, rises, covering the platform as:*

THE CURTAIN FALLS SLOWLY

William Witherup

A LETTER TO ABC

'The Day After' Editors
American Broadcasting System
1330 Avenue of the Americas
New York, New York 10019

Dear Editors:
Your program on nuclear war seemed to shock some people.
I was not one of those. I was with it until the missiles went off
and the explosions were simulated. The simultaneous firing of the
missiles was indelible. You should have kept *in* the excised footage
of Hiroshima! You also should have simulated pictures of Russian
men women and children dying. And bled those in. We all need
to vomit at the mere *thought* of missiles. As long as the Russian
people are seen as dehumanized and as abstractions, the four thugs
you had on the following panel discussion, aka Kissinger, Buckley,
Scowcroft, McNamara, will be able to justify their Machiavellian
synaptical switching that passes for 'thinking'. And will go on
blathering till that nuclear Hell blisters us all, supporting nuclear
parity, a concept that in itself is mind-boggling.
After the firing of the missiles the program degenerated into
soap opera, starring the noble Dr. Robards as he rots away. There
was no dark winter, as Sagan and other scientists predict. There
was no vomitting, shitting, rotting, no actual *stink*, as a colleague
of mine pointed out. There was no *real* death. It became *General
Hospital*. Lots of work for the makeup department and the
styrofoam model makers. How long did it take to cut up all that
rubble?
The script, the dialogue, was inane. The question is, can
intelligent life be on TV?
If you would really like to do a service for humankind, make
a three way program with the United States, Japan and Russia.
Check out the Japanese book, available here through Pantheon,

Unforgettable Fire, drawings and statements by Hiroshima victims. Here's a book will make you weep, my friends. Take your cue from this, have more courage next time. Americans need to face (1) that Russians are human, (2) that *we* started the nuclear arms race and we are the ones raising the ante and (3) the dropping of the bombs on Hiroshima and Nagasaki, were crimes as vicious and unthinkable as those done face to face in Auschwitz, Belsen and Dachau.

I found it ironic that Carl Sagan was the only panel member to mention computer error, and that most of your black slugs were filled by computer advertisements! We are going to be barbecued by either computer error or pathological act. I was in the USAF Security Service, with obeisance to Catch-22, twenty-five years ago. I monitored, from the island of Crete, home of one of the Goddess cultures, Russian commercial air traffic in the Caucasus. My Arabic-speaking colleagues listened in on Lebanon and Syria. Nothing has changed for the better. The bloodshed has increased and we have more missiles. I saw, even then, plenty of pathological activity within my own supposed elite, both officer and enlisted. Do a drama on how an officer cracks up, because of problems at home, in a missile silo command. That will scare the socks off anybody. Hell, I'll even write it for you.

Your panel was loaded with assassins and apologists for administration bathos and self service. The only human beings on it were Koppel, Sagan and Weisel. Where was a woman? Where was Dr. Helen Caldicott, one of the most humane and courageous and articulate anti-nuclear spokespersons on the planet? She said in a speech here several years ago that she had been trying to get on the major networks for years with her message. If she wasn't available, which I doubt, why wasn't there another woman of equal intelligence and righteous wrath? Were you afraid a woman would show up the masculine imbecility for what it is?

You were so worried the film would be political that you denuded it. And then as a sop to the far right and to the administration, you gave us *The Four Thugs Plan Nuclear War*, introduced by that administration zombie, Thick Soles Schultz.

I, sirs and madams, do not usually watch television. I think the medium is an abomination. It does not serve thought and it provides nothing you can't find in a book, whether novels, poems, histories or travel books. Along with missiles, it is civilization's worst shuck. However, as television will most probably continue to exist as a cocaine for the mind, it is time for the networks to be more responsible. The old saws: profit over thought, money before consequence and make-a-buck-anyway-you-can, were changed in 1945 when those alchemists in the Devil's employ mixed up their wormy batch. Unless you get more political, meaning air time for liberal as well as conservative thought, we will all blister in the red-gold alchemical fire!

Why not a documentary on Hiroshima on prime time? A documentary on how the everyday Russian lives? Spend five of your so-called precious seconds of air time with a camera focused on a Russian child's face, and ask the question then, can we even consider firing one nuke? If it means losing some sponsors to save your souls, make the obvious choice. We no longer have *time* to mess around with the mental machinations of the Buckleys, the Scowcrofts and the Kissingers. Have more courage, for all of our sakes.

I have gotten worked up — and I could as easily and justifiably be writing to CBS or NBC — because television is the major opinion influencer in this country. But *real* thought, *real* concern, *real* debate, is relegated to the alternate channels, such as KQED here in the San Francisco Bay area. But most people watch the major channels, let's face it. As Jerry Mander points out in his book, *Four Arguments Against Television*, television exists for the sake of the advertiser and not for the sake of the viewer. It is time to reverse that process. If we must live with this plastic and glass Baal, we deserve better information, true dramas, debate in depth and a disaster film that moves us to action.

In 1945 I was 10 years old and living in Richland, Washington, the community that houses most Hanford workers. My father was a blue collar worker who helped, either directly or indirectly, mix the batch of plutonium that got stuffed into Fat Man and that shat fire on Nagasaki. We all thought it was great. Hooray for our side!

There are no sides left. It is imperative we take the Buddhist position that all life is holy, the least cricket on the sill, the mouse behind the drywall. Remember the face of the Russian child I proposed above. Make it your mission and responsibility to program truth, in the name of all life on this planet.

William Witherup
November 21, 1983

Post Script: ABC answered my letter with a standard postcard that said, in effect, "thank you for your response and support of *The Day After*."

William Witherup

TO MY FATHER

To My Father

who burns with prostate cancer.
Carried plutonium home in his underwear,
potent ashes of Nagasaki.

"For Christ's sake, Dad,
you went to work daily out of love,
but did the Devil's job.
You guys stoked Hell's ovens,
brought back deep shadows in your pails.

All the Geigers can't count
how much your children love you,
or measure thirty years of labor
smoldering in your work pants,
or monitor sperm spitting across centuries,
igniting everywhere karmic fires."

William Carney

from **CITIES**

(3 sections of a 12 part
poem on nuclear warfare)

III. The Silo

You get there along roads that section
land, a minute at a time, precise square
miles of corn, wheat, barley, sunflowers
surging softly as the ocean once
rode this terrain. How these geometries
amaze: grid tightens eastward into
cities, taproot to transmitting
kernel, your own mind recollecting
diatoms of all dimensions settling,
soft flakes of light, into eventual
stone: this gathering, this memory
the foundation of wide harvests,
limestone buildings and crushed gravel roads.
It's dawn. From the horizon rise
cylindric silos. The rhythm now
picks up phone poles, flashing, then the swoop
of wires like a goldfinch in between
communicating town to town,
quick exclamations adding up to
one plain statement at the core of each
community: grain nucleus,
acropolis of grain stored up from
intervening countryside.

                    Now grid
again the air, imposing chain link
strands as if this bounded land were tilted
up, abstracted, punched through like a sieve.

You hold this to your eyes. Prepare
credentials.

Stop.

NOTES. U.S. NUCLEAR PREPAREDNESS.

Omaha, Nebraska.
the readiness is all.

invert now
imagery of aspiration. draw
horizon in. dark circle sunk
into pitched plains.

a sun collapsed on
cindered self bores down through time a hole
like this, worlds reeling into it.

you
spiral down steel staircase,

missile hung
like pupa waiting,

round and round, thick
woven silence deadening approach.

as
cranes once thunderous brought down this sky,
lines

untangled, recombined,

now twist
in toward mute vanishment.

as spider
dizzying spins out itself.

as bats
return clockwise to a dark place.

as

snow, warped cyclops storm, blind whiteout through which
men will circle till they drop.

air, bear

this weight.

the way hear tell a man once
hung legs churning over tidal
vortex, strange waters he had ventured
in,

now grasping his last hope these straining
roots hands chanced upon.

you're losing it.

mirrored metal wall bangs back and forth
the image and reality,
beautiful

distortions

like the deer
antelope and mammoth figuring
forgotten magics

of fecundity

and kill.

you turn to place palms flat on
wall, search seam or crevice, fly-like, to get
hold of.

breath registers on the surface,
disappears, your own face

comes and goes

then others knotted, dense packed, struggling
conglomerate flesh

mouthing to break through

to you.

and at your back, hissing
escaping oxygen, far down slow
roar begins

       as in incoming shells
the ocean curls.

NINE.

       fire flickering.

just natural. we've always been

       this way.
the cave piled up with calcium.

       the way
kids take to a computer game.

       as if
long gone from off the earth, huge bear shagged
as oak wood prominence, uprushes
from the cave's throat scattering

       trapped men
like leaves in front of winter

       brushing
them aside, gray cortex splattered on
gray stone.

EIGHT.

       Agamennon had it.

gets me right here in the gut sometimes
deep down.

       the hollow horns.

       proud bronze
projectile enters at the cheek, just
under left eye, crashing through clenched teeth and
out part way the neck

          miraculously
severing

      neither trachea nor
spinal cord. he falls

        still breathing
and aware.

       they found at Troy forty
circling cities (where now uncounted
grasses pulse again)

       naming them
horizons.

SEVEN.

    set stone to stone.

         take
charcoal, saltpeter, sulfur.

        swallow
hard

  (the black spore bursting into life)
feel

   inside the cell

      walls permeable
Constantinople

     the explosion
inside

   out

    cells screaming separations
as a jet

   end over end

                down
city canyons.

                this prime equation.
1453. *no stopping it.*

SIX.

        just have to hold our own.

                        two years
before Plymouth, eleven after
Jamestown,

                similarly an expression
of spiritual fragmentation,
secular expansion,

                an exploding
world.

        this nation born of.

                        and numbers:
30 Years War. 7,000,000 Dead
War.

        and most of these civilians.

                        caught
up in

        slush and sleet they cannot
move

        for malnutrition, skeletal
or (sure sign) stomachs full

                        of air or
corpses bloated, wide-eyed, quiet. as
maggots in a mass grave

                writhing fruit
drink red.

    numb numbers.

                    Westphalia

1648, pieced Europe
into states, each granted rights to war
and taxes.

    temporal sovereignty.

the human rule

      of space and time.

                FIVE.

take your average individual
lying low,

      bogged down, scared

             stiff, you stick

a flag up

      over him (whips furious)
he'll fight like hell, anything

           to keep

the feeling strong.

      the isolated

shots ring out, one by one, one following
another.

      sweat crawls over you like

insects.

    take the American

Revolution, guerillas, freedom
over all else,

      every man his own war.

take French liberty, imposing
compulsory military service
to salvage revolution.

take Prussia
which organized a) peacetime conscription;
b) war is politics; c) war is all
out, a romantic construct

(look
again at Delacroix and Wagner):

Lorraine won in six weeks.

breathtaking.

take the lone man,

seventeen, blondish
hair, slight wave cut smartly over
forehead, knowing and uncertain eyes
alive

as told all out the hundred yards
against machinery

flashing *brighter*
than a thousand suns.

FOUR.

as lit
apartments or entire city
burning cold with them

wide fields of stone
return the dying sun.

unlid the grave,
the warm life under each flames out.

count each:

gallipoli: two hundred
thirteen thousand nine hundred eighty.

antietam: 22,000.

mukden:
160,000.

verdun:
330,000.

the somme:
1,000,000.

stalingrad: 2,000,000.

korea: 5,000,000.

first world war total:
40,000,000 dead.

second world war:
60,000,000 dead.

        numb numbers. cold.

what is incomprehensible must be
experienced.

        crossed soldiers, gift-tied, sent
away.

    ticking half-lives massed again.

            THREE.

dachau	sachsenhausen	buchenwald
mathausen	flossenburg	ravensbruck
auschwitz	neuengamme	gusen
natzweiler	gros rosen	lublin
niederhagen	stutthof	arbeitsdorf

TWO.

    hamburg

        stuttgart

           dresden

                guernica

berlin

    cologne

        dusseldorf

           london

coventry

    tokyo

        perfect

release:

    distant,

        casual

           as rain, these
hard accumulations

        end over
end

    through pliant air

        reptilian
descend,

    soft constrictions of cold breath
left rising from

        the surfaces of things.
snake must got his tongue.

        hiroshima.
nagasaki.

    ONE.

    now hear this
mycelia of silence

                    spreading
through you, covering

                         your surfaces
the way clouds mildew earth.

                              the way men
strain in silence nearing laboratory
breakthrough

              (and the world waits quietly
for word).

              the way in institutions
persons piecemeal feed out mind, thin line
sunk into

        tumultuous silence
nothing answering, reel and chum much
as they may.

              you know what's next, how

two mile circle. gamma radiation
kills outright. cells droop like Dali clocks.

how eight mile circle. 400 mile per
hour wind avalanches buildings,
transforms everything to missile.
people driven as nails or blind snow.

how ten mile circle. fireball blinds
anyone caught looking. flesh cooks, laced
by its surroundings. this page ignites.

how thirty mile circle. burning dark
snow descends, *protracted afterburst*,
a trillion hiroshimas in the cells
of anyone exposed. each person
in decay, internally, in merger
with their own echoing creation.

how circles of indefinite
diameter. electromagnetic pulse
kills all communication.

how interpenetrating circles.
multiply. one megaton by
seven thousand megaton attack
to fifteen thousand megaton
mutual exchange, a *saturation
bombing* of two continents, towns down
to fifteen hundred (Housatonic,
Bethel, Cloverdale). *local effects*
like pebbles in a pond, each city
grown to join with all others
in a wash of fire, radiation, shock.

how circles of worldwide necropolis.
from carcasses of mammals, carcass
hills, the seepage into oceans
starts, and exponentially
the populations of bacteria
bloom cyclic waves *ad nauseum*.

how atmospheric circles, circles
of air. the dust from this fight rises, spreads
radiation earthwide strong enough
to mutate who knows what future
generations. blocks significant
sunlight cooling (maybe trapping, heating
up) till climates, ice floes, oceans
also mutate. finally recombinant
with ozone, depleting seventy
percent, allows in ultraviolet
sunlight now becomes the blinding flash
steadily intense for thirty years
on all surviving grain and retinas.

ZERO.

    Feel then one last time your
fingers on the missile's skin, sweating
condensation cold the way antarctic
metal sticks to you, burning, stripping
flesh away: reach now toward this
absolute, all motion stopped: inside
hungry for your touch, the tonguing fire
roars into awareness lifting every
language skyward: ride, ride this high craft
clean out into empty apogee
then turn—the earth suspended past belief
beautiful and brief—then hurtle home.

V. The Scientist

Outside the Cafe Dante traffic
streams. Delivery trucks and buses
lumber like herds across a Pleistocene
savannah tawny with wide morning
light. People descend, deliveries
are made. He stirs and spreads the manuscript.
The cosmos in a coffee cup comes
clear, unravels, swirls again toward
tighter mystery. Breath moves upon
the surface of the deep.

if I had

never studied whales.

The holocaust
for dinosaurs occurred when time long gone
the stars went wrong. Asteroids gavelled earth
till numb dust shrouded out all warmth.
During that carboniferous night
green plants which once had shot a hundred feet
through warm, moist air on stalks as tender
as asparagus, collapse to spore.

he's got the subject right at least.

Diplodocus and Brontosaurus,
heaped mountainous, erode away.
Meat-eaters, first bloated, stumble soon
on bones picked clean: in death its prey see
high Tyrannosaurus overthrown.
And under all, nocturnal scavengers,
tunneling intelligence, small mammals
make way through the reptilian overload
toward their eventual dawn.

Steamed milk
pressured toward pure pleasure, the perfect

cappuccino takes off behind him
like a jet, erect.

          The issue isn't
death. If anything, extinction
proves death's final failure, death again
life's fundamental adaptation to
a changing world, over and again
regrouping as the planet spins out
fluctuating destinies. Imagine
sunlit ocean plankton huddled up
against intensifying salt or
current. Snowballing time accumulates
that sexual pulse in untold zygotes
held bustling as cities, every cell
the self-same individual song.

             whales talk
ten thousand miles apart, one saying
to another half way round the planet
'I am here.'

          Light lives in the areca
palm like neon. He looks at it,
his eyes a photosynthesis
equally intense. Dust hums and trembles
in the current.

          Nor is knowledge
what went wrong, much as people scapegoat
science. They turn to us their guilt. To think
the brain analogous to fangs
so large they'd choke the feeding sabertooth
explains our missiles only.

            twenty
years obscure, pure research, then must be
some shadow network picks up possible
significance. the money starts
to flow.

More like Stegosaurus, its
spiked armament a tail so weighted
it drags back more neurons than the brain
contains. Contol is vested furthest from
perception.

no problem anymore
with publication. mainline results
direct to Tennessee.

He studies
the collapse of newsprint columns next
to him, the heads each day absorbing
more black ink.

In blind hope too they turn
to us. In space in time we'll live inside
technology. The way green plants
anticipated atmospheric
oxygen millennia before
the first crustacean crawled aloft, or we
live now within these words, capsuled
reality.

the way an eagle
out of nowhere dives an osprey.
pirating the fish first meant to feed
whole nestfuls.

Deeper escape they want,
a cosmos able to excuse, dispense
pure entropy. They heap their offerings
then pray us prove that easy prophecy
finally the truth.

now they can tell
precisely the coordinates of
every submarine in every ocean.
black pods pregnant with malevolence.
the perfect defense. who could argue

otherwise, all the uncertainty
now gone.

      The woman he's been watching
quickly stands to leave, her dress backlit
like a cathedral window.

           In fact
the universe still waits the word
from us, uncertain at its core.

           but why,
if in defense, such secrecy?

           When first
Oppenheimer at Los Alamos
thought his one atom poised to trigger
aerial reactions torching earth
into a star, he hit it close enough.
Such relativity—'everything
changed except our thinking'—leaves us now
profoundly free.

          so then suppose
one day empanelled papers in his lap
shout out perfected capability.
the pressures would be too immense.
he'd play the odds, he'd engineer a way
to use the thing.

          Biting into light
and ordinary matter we've now found
a density of power able
to darken everything that it began. The power is not evil.
We got here just by looking. The way
out is the way in. We need only
to see clearly these abstractions, blips,
trajectories mean plain and simple
death, death one breathing person at a time
in magnitudes of billions, those deaths

multiplied time over unseen time
by every possible alignment
of those billion gametes streaming through
each person of those billions now
alive. This much is true. This much is
in our power.

He fishes for a dime.
The man at table 21 adjusts
his headset.

The number at the Globe.

IX. The Speech

Early this morning I received word
that five hundred Soviet advisors
have joined Iraqi forces
in their CONTINUING AND UNPROVOKED
attempts to dislodge the United States
Marine Corps units I have charged
with protecting American oil
interests in the deserts south of Baghdad.

I have responded by issuing
a CONTINGENCY order for the field
use of small caliber 203
and 155 mm
Howitzer nuclear artillery.

I have also placed on full alert
status the entire strategic
nuclear arsenal of this nation:

1,114
Minuteman and *Titan* ICBMs;
417 B-52
and FB-111 bombers;
744 *Poseidon*,
Trident and *Polaris* SLBMs;
22,000 tactical systems.

Let any enemy consider
well this poised consequence of their own
careless acts. If forced to it we will
mince more than words before this day is done.

Grave as these decisions seem, we have good
reason for them. LET ME SET STRAIGHT

for you the intricacies which led
us to this point.

          First, our national
interest in Persian Gulf oil is clear.
Iraq alone supplies somewhere in
the neighborhood of three percent of
our consumption: oil which not only feeds
our freeways and warms our homes, but
provides a VITAL STRATEGIC RESOURCE
without which this country could sustain
no war of more than ninety days'
duration. Let us heed the lesson
Rommel etched in these same desert sands.

Secondly, the Soviet threat must
be met. Our words must be born out by
a STEEL WILLINGNESS TO ACT. The fact
that we've contained so tightly Russian
aims for forty years bears witness to
our rightful vigilance.

          Thirdly,
we are engaged already in global
battle, at stake the minds and hearts of men.
The example we provide today
of the UNBENDING DETERMINATION
of free men to preserve the planet's
freedom will not be lost.

          The evil
of the communist experiment
with this most basic element
of human nature we will in the end
eradicate.

REST ASSURED your nation's
course is justified. The very dangers
of this day prove the correctness of
our military readiness. I trust
this moment to be forge and crucible
of renewed national unity.

I AM PROUD TODAY to serve as your
commander-in-chief. I AM PROUD
of the power—as infinitely
destructive as it is minutely
honed—lying here even as I speak
the merest reach away. I AM PROUD
of the American people whose high
ideals and deepest ingenuity
have freed this power. I AM PROUD
that we're the ones chosen to wield such
limitless capacity.

We hope
against hope not to have to use it.
But we must not fear its use. For what
other reason did God entrust this gift
first into the hands of free men?

In simple truth this is a moral
world, a moral universe we live
within. There still is right and wrong, good
and evil. And we as yet remain
a moral nation, a nation armed
with truth, allied with God, fortified
by an unyielding belief in
the ultimate freedom of mankind
to direct his final destiny.

THERE IS NO HIGHER LAW than this.
We will live free—or die free if we must.

We needn't die. I'm confident
this show of our resolve will turn
around the Russian bear as has proved true
before. But here I turn to you,
the American people, MY UTMOST
PRAISE AND ABSOLUTE FAITH. I draw
my strength today unquestionably
from your own willing, free consent.

                                      In this
new style of war, this war of nerves,
this living-room war, the captive
populations of two continents
face off across uncomprehending
void. We are all in the trenches
this time. We all now face THE SUPREME
SACRIFICE. It heartens me to know how
hardened all of you have gotten to
these final tests of human courage.

Should push come to shove, I'm sure also
that each of you have been observing good
basic civil defense. National
survival may depend on little
steps taken toward your own survival.
ABOVE ALL ELSE AVOID looking
directly at a nuclear event.

When I leave the air today my image
will be superseded by the stars
and stripes. Throughout the night the flag
will mark those stations keeping you
informed. All other sources of
communication will be blackened.

You may therefore imagine this single
image waving proud and clear above

us all. Think then of that earlier
flag, its waves the brilliant coils of
a snake, its plain embroidery
DON'T TREAD ON ME. The American
rattlesnake's unique in all the world.
It gives fair prior warning when disturbed.

This afternoon, the world should note:
we are disturbed. This is our warning.

Jed Rasula

THE FUTURE PERFECT

After all, what did they call it — the Gimmick,
drummed up by the Longhairs — "Little Boy" &
"Pumpkin," names of the Bomb. Nagasaki, Hiroshima, victims of know-how, still come apart
in the dark, scattering larval silhouettes
behind the retina, now I lay me down to sleep.

*

Detect and interpret corrosions out of space:
they carry the news long gone.
Look out at the stars: look back in time
— these are one & the same.
Quasars no longer exist, but their transit
makes us ourselves. We be-become.
If magic snakes into their lingering tones
how will we know? Or who? Who's slipped inside
on a wick or a jet, a radio shiver
gliding through hypnotised leaves,
through peeling layers of memory
thinned out, becoming transparent,
wandering out in single cells, brain drifts by
in dwindling herds, blurred and sluggish
with dormant atomic sleep, aroused by electrical laws,
commanding suns with a string of zeros —
who passes through conscious results and lands on the map.

*

I walk about,
the stars change position above me:
we swallow the pact.
Three degrees above absolute zero
the earth is bathed in sound.

And we who catch this long gone sound of creation just
    reaching our ears
are bundles of after-effects,
not created or plucked but cooked, chunks of a star
exploded and then set adrift
and made the sun and were the world and puzzled the cause.
What matters is *extremely hot.*
"We were" it seems to say,
deceived by the present tense.
The present tensed in thought concurs, and blurs.
Already gone when it gets here, it seems to have *said.*
But what would it say?
— "we are" wherever it was when it "said"?
And how did it know we would listen, or hear?
The future perfect:

it will have been.

Jean Gonick

NUCLEAR ANXIETY, PAST AND PRESENT

Because I am 33 and have no children, I don't often get a chance to meet or talk to kids. However, when I do, their preoccupation with nuclear war is obvious; it reactivates my own anxiety. Why is the fear of a 10-year-old so much more intense than an adult's? Is it because I've had a chance, if not to grow old, at least to grow up?

In 1960 I was in fifth grade and was subjected, along with my classmates, to the absurdity of air-raid drills. Although not usually rebellious, I did rebel against this exercise by refusing to crouch under my desk with my hands over my head. "If I know the bomb's coming, I'm going home to my mother!" I insisted, while being escorted to the principal's office. Why should I await death with Mrs. Watters and the fifth-grade class of Wildwood Grammar School when I could die with my mother at home? Was it possible that the principal didn't know that we would all surely die? Once seated in the principal's office, I repeated my stance: "Getting under the desk won't help when the whole school blows up," I said. Somehow I sensed that I wouldn't be seriously reprimanded for this lack of cooperation. I was confident that I was right, and that they knew it. I was also confident that, in the face of death, any punishment inflicted on me by Wildwood School was small potatoes indeed.

The girls in my class all feared "The Bomb" — and always in the singular form, as if one lone bomb would eradicate the United States from the Atlantic to the Pacific. The fifth-grade boys may well have had a more literal comprehension of how world destruction worked: they were still carving swastikas (ignorant of their significance) into their wooden desks, and each of them could imitate every audio effect from World War II. To be honest, I don't recall the boys voicing any fear at all about the bomb —perhaps they considered it just one more war game. Or perhaps they merely suffered their anxieties in silence, as boys in 1960 were wont to do.

My girlfriends and I, though, were openly panicked. Every low-flying plane sent us to the window and sometimes under the bed. "Will it happen today?" we wondered. "Could that plane be the Russians?" It was a daily, constant possibility. Each time we heard a test of the Emergency Broadcast System (and it seemed like so many, many times), we pushed our young imaginations to the limit. "This is just a test; this is just a test," the announcer would say. We would think: What if it were real? How would it feel?

We felt positive that someday it would be real, and just as the announcer rehearsed his dispensing of the news, we wanted to accurately rehearse our reaction. It was titillating, in a horrible way, to so intentionally flirt with fear — much like sneaking to the Grand Lake Theater to see the latest Vincent Price horror movie. The movie was fantasy, the Russians were real, and both were awful.

Our attention to these ominous emergency broadcast tests recalled an earlier ritual: the "consider infinity" game. I'd sit outside with my overnight guest and we'd stare at the night sky. How far did the sky reach? Was there a wall? What was behind it? We'd ponder these questions until it felt uncomfortable then rush back into the house to work on forgetting this awesome imaginative stretch. Infinity and world destruction were equally inconceivable, try though we might to make them otherwise.

"What would you do if you knew the bomb was going to drop in exactly one hour?" we often asked each other. It was the most serious of games, completely trivializing kickball and Monopoly. It was even more complelling than the old standard: "What would you do with a million dollars?" A typical fifth-grade answer was: "I'd eat a giant salami sandwich with lots of mayonnaise and drink two root beer floats." This seemed a logical final joy. In sixth grade, junior high loomed closer and our preoccupation changed. The new answer: "I'd tell Tom Harris that I like him." And then, forget that pallid wish: I'd tell Tom Harris that I love him!" My blondest and prettiest friend already wore her first bra and knew precisely what she wanted to do: "I would lose my virginity — I'd just find some boy and do it!"

Far from shocked, the rest of us admired her directness, her courage. Standing on the brink of womanhood in our first nylons and T-strap shoes, we shared her lust for the future. The Russians just had to wait at least five more years: It was unthinkable to die before making out to a slow dance, going to a drive-in movie with a boy who had a real driver's license, and wearing White Shoulders perfume with permission.

Wanting fervently to reach adulthood, we pleaded with our parents to build fallout shelters. *Life* magazine, to which everyone subscribed, carried huge spreads on the different models springing up all over the country, we pointed to *Life* and argued for our own. "I know we can afford it — we have a dishwasher!" was the middle-class cry. "You can take it out of my allowance from now until my senior year!" What good was an allowance anyway if you weren't around to spend it? I never knew anyone who actually built a fallout shelter; our parents all seemed to think it unnecessary and we wondered why. Was it because they didn't believe World War III would happen? Or were they all selfish people who, having lived out most of their own lives, were unconcerned about our getting to do the same? A chilling thought.

Increasing media coverage of the Cold War taught us that the bomb was indeed not singular and that radiation was deadly. Once upset about living in a target area ("Mom, couldn't we move to Ohio?") we decided that a target area was probably the best place to be. "It'll be over real fast for us," we comforted each other. "Maybe it will happen in the middle of the night and we won't even feel it." No nuclear naivete for us — we were becoming educated.

I combed the newspapers and magazines for the slightest reassurance, particularly random signs of humanity in Nikita Khrushchev. Nikita and I were on intimate terms. My scrapbook had one page devoted to 'My Enemies" where three photos and names were displayed: my older sister (for the usual sibling reasons), a girlfriend down the street with whom I had frequent quarrels, and Nikita himself. I had clipped his picture from the Oakland Tribune and included him on this most personal of lists. He was going to kill me, wasn't he? When I read about his wish to see Disneyland, I was briefly calmed. Any man who wanted to go to Disneyland couldn't be all bad — he couldn't really push that button.

Adolescence arrived, as did the Beatles, and nuclear war receded from my consciousness. Reminders presented themselves at pivotal times: As my friends and I did eventually leave our virginal states, there was a distinct satisfaction in having "beaten the clock." I think we were somewhat amazed to complete any rite of passage: to become 21, to vote, to order a drink. All that fear for nothing? We were safe after all?

Still, the threat of world destruction was always there. I stood before the Taj Mahal last year and surprised myself by thinking: "This would be a terrible loss!" I considered the arbitrary nature of The Bomb: It would destroy the Taj Mahal as unwittingly as if did all the McDonalds in America. A 4000-year-old culture had no more immunity than one of 200 years. Seniority meant nothing.

"What would you do if you knew you had an hour to live?" my peers might ask each other now. Well out of grammar school, we are all too aware of the futility of evacuation or of trying to reach loved ones. Present company will serve as intimates — would indeed become intimates at such a time — and, foregoing the hedonism of a root beer float, we'll probably open a bottle of Scotch. I am afraid now, but the fear is outweighed by an over-whelming adult sorrow: a grief for the waste of the world, not just for my own life.

There is no question in my mind that a child's terror surpasses an adult's. I know that this all felt much worse when I was 10 years old and living in an innocent time frame. Adults are convinced of their mortality. Children are not, nor should they be — this is partly what makes them children. To be one today, deprived even of the panacea of fallout shelters, would, I think, require unfathomable courage.

HOW DID WE GET HERE?

MISSILEMEN

missile thrush: A European thrush, *Turdus viscivorus*, that eats berries, mainly of the mistletoe.

misshape: To shape badly; deform.

missile: 1. Any object or weapon that is fired, thrown, dropped or otherwise projected at a target; projectile. 2. A *guided missile* (see). 3. A ballistic missile (see) From Latin *missilis*, from *mittere* (past participle *missus*), to let go, send.

missileman, -men: A person skilled in the design, building, or launching of ballistic missiles.

missing: Not present; absent; lost; lacking.

missing link: 1. A theoretical primate postulated to bridge the evolutionary gap between the anthropoid apes and man. 2. Something lacking but needed to complete a series.

mission: 1. A body of persons sent to conduct negotiations or establish relations with a foreign country.

*

"Well, it's over," said Lisa, taking her mother's hand. Gradually the woman became calm.

"Anyway," continued Lisa, "I think wherever there is love, of *any* kind, there is hope of salvation." She had an image of a bayonet flashing over spread thighs, and corrected herself hastily: "Wherever there is love in the heart."

"Tenderness."

"Yes, exactly!"

They strolled further along the shore. The sun was lower in the sky and the day cooler. The raven came skimming back, and a shiver ran up Lisa's spine.

—D.M. Thomas,
The White Hotel

*

When we are mad with fear about nuclear weapons and their possible use, our world changes. We realize that any child can read the front page of the newspaper and see that countries are buying and selling nuclear weapons; that a world lawfulness is non-existent, and that no one has advanced any solution for the containment or abandonment of instruments of global destruction. Children look to us with assurance that they may live to grow up, and we cannot assure them. We cannot even begin to explain how we got in this dilemma, and so we begin a kind of study — first, of the weapons themselves, acquainting ourselves with exactly how many there are, of what vintage and caliber, and where they are; then, by retracing the history of weaponry, war, and soldiering. The nuclear dilemma is both an external problem of a gung-ho economy that made too many of (to some minds) an exciting thing, and an internal problem of a national, cultural lack of self-scrutiny, a lack of self-reflection. None of us came on this stage barehanded. We are all products of parents and towns who had totally different attitudes towards war, national sovereignty, kicking ass, the military, and peace. Partly because we have lived through the sixties and we saw families and generations torn apart by differing opinions on Vietnam, we are now laid bare. Our political skeleton, in the eighties, is beyond stereotype: not all military men are hawks, not all poor people are liberals. We can each take our own background and poke through it awhile and come up with the differing sets of attitudes which helped to create this mess. If we keep on this, if we don't turn our backs and think someone else is going to solve it — and many of us are bolt upright with fear precisely because we realize there are at present no good answers — we might work, culturally, a fabric like a beautiful knitted shawl, of people honestly committed to bearing responsibility for the nuclear dilemma and finding a way out of it into brighter woods.

*

We all stand in some relationship to defense weapons: to their making, to their planning, to their use, just as we all stand in some relationship to the other great issues of our lives — to war, to love, to relationship, to death. This commonality gives us a measure of hope now, as it gives us positive *esprit* at other hard times. Countries, nations have been very wrong before — in our time, Hitler's anti-semitism and the detonation of the bombs obliterating Hiroshima and Nagasaki rank as major cultural horrors difficult to fathom or surpass — but humankind has never been so wrong, so misguided as a whole species that it made possible the ending of all life forms on the planet.

The cool and precise military strategist stands under the shadow of nuclear weapons just as much now as the farmer in his field, the small-town cheer-leader, the military wife dutifully accepting yet again another assignment, the thousands of ordnance clerks who just "send the power down the line." Warriors, both conservative and liberal in their political sentiments, create weaponry, but we all become its victims. There is no division between warriors and victims in war, least of all in thermonuclear warfare. Although the buying and selling of nuclear armaments is a major source of foreign capital for the United States, no one would make *any* money at all in a nuclear war; no one would profit.

*

My people lived in a place that had its entire reason for being as a mining town. Although they weren't miners themselves, that was the culture and the dominant energy in Denver in the years since its founding in 1858 and through my childhood in the forties and fifties.

My father was a writer and a publisher. He made a wooden pony for me out of a square box, with stirrups and a saddle. He bought me a cowboy outfit with boots and a cap-gun and fringed leather chaps. He sat among the evergreens in the cool, quiet tree-graced backyard of our Denver house in back of a goldfish pond and chipped away at a huge marble polar bear because the main thing he liked to do was carve animals out of wood and stone.

Denver, the West, 1954: Fifth grade. I played with a best friend in her bomb shelter under the steps of their house. It was stocked with shelves and shelves of Campbell's soup. We did not 'duck and cover' in school. Denver was an arrogant boom town, dominated by the wealth of its natural resources: gold, silver, grass, water, wheat lands, climate, coal, scenery, skiing and vacation-land (developers), oil, uranium, plutonium, shale oil, natural gas. Most dominant for my father were oil, natural gas, and uranium, in that order. He was tantalized by the future of shale oil but didn't live to see its development, its particular boom and bust. The discovery and frenzied exploitation of resources followed a course independent of the national economic cycle. The draw to pour money into any one of them might be dampened by conditions out of state, but the minerals were still in the ground, no matter how the stock market performed. Thus Denver had that super-ciliousness, that insular arrogance which comes when the means of one's fortune are close at hand rather than imported. Denver was a center for distribution in the west, distribution to towns that were so much more rural that it got back from them not new infor-mation, but reified versions of the image it gave out. What I am reaching for is an explanation for the insularity of my people — why the country at large, world and foreign politics, seemed so outside their ken. The Denver I see in the headlines now is a town where many people carry loaded pistols in their glove compart-ments to fight and argue over injustices on the highway. Immediacy of intent without self-reflection seems always to have been a prereq-uisite of growing up in Denver.

My father was involved in land. He cared about its past, its present use and ownership, the people on the land, and what was underneath and could be brought up. He never tried to own land himself. He was content to document the buying, selling and leasing of gas and mineral rights in his magazines, and he cared about the quality of the deals. He knew who was screwing who, although he did not always report on it. In a book written for Indian tribes (to help them get more control over the licensing of their mineral rights), his language reveals how he viewed the large drilling companies which eventually bought up small operators — the readers of his magazine:

". . . it is important to keep the independent operators from being completely shut out by the very big companies. Restless and aggressive little operators, the independents, manage to put together drilling deals to get even the least likely areas tested, and in more than a few instances it has been the independent who has opened up an important new oil field or launched a 'play' that causes intensive exploration over a large area. It was an 'independent', the Kerr-McGee Corporation of Oklahoma City, which brought in the sensational new Navaho oil discovery in Apache Country, Arizona, appropriately named by the Navahos *Dineh bi Keyah*, 'the people's field.' "

This is how it seemed in 1967 to my father, who saw the world in categories: "independents" and "very big companies". The independents slowly became very big companies. By the time Karen Silkwood got to Kerr-McGee five years later, it was as big and dirty a factory as there was in the western world. My father would not have understood (if he had lived long enough), but all the warning signs were there. Companies like Kerr-McGee were all smiles and handshakes when drilling on Indian lands, but pure malignancy when it came to caring about sacred sites or human beings.

The Oil Reporter was on the side of progress and unexamined growth; it sported a bright red and white cover usually featuring a piece of drilling equipment or a new kind of rig. Selling the cover meant the whole issue was paid for. My father made long, meandering trips down to the four corners to sell ads for *The Oil Reporter*, but no matter how many he sold, the government "partnership" with large oil firms squeezed the small operator out.

Uranium, the magazine he started when *The Oil Reporter* declined, seemed over and done with in a minute. He took a group of investors around the world to look at uranium holdings in South Africa, in Australia, in New Zealand. The AEC was moving quickly to sew up domestic uranium production just as my father was getting on to the big story of who owned what and the incredible wealth in holdings it might involve. There was a sudden dearth of information. My father must have reeled back, struck like an insolent child for presuming he could be in on this story, for presuming there would even be independent investors who were not large companies or the government. He turned to other "projects": a vanity biography of a "Uranium Queen," a white-haired old lady named Stella Dysart; an arts magazine. Then he declared bankruptcy. The face of oil, uranium and natural gas exploration had changed. No one needed his magazines or directories, no one gave a hoot about independent little operators.

The use of the elements which came to make nuclear power plants and nuclear weapons wasn't discussed while they were being made. The fifties were post-war years of research, exciting exploration and manufacture. The atom was "friendly". How a nuclear reactor worked was a diagram to be drawn by school children: the rods and the cones are inserted in the huge square here, the chain reaction was shown by many asterisks connected by arrows. That meant, it can go on and on and *on*. . . . I drew such a report; I remember being challenged to figure it out in the same way a school child attacks any problem. I made, with exactly the same diligence and concentration, a report on the instruments in a symphony orchestra, and later in the year a journal of an eleven-year-old girl (my counterpart, I imagined) living in an Egyptian palace in the year 1400 B.C. during the reign of Tutankhamen.

My father was walking along hillsides in Utah, Colorado, New Mexico, South Africa and Australia listening to their secret with a geiger counter. When the needle began swinging and the static increased, it also meant he was absorbing more radiation into the bone marrow of legs which were already weak from a childhood bout of polio. When he died in 1974 of "a perforated ulcer" one doctor suggested there may have been as many as five different forms of cancer. No one sat in the hospital reflecting on the effects of plutonium, which has a half-life ranging from twenty minutes to seventy-six million years.

*

My father had a business associate who had more or less lost touch with a child from a first early marriage. By a chance occurrence I came upon the family history of this child:

George Scott Brewster V was born on July 21, 1921. He had a B.A. and an M.A. in physics from Princeton University

(1945) and Florida State University (1949). His Ph.D. in Meteorology was from Renssellaer Polytechnic Institute. He attended Navy school in California, saw sea duty in the Pacific, and, after the war, eloped with Harriet Chester Mims (Sweetbriar College). They were married on June 2, 1947 in Aspen, Colorado.

From 1948 to 1950: Optic Dynamics Lab — developed infra-red aerial camera with light-intensifying lens. From 1950 to 51: Meteorological Division, National Health Facility, Bethesda, Maryland. From 1952 to 53: Los Alamos Energy Range — mapped explosives testing sites. From 1953 to 55, Hughes Aircraft Corp. — tested high-altitude equipment; from 1955 to 59, Overseas Research Associates (Army), Washington, D.C. — developed tactical communications nets, tested war games simulating nuclear battlefield (data later applied at HQ US-European Command, 1960-66). From 1960 to 61: Systems Reconnaissance Institute, Dow Chemical Company; from there to Stanford Research Institute until 1967 (from 1964 to 69, assigned to Germany to develop operational model for new command center and emergency backups). 1967: assisted Egyptian Government in resource management, budgetary liaison (mission curtailed by '6 day war'). From 1968 to 1977, Los Alamos again, developed "alternative" energy projects, consulted with Navajo Tribe on coal gassification and uranium development. From 1974 to 77 he was an economic consultant to the Navajo Tribal Council while representing LAER at DOD and AEC. From 1975 to 1979 — held seminars for upper-level diplomatic and military staffs, JCS, NATO. Then from early 1970 through 1980 he established and managed the "Kuwait Project Team." In 1979 he formed his own company: Los Alamos Gas and Energy Associates (independent consulting on radioactive waste management, geothermal development, and hydro-thermal commercialization). In 1978 he became (and remains) an analyst for the Institute for defense, Washington, D.C., specializing in operations coordination of "Command-control-communication-intelligence" (C³I) systems for U.S. Unified Commands.

*

Such is the tenor of American life in the post-war era: George Brewster was an exemplary son. His easy sally between government and private industry, the way in which aerospace, Air Force, upper air studies, reconnaissance systems, and "doctrinal studies on electronic warfare" are woven together speaks of the way in which our military, private industry, and foreign governments collaborate. Where was George Brewster? Probably flying on a private jet between the simultaneous positions and commands he held. In one uniform he was a private consultant to the Navajo, the Arabs; but he could return from his motel the next day bearing his briefcase of Joint Command priorities.

This George Brewster was not a man worrying about the ethical and moral consequences of nuclear armaments. He was concerned with the building of systems, able to emphasize technical accuracy and objectivity, concentrating attention on questions of detail which could be reduced to quantitive calculation. Factual analysis, rather than moralistic judgment, was his ballgame. In the times in which George Brewster did the things listed on his resumé, he was seen, and saw himself, as building a safer country, "making the world safe for democracy." He did not think he was doing anything wrong, any more than Teller or Oppenheimer or a thousand other similar research scientists did who were involved not only in research but "planning and command." Perhaps the only thing they or any of us have done wrong is to isolate our tiny segment of the whole from the total fabric, which has seemed to absolve us from taking any responsibility for the ethical and moral issues surrounding the use of the finished products.

There are no exogenous war chiefs. American military men (and women) come from the best families, the best schools. They have all written heartfelt papers on ethics and justice. Once George Brewster came to Denver on assignment to explore sites to store nuclear wastes. He had been searching the Southwest on this grail, and he dropped in at the house of one of my father's close friends for dinner and announced that he had found the perfect place: Carlsbad Caverns. He proclaimed this with the same pride (no doubt) he had presented earlier achievements.

After all, he was annointed. We were mere civilians. And we lacked his background in math.

*

It is against this background that the present symptomology plays itself out in a repetitive minimalist dance. *For every action there is an equal and opposite reaction*: In almost magical payment for the lack of fear and concern my people showed towards others during World War II, McCarthyism, Hiroshima, Vietnam or now on into the crimes of Khomeini or the subjugation of Poland and El Salvador, I seem to be putting in my time studying the pathologies of fear, desire and aggression in pornography and nuclear armaments. When we drove by Rocky Flats on our way home from our summer house in the foothills of the Rockies, engineers were tooling the plutonium components for nuclear warheads. Rocky Flats was a barbed-wire expanse of flat plain with no visible signs on it, not much different from the other great areas of property the government owned in the Southwest and West. No one knew what happened there and no one cared. No one gave it a thought, on any of the soft warm summer nights we passed by.

The disease I carry now is compulsive and obsessive. It is on the order of "Step on a crack, you'll break your mother's back," a childhood game with particular appeal to obsessive personalities. In the midst of a little happiness, doing some mundane domestic task like hanging out the laundry in the sun, or reaching for a corn seedling to put in the rich dark earth, I'll immediately have a vision of nuclear winter. No sun. No vegetation. People incurably sick, starving, no medical care, everyone eventually dying. Total rubble, people picking their way through buildings reduced to huge piles of brick and concrete, a stench in the air so strong one cannot breathe, and a continual parching thirst. The vision comes without conscious direction on my part, and feels like a collective fear— perhaps the fear of others who don't fear, often enough to account for all those people in my past in Colorado who never thought of the consequences of so many nuclear weapons poised and ready to explode, and all the people now who still don't think of it because they are lulled by different and more benign illusions. I can tell the fear is compulsive because it is similar to the disorder which causes the compulsive personality to read the same page over again: it's a feeling that if one could think themselves out of this, there would be a way out. I *long* to escape this particular neurotic problem. It happens when I wash the dishes and look out the window to the newly planted yard with pleasure. As I become more aware of the actions of this administration and views of the United States from abroad, the fear becomes a motivating force, an informed awareness rather than a panic reaction. But I can't help watch also, very carefully, the forms of awareness of people like the ones I came from in Colorado, who profit at the expense of others . . . whether they be colonial or in-house business interests, conglomerates or mining engineers squeezing out rural farmers for the next homestead open pit gold mine. I would not be playing this compulsive game in my head if the cultural climate were not wound up in a kind of mindless blind-folded stance not dissimilar to the "Friendly Atom" Walt Disney portrayed in the fifties. The equal and opposite reaction is a kind of carrier cancer brought on by the presence of so many nuclear weapons in a cultural climate which seems to sanction and feed on violence. The Jungian psychiatrist Robert Sardello has commented that even if the bombs don't go off, we will, until they are rendered powerless, be dominated by the fear of their detonation:

> "When the forms of mass consciousness reach a critical state, the conditions for nuclear annihilation are present, whether or not the bomb goes off."

*

We try not to sit in judgment. We try to have some compassion, some understanding and sympathy for a different era. We are irritable and it shows.

Men happy to get back to work after the war. Women willing to give back their jobs to the men who had left them, to move back into the home and be a mommy again; happy to have a father back home. The fission scientist was the cream of the crop: paid research, highly motivated by the Great War and Hitler's ravages, *never again*. Suddenly, everyone was building and moving again in a post-war economy. Men were selling cheaper cars and everyone wanted one and could afford one; people moved to new suburbs which seemed so quiet, so calm after the city. Science was the progenitor for the marketing of all kinds of products: dacron, nylon, new synthetic plastics, metallic blends. The lines between research and planning, design and manufacture blurred easily because one advancement made another possible. In the early fifties there were so many advancements in how products were made, and the rapid rate at which they could be made. Best of all, the economy inflated cash for people to buy them. Advancements combined, like tributaries of rivers, to accelerate technology and make previously expensive items much cheaper. The fact that fission weapons could be made more cheaply and smaller, yet with still greater power, opened markets abroad for those who wanted nuclear power in general and nuclear weapons in specific. The man in the street did not make distinctions between nuclear power and what it could be used for. The friendly atom, assumed a part of the economy by every administration that came and went, joined with first the large computers, and then with the semi-conductor revolution. The specs became at once more complicated, more precise, more detailed, and to the engineering scientist, more intellectually interesting with the introduction of the micro-chip. Companies which had lost out on their original markets (Singer Sewing Machines, for example, when women went back to work and stopped sewing at home) invested in two sure-fires: nuclear defense industries *and* micro-chip technology. All the timing devices could now be fitted to a tiny chip to make even cheaper, smaller, still just as powerful "vehicles".

By 1983 the distinction between the research, design, and manufacture of defense weapons had so blurred to the public eye that it was hard to decide who was most responsible for their presence. When the press and a group of Catholic clergy asked some Livermore Laboratory designers if they felt responsible for making the world *less safe*, for ringing the world with death machines, they were astonished. They replied that they were making the world *more safe.* Their pride was assaulted, they implied, they had done nothing wrong. Such news items pointed up a growing awareness and suspicion of the double-think of deterrence, which a now more-watchful public began to follow like an odor of molding, still–damp laundry traced to the dryer where someone forgot it for years. Ronald Reagan told everyone he was in favor, for example, of the idea known as "build-down," where two old nuclear devices would be destroyed for every new one built. Critics pointed out that the new devices are at least twice as deadly—"destabilizing" is the word used by weapons experts— as the ones they replace, so nothing is gained. We came to understand, slowly, that he wasn't really in favor of less weapons, but would always want more.

So, here we are. We have a product that threatens life on the planet which is being manufactured, sold, exported, and stockpiled for our own use by people who just think they're doing just what capitalism intended—making a good product and sellin' it. No *other* manufacturers worry too much about results. Products are recalled *after* people have died: *Rely,* a fan-shaped menstrual tampon was so massively absorbent it caused toxic shock poisoning and killed a number of women before it ceased production; DES left a generation of women in doubt about their health; any number of pesticides and anti-biotics. *Consumer beware* is the name of the game in America. Defense weapons are a hard product to recall because there is no global equivalent to an FDA. The Atomic Energy Commission is a ludicrous watchdog for the planet.

Change has to come, I am convinced, from the bottom up. Small specific changes of consciousness in many places at the same time make, finally, a national movement. Any other kind of change easily becomes part of the polarizing political process wherein even people who might agree with one another find themselves adopting radically opposed solutions.

Take, for example, the present cultural reaction towards abusive pornography. There is a fairly large proportion of educated men and women in America who now regard some kinds of pornography as culturally unhealthy. This hard-core porn is considered damaging because it fosters attitudes about women (and children, where kiddie porn is included) which make normal healthy sexual and non-sexual interaction with women difficult. Yet the dilemma of First Amendment violations is so great that the first attempts at legislation (introduced by Andrea Dworkin and Catherine MacKinnon, for example, in the Indianapolis and Minneapolis City Councils) simply run into the old wasps' nest of freedom-of-choice issues: people should have the right to choose their form of entertainment, even if that form includes images which have as their intent the brutalization, demeanment and violation of women and children. The process of introducing legislation is a years-long one of continued refinement, but we can expect during the process a raft of polarizing reactions—to the extent that liberal male lawyers, often well educated themselves, pit themselves against feminists, and the general population looks from one to the other to see who is most bearable. Both positions become distorted, too extreme, and the common citizen identifies with neither.

When people act at the local level on a smaller scale, this polarizing process doesn't happen so quickly. On the main incoming avenue in Berkeley, for example, prostitutes openly soliciting and turning their tricks in cars in full view of pedestrians and home-owners have been hounded by teams of local residents aghast at this open trafficking in their neighborhood. These ordinary townspeople, led by a Protestant pastor from a local church, feel outraged that their sidewalks should not be safe for their children to walk on, and that they and their children should have to see, at such close view, the prostitute's world. In other parts of the country adult bookstores and movie houses have been closed by neighborhood merchants denying lease renewals. But there is only so much that can be done. In an age of satellite t.v. and rocket-delivered weapons it is hard to focus on neighborhoods. A prosecutor in a recent teen satanic drug cult incident on Long Island, New York, (in which one arrested teenager later took his own life) pointed out that parents and law enforcement officers were missing the obvious: these were not kids seriously involved in a satanic cult or with any interest at all in occult matters. They were affluent bored youth with free access to drugs who had been watching the popular MTV punk rock videos, which deliver drug-high satanic/vampiric imagery. The producers of these MTV videos saw a lucrative market, just as the San Francisco-based Mitchell Brothers did when they started creating sleezy sex films and "Copenhagen Live" sex parlors—and just as the manufacturers of nuclear weapons did when they realized that small, cheaper, just-as-explosive nuclear tips could be sold to developing nations. If no one opposes these products, they just go right on being made. They find their market. It's no wonder that every business feels justified in ignoring ethical or moral scruples, when the government broadcasts in a clear loud voice, administration after administration, that the manufacture, sale and distribution of massive weapons which would assure planetary destruction, if used, are a perfectly fine way to balance the budget and make a living. The whole planet is now being treated as a gross national product instead of a series of ecosystems and neighborhoods.

Social change activists working within the nuclear freeze movement are involved now in "conversion plans" for the defense industry. Perceiving that one of the main obstacles to the halting of the manufacture of nuclear weapons is that all the contractors down the line involved in the process would be put out of work, anti-nuclear activists have been holding conferences and drawing up papers which might suggest alternative uses of nuclear technology. People don't necessarily want to make nuclear weapons, they want to make *something* that is at the same high level of technical expertise and rate of pay as the weapons. We have converted once before—from a war economy based on defense industries to a peace-time economy. Someday, to survive, we will have to do it again.

*

During the later years of the Vietnam War, when I was a young mother in a mid-western university town, I belonged to a women's peace group. I belonged mainly so I could find friends to talk to about matters other than children. Such groups have continued during the last fifteen years. Dr. Helen Caldicott founded one of them, Women's Action for Nuclear Disarmament.

Their work now is much more ambitious and has the potential for totally changing the face of western culture. They have become increasingly involved in a many-generational education peace curriculum involved with not only stopping the production of nuclear weapons, but educating children and adults on alternatives to violent inter-personal behavior.

Is fighting a normal activity? Is violence a good way to resolve conflict? If your father thinks kicking ass is what being a good father is, does that mean you will do it too? If you have been beaten and abused as a child, will you drift more easily into hierarchical highly disciplinary career worlds like the Marines and the Army? For the first time in this culture, abused children and abusive parents are learning how to cope with one another without hitting. For the first time in this culture, battering husbands and wives are attending workshops devoted to coping with anger without beating up a spouse or child. How can one cope with their own anger and the anger of another?

Relaxation exercises, stress reduction, anger journals, conflict management are all counselling methods used by domestic violence therapists. These are all excellent methodologies, but they presume an interest and ability to use therapy on the part of the client, and they are mental, psychological, verbal approaches. The internal martial arts are an exciting way to work with this same territory because they involve physical work, a physically exhausting outlet while at the same time teaching people a new way to look at the violence in themselves. They give people a means to recognize their suppressed aggressive energy towards an opponent and act it out in a safe place—while training in a martial art. So many people who have problems with anger are alienated from conventional therapeutic methods, which presuppose a doctor/patient relationship, rather than the master/student relationship of the martial arts. In my own study of aikido I am learning not simply how to compete with myself and others, which I would learn in any sport, but how I arrange myself to ward off fear and violence. I interact in each session with a number of partners around issues of anger and aggression, while continually studying myself: the ways I hold myself physically, the ways I tend to learn or jump ahead to mimicking a move rather than internally feeling it, the ways I preen and compete rather than really focus on my partner.

Often people are attracted to aikido, as to the other martial arts, because they want to be able to defend themselves if attacked on the street. Aikido is not much against a gun, but it trains the mind to let go of fear and competitiveness. It brings a psychological component to its discipline of learning moves, throws, holds, rolls. These moves help a body react which might otherwise go limp in terror. When I am in confrontation with a friend, a spouse, a boss or a child, they help me to slow down and watch what is happening rather than feel I must strike or take flight. I view this training as midway between therapy and a competitive sport, but essentially serious about something completely discrete to itself: it is training in the proper way to channel energy outward towards a partner or opponent without losing connection to a rooted sense of myself.

Aikido doesn't claim a long history. It was originated in the 1930s in Japan by Morihei Ueshiba in direct opposition to karate, a usually more deadly self-defense technique in which the practitioner is taught to block his opponent's attack and then deliver a destructive counter-attack that will cause serious injury, and judo, a competitive sport where two contestants unbalance, throw and then pin an opponent to the mat with sweeping foot motions and various holds and throws. The difference between aikido and these other two is that aikido is a self-defense art in which the practitioner aims to protect one's self without injuring one's opponent. All these trace their roots back to a connection between Zen and the order of the samurai, *bushido*, the medieval code of chivalry. In aikido the practice and training with a partner which sharpens self-knowledge and introspection rather than straight competitiveness is presently more developed than in karate or judo or kendo.

Aikido functions as an insightful psychological system in which the tension and aggression of normal daily life can be studied and watched in one's self; it is the first physical system I have encountered in which energy other than strength and power are used to motivate movement. George Leonard describes this connection with zazen in aikido in the foreword to Taisen Deshimaru's *The Zen Way to the Martial Arts*, as he quotes Master Deshimaru:

> . . . zazen does not mean ecstasy or the arousal of emotion or any particular condition of the body or mind. It means returning, completely, to the pure normal human condition. That condition is not something reserved for great masters and saints, there is nothing mysterious about it, it is within everyone's reach.
>
> Zazen means becoming intimate with oneself, finding the exact taste of inner unity and harmonizing with universal life.

When people study aikido with this approach (fully realizing, as so beautifully depicted in the film "The Karate Kid" that "there are no bad students, only bad teachers") they are making a long-term investment in the belief that if they can change their own attitude towards violence, they can deal more effectively not only with external violence at large but with their own aggression. This is close to a square–on confrontation with the shadow, the part of the self that has no way to find expression in daily life. When I practice a hold with my partner I am facing both my own fear of attack and my desire to attack, at the same time reaching to my self for a certainty and confidence that will dispel fear but not substitute bravado and competition in its place. If I am not comfortable with myself, I will be ineffective in sensing where my partner's strength is coming from and he or she will easily topple me. There is no hope held out in aikido for universal love, life everlasting, people necesssarily being good to one another, or ultimate understanding with one's enemy. Aikido is at the other end of the spectrum from born-again Christianity. It does not presuppose commonality, or particular good will on the part of other humans. Aikido pursues self-honesty in the belief that if humans understood themselves better, they could manage conflict with each other more effectively.

In aikido you facilitate your opponent. You help him on his way out of your way. Your strength to make him stop interfering with you comes from intense concentration on one movement—for instance, a wrist twist—that does not rely on pure physical strength. You are comfortable with yourself; you center yourself before you even try to contact him. You don't become embroiled in him, too concerned with his pain or comfort, or his welfare; you don't even become involved enough in him to want to kill him or really hurt him. Those intentions are viewed only as your projections of your fear of him. You want the best for him, because he is a member of the human species; you try to move him along on his way. Every day we come across people who are toying with us whom we must move along: the therapist must move along the manipulative patient, the wife must keep from becoming embroiled in argument with husband or child, the bus driver must keep the people moving along and the bus moving along. Standing back and letting someone find his own way is a different form of power than domination. In aikido the power of an attack is redirected safely and forcefully by a prospective victim joining with its motion and taking control of its force. The people who are attracted to this form are game for grappling with their fear of violence (which is exposed) and their fear of their own force. They want, primarily, to feel safe, but they want also not to feel like victims. They understand that you can't be nervous or anxious or emotional and feel safe. You have to be like water, reflecting clearly whatever is there, and yet not losing the shape and form of what and who you are.

On the airplane to Denver recently I sat next to two cultural types who reminded me of who is out there in America and the difficulty of changing the vision of the future of America. For two hours on the way to Stapleton Field I chatted amiably with a contractor from Omaha who was returning from supervising the construction of an off-shore oil rig the size of a ten-story building in the waters west of Vallejo. He was happy to have someone to talk to; so was I. We drank soft drinks and munched sandwiches, over the Sierras, the great desert, and finally, the Rockies. What did he think of the nuclear dilemma? Of children not sure they would live to grow up? Did he feel any national embarrassment at having a nuclear capability now to destroy the planet one hundred and sixty times over? His thoughts on these matters were very clear, and he was happy to talk about them.

"I read that kids were having real bad dreams about nuclear

war in one of the newspapers I read, I forget which one—is that true? I couldn't figure out if that was true or not. I read about twenty newspapers a week, so I never know which one I read something in. But we have to keep up building better weapons because ours are about twenty-five years out of date. We have to be up-to-date. We can never let down our guard. You ever buy a computer? It's like that. There's new hardware constantly coming out and you've got to have the best, it's like that with weapons. Of course the Russians'll get the jump on us if we don't have the best hardware, and we don't, now.

"Y'know, they've never retracted that remark they made in the sixties about wanting to take over the world. Things'd be different if they would. Sometimes I just think of that remark and I feel a chill up my spine. They only respect force and might. They don't screw around with Reagan, that's for sure; Carter, they just walked all over him. He didn't inspire their respect. Our church and university in Omaha has some special ties with Afghanistan— we were involved in a lot of exchanges with a department of one of their universities and we've followed the fate of a number of families who've been very hurt by the invasion of Afghanistan. You can't make peace with people like that — all you can do is hope they respect your ability to hurt them. We can't ever let up."

On the way back from Denver I sat next to a mother and daughter. They had never flown before. They were tremendously excited, smiling, cheery, playing games with one another. They were not talkers, as more seasoned travelers often are. They were involved in themselves. They reminded me of the people in the country for whom politics is not an interesting subject. It takes a certain set of personal resources to collect information and keep track of enough facts to make sense out of politics. This mother and daughter, sunny and light-hearted as they were, seemed to me to be people who barely followed the international issues of the day. They could have been the charming family of the blustering Republican I sat next to on the way to Denver, whose politics were reduced to a hardline "might is right," " bigger is better" set of attitudes.

In *The March of Folly* an exasperated Barbara Tuchman

writes, "Why do we invest all our skills and resources in a contest for armed superiority, which can never be attained for long enough to make it worth having, rather than in an effort to find a *modus vivendi* with our antagonist — that is to say, a way of living, not dying?"

The outlaw Josey Wales (played by Clint Eastwood in the film of that name) rides into the camp of Ten Bears, the Comanche chief. He tells him that he and his friends will not be driven from their land by the Indians; they have been chased across the country and they have no where left to go.

"Then you will die," says Ten Bears.

Josey nods. "I came here to die with you. Or live with you. Dying ain't so hard for men like you and me. It's living that's hard — when all you've ever cared about's been butchered or raped. Governments don't live together; people live together. With governments you don't always get a fair word or a fair fight. Well, I've come here to give you either one, or get either one from you. I came here like this so that you know my word of death is true — and that my word of life is then true. The bear lives here, the wolf, the antelope, the Comanche— and so will we. And we'll only hunt what we need to live on, same as the Comanche does. And every spring when the grass turns green and the Comanche moves north, he can rest here in peace, butcher some of our cattle and jerk beef for the journey. The sign of the Comanche, that will be on our lodge; that is my word of life."

"And your word of death?" asks Ten Bears.

"It's here in my pistols. And there in your rifles. I'm here for either one."

"These things you say we will have, we already have."

"That's true," says Josey. "I ain't promising you nothing extra. I'm just giving you life, and you're giving me life. And I'm saying that men can live together without butchering one another."

Ten Bears ponders this and then speaks. "It's sad government's are chiefed by the double tongues. There is iron in your words of death for all Comanche to see. And so there is iron in your words of life. No signed paper can hold the iron. It must come from men. The word of Ten Bears carries this same iron of life and death.

It is good that warriors such as we meet in the struggle of life. Or death." He pauses, takes out his knife and slashes his hand. "It shall be life!" The two men ride closer, and Josey takes out his knife and cuts his own palm. They press their bleeding hands together.

One is a different kind of friend with an antagonist than with a compatriot, but one is still a friend. All through my childhood, since 1944, the world has been falsely divided into friendly and unfriendly nations. But it is only with those friends that are also enemies that we can learn anything about ourselves and make a real peace.

*

As I go about the garden and the house doing the routine tasks any women does, I don't regret my compulsive almost mantric-like visions and thought about nuclear war. In such thoughts are a first awareness about it as a real possibility. In such terror is probably imbedded conscience and an awareness of responsibility: I, like so many others, entrusted our safety to others, who did what they thought was correct. Maybe they weren't right. When one takes on one's own heritage and connection to a collective guilt, admits one has had a hand in creating the problem, a massive amount of internal, personal energy is mobilized to help solve the problem. The problem *is* solvable (although perhaps not in time) if enough people become involved in thinking through our posture. Leaving such matters to "specialists" has resulted in technology in a moral vacuum. It is very much our business.

A sizeable number of born-again Christians now think that it doesn't really matter if the world is annihilated, since they will be saved in a last judgement. It is the same arrogance and selfishness Americans show in appraising the world as better and worse "markets": "Why do business with the Russians? (or the Guianans)—They're a lousy market." Only an individual and cultural transformation of values can combat the present double-think of the Reagan Administration ("We need to stockpile chemical weapons in order to prod the Soviet Union into a chemical weapons agreement destroying chemical weapons and banning them throughout the world"). We need to raise a generation of people who value internal spiritual and psychological growth and who are capable of other options for the effective communication of anger besides cold-war threat behavior and violence.

In aikido one learns to use the energy of the opponent to facilitate that opponent on his way out of your way. The strength to make him stop interfering with you comes not from your physical strength, but your concentrated focus and energy. You are centered. You are comfortable with yourself and *grounded* (a word, admittedly, the human potential movement never let go of once it found). We have done two things wrong in our dealings with the Soviet Union: we have alienated our opponent so much that we have lost the basic avenues of commonality which would forge a closer relationship, and we have adopted methods of arguing which stifle discussion and never let us know even how our opponent is thinking. We need to go back and teach ourselves the right ways to argue — not to lose our ground and our aims, but to hear one another out and be heard. And we need to go back and learn how to fight honorably. A closer touch with one another, especially when we argue, and a fuller sense or our place among the creatures of the natural world might help us back off the brink. We are there for a reason, and we have been a long time coming.

Embedded in the sheer terror one first experiences upon becoming fully aware of nuclear peril lies a modesty which may be the beginning of constructing a new order of self-honesty free of some of the arrogance and deceit we've wound ourselves up in, tight as a ball. We need to be able to tell our children that there *is* a way to deal with an enemy without destroying ourselves and them and the whole planet. The children who can be reassured about nuclear holocaust are not those whose parents will not speak of it, but those whose parents have made it a central issue to solve in their lifetimes.

VORTEX GAUDIER-BRZESKA.
(Written from the Trenches).

NOTE.—The sculptor writes from the French trenches, having been in the firing line since early in the war.

In September he was one of a patrolling party of twelve, seven of his companions fell in the fight over a roadway.

In November he was nominated for sergeancy and has been since slightly wounded, but expects to return to the trenches.

He had been constantly employed in scouting and patrolling and in the construction of wire entanglements in close contact with the Boches.

I HAVE BEEN FIGHTING FOR TWO MONTHS and I can now gauge the intensity of Life.

HUMAN MASSES teem and move, are destroyed and crop up again.

HORSES are worn out in three weeks, die by the roadside.

DOGS wander, are destroyed, and others come along.

WITH ALL THE DESTRUCTION that works around us **NOTHING IS CHANGED, EVEN SUPERFICIALLY. LIFE IS THE SAME STRENGTH. THE MOVING AGENT THAT PERMITS THE SMALL INDIVIDUAL TO ASSERT HIMSELF.**

THE BURSTING SHELLS, the volleys, wire entanglements, projectors, motors, the chaos of battle **DO NOT ALTER IN THE LEAST,** the outlines of the hill we are besieging. A company of **PARTRIDGES** scuttle along before our very trench.

IT WOULD BE FOLLY TO SEEK ARTISTIC EMOTIONS AMID THESE LITTLE WORKS OF OURS.

THIS PALTRY MECHANISM, WHICH SERVES AS A PURGE TO OVER-NUMEROUS HUMANITY.

THIS WAR IS A GREAT REMEDY.

IN THE INDIVIDUAL IT KILLS ARROGANCE, SELF-ESTEEM, PRIDE.

IT TAKES AWAY FROM THE MASSES NUMBERS UPON NUMBERS OF UNIMPORTANT UNITS, WHOSE ECONOMIC ACTIVITIES BECOME NOXIOUS AS THE RECENT TRADE CRISES HAVE SHOWN US.

<u>MY VIEWS ON SCULPTURE</u> REMAIN ABSOLUTELY THE SAME.

IT IS THE <u>VORTEX</u> OF WILL, OF DECISION, THAT BEGINS.

I SHALL DERIVE MY EMOTIONS SOLELY FROM THE <u>ARRANGEMENT OF SURFACES,</u> I shall present my emotions by the ARRANGEMENT OF MY SURFACES, THE PLANES AND LINES BY WHICH THEY ARE DEFINED.

Just as this hill where the Germans are solidly entrenched, gives me a nasty feeling, solely because its gentle slopes are broken up by earth-works, which throw long shadows at sunset. Just so shall I get feeling, of whatsoever definition, from a statue ACCORDING TO ITS SLOPES, varied to infinity.

I have made an experiment. Two days ago I pinched from an enemy a mauser rifle. Its heavy unwieldy shape swamped me with a powerful IMAGE of brutality.

I was in doubt for a long time whether it pleased or displeased me.

I found that I did not like it.

I broke the butt off and with my knife I carved in it a design, through which I tried to express a gentler order of feeling, which I preferred.

BUT I WILL EMPHASIZE that MY DESIGN got its effect (just as the gun had) FROM A VERY SIMPLE COMPOSITION OF LINES AND PLANES.

GAUDIER-BRZESKA.

MORT POUR LA PATRIE.

Henri Gaudier-Brzeska: after months of fighting and two promotions for gallantry Henri Gaudier-Brzeska was killed in a charge at Neuville St. Vaast, on June 5th, 1915.

Freeman Dyson

WEAPONS AND HOPE (excerpt)

From "Scientists and Poets"

Some of the people who worked under Oppenheimer at Los Alamos asked themselves afterward: "Why did we not stop when the Germans surrendered?" For many of them, and for Oppenheimer in particular, the principal motivation for joining the project at the beginning had been the fear that Hitler might get the bomb first. The Germans had a large number of competent scientists, including the original discoverers of nuclear fission, and a secret German uranium project was known to exist. The danger that Hitler might acquire nuclear weapons and use them to conquer the world seemed real and urgent. But that danger had disappeared by the end of 1944. Nobody imagined that Japan was in a position to develop nuclear weapons. So the primary argument which persuaded British and American scientists to go to Los Alamos had ceased to be valid long before the Trinity test. It would have been possible for them to stop. They might at least have paused to ask the question, whether in the new circumstances it was wise to go ahead to the actual production of weapons. Only one man paused. The one who paused was Joseph Rotblat from Liverpool, who, to his everlasting credit, resigned his position at Los Alamos and left the laboratory in December 1944 when it became known that the German uranium project had not progressed far enough to make the manufacture of bombs a serious possibility. Twelve years later Rotblat helped Bertrand Russell to launch the Pugwash movement, an informal international association of scientists dedicated to the cause of peace. From that time until today, Rotblat has remained one of the moving spirits of Pugwash. The reason why the others did not pause is to be seen clearly in Oppenheimer's assurance to General Groves, written on October 4, 1944: "The laboratory is acting under a directive to produce weapons; this directive has been and will be rigorously adhered to." Oppenheimer had accepted on behalf of himself and his colleagues the subordination of personal judgment to military authority. The war against Japan was still raging. To step aside from the production of a decisive weapon, while soldiers were dying every day in the Pacific Islands, would have seemed like an act of treason. It was wartime, and in wartime the ethic of the soldier, "Theirs not to reason why," prevails.

Fighting for freedom. That was the ideal which pulled young men to die in Spain, to take up armed resistance against Hitler in the mountains of Yugoslavia, and to go to work with Oppenheimer in Los Alamos. Fighting for freedom, the traditional and almost instinctive human response to oppression and injustice. Fighting for freedom, the theme song of the Spanish war and of World War II from beginning to end. Cecil Day Lewis wrote in 1937 a war poem called "The Nabara," a long poem, perhaps the only poem which adequately describes the spirit of those who went to fight against hopeless odds in the early battles of the Second World War, even though the poem was written before that war started. "The Nabara" is a dirge for fifty-two Spanish fishermen, the crew of an armed trawler which lost a battle against one of Franco's warships. It is also perhaps a dirge for all of us who have chosen to fight for freedom with the technologies of death. I quote here a few of the concluding stanzas:

> Of her officers all but one were dead. Of her engineers
> All but one were dead. Of the fifty-two that had sailed
> In her, all were dead but fourteen — and each of these
> half-killed
> With wounds. And the night-dew fell in a hush of ashen
> tears,
> And *Nabara's* tongue was stilled.
>
> *Canarias* lowered a launch that swept in a greyhound's
> curve
> Pitiless to pursue
> And cut them off. But that bloodless and all-but-phantom
> crew
> Still gave no soft concessions to fate: they strung their
> nerve

For one last fling of defiance, they shipped their oars and
    threw
Hand-grenades at the launch as it circled about to board
    them.
But the strength of the hands that had carved them a
    hold on history
Failed them at last: the grenades fell short of the enemy,
Who grappled and overpowered them,
While *Nabara* sank by the stern in the hushed Cantabrian
    sea.

They bore not a charmed life. They went into battle
    foreseeing
Probable loss, and they lost. The tides of Biscay flow
Over the obstinate bones of many, the winds are sighing
Round prison walls where the rest are doomed like their
    ship to rust —
Men of the Basque country, the Mar Cantabrico.

For these I have told of, freedom was flesh and blood —
    a mortal
Body, the gun-breech hot to its touch: yet the battle's
    height
Raised it to love's meridian and held it awhile immortal;
And its light through time still flashes like a star's that
    has turned to ashes,
Long after *Nabara's* passion was quenched in the
    sea's heart.

This poem appeared in Day Lewis's *Overtures to Death.* It
resonated strongly with the tragic mood of those days, when the
Spanish war was slowly drawing to its bitter end and the Second
World War was inexorably approaching. When I was in high school
in 1938, our chemistry teacher Eric James, who was the best teacher
in the school, put aside chemistry for an hour and read "The
Nabara" aloud. He subsequently became famous as a university
vice-chancellor and is now sitting in the House of Lords. I can
still hear his passionate voice reading "The Nabara," with the boys
listening spellbound. That was perhaps the last occasion on which
it was possible to recite an epic poem in all sincerity to honor the

heroes of a military action. At Hiroshima, the new technology of death made military heroism suddenly old-fashioned and impotent. After Hiroshima, Day Lewis' lofty sentiments no longer resonated. The generation which grew up after Hiroshima found its voice in 1956 in the character of Jimmy Porter, the young man at center stage in John Osborne's play *Look Back in Anger*. Here is Jimmy Porter, griping as usual, and incidentally telling us important truths about the effect of nuclear weapons on public morality:

> I suppose people of our generation aren't able to die for good causes any longer. We had all that done for us, in the thirties and the forties, when we were still kids. There aren't any good, brave causes left. If the big bang does come, and we all get killed off, it won't be in aid of the old-fashioned, grand design. It'll just be for the Brave New nothing-very-much-I-thank-you. About as pointless and inglorious as stepping in front of a bus.

Jimmy Porter brings us back to where Haldane left us in 1924. The two world wars seemed totally different to the people who fought in them and lived through them from day to day, but they begin to look more and more alike as they recede into history. The first war began with the trumpet blowing of Rupert Brooke and ended with the nightmares of Wilfred Owen. The second war began with the mourning of Day Lewis and ended with the anger of Jimmy Porter. In both wars, the beginning was young men going out to fight for freedom in a mood of noble self-sacrifice, and the end was a technological bloodbath which seemed in retrospect meaningless. In the first war, the idealism of my uncle perished and the hand grenades of my father survived; in the second war, the idealism of Joe Dallet perished and the nuclear weapons of Robert Oppenheimer survived. In both wars, history proved that those who fight for freedom with the technologies of death end by living in fear of their own technology.

From "Russians"

After the Mongols, invaders came to Russia from the West — from Poland, from Sweden, from France, and from Germany. Each of the invading armies was a horde in the Russian sense of the word, a disciplined force of warriors superior to the Russians in technology, in mobility, and in generalship. Especially the German horde invading Russia in 1941 conformed to the ancient pattern. But the Russians had made some progress in military organization between 1238 and 1941. It took them three hundred years to drive out the Mongols but only four years to drive out the Germans. During the intervening centuries the Russians, while still thinking of themselves as victims, had become in fact a nation of warriors. In order to survive in a territory perennially exposed to invasion, they maintained great armies and gave serious study to the art of war. They imposed upon themselves a regime of rigid political unity and military discipline. They gave high honor and prestige to their soldiers, and devoted a large fraction of their resources to the production of weapons. Within a few years after 1941, the Russians who survived the German invasion had organized themselves into the most formidable army on earth. The more they think of themselves as victims, the more formidable they become.

The Russian warriors are now armed with nuclear weapons on a massive scale. The strategic rocket forces of the Soviet Union are comparable in size and quality with those of the United States. The Soviet rocket commanders could, if they were ordered to do so, obliterate within thirty minutes the cities of the United States. It therefore becomes a matter of some importance for us to understand what may be in the Soviet commanders' minds. If we can read their intentions correctly, we may improve our chances of avoiding fatal misunderstanding at moments of crisis. Nobody outside the Soviet government can know with certainty the purposes of Soviet deployments. The American experts who study Soviet armed forces and analyze the Soviet literature devoted to military questions have reached diverse conclusions concerning Soviet strategy. Some say that Soviet intentions are predominantly defensive, others that they are aggressive. But the disagreements among the experts concern words more than substance. To a large extent, the disagreements arise from attempts to define Soviet policies in a language derived from American experience. The language of American strategic analysis is alien and inappropriate to the Russian experience of war. If we make the intellectual effort to understand Russian strategy in their terms rather than ours, as a product of Russian history and military tradition, we shall find that it is usually possible to reconcile the conflicting conclusions of the experts. An awareness of Russian historical experience leads us to a consistent picture of Soviet policies, stripped of the distorting jargon of American strategic theory.

The two experts on whom I mostly rely for information about Soviet strategy are George Kennan and Richard Pipes. Their views of the Soviet Union are generally supposed to be sharply divergent. Kennan has a reputation for diplomatic moderation. Pipes has a reputation for belligerence. Kennan recently summarized his impressions of the Soviet leadership as follows:

> This is an aging, highly experienced, and very steady leadership, itself not given to rash or adventuristic policies. It commands, and is deeply involved with, a structure of power, and particularly a higher bureaucracy, that would not easily lend itself to policies of that nature. It faces serious internal problems, which constitute its main preoccupation. As this leadership looks abroad, it sees more dangers than inviting opportunities. Its reactions and purposes are therefore much more defensive than aggressive. It has no desire for any major war, least of all for a nuclear one. It fears and respects American military power even as it tries to match it, and hopes to avoid a conflict with it. Plotting an attack on Western Europe would be, in the circumstances, the last thing that would come into its head.

Pipes is a Harvard professor who has been on the staff of the National Security Council in the Reagan administration in Washington. He stated his view of Soviet strategy in a recent article with a provocative title: "Why the Soviet Union Thinks It Could

Fight and Win a Nuclear War." Here are a couple of salient passages:

> The classic dictum of Clausewitz, that war is politics pursued by other means, is widely believed in the United States to have lost its validity after Hiroshima and Nagasaki. Soviet doctrine, by contrast, emphatically asserts that while an all-out nuclear war would indeed prove extremely destructive to both parties, its outcome would not be mutual suicide: the country better prepared for it and in possession of a superior strategy could win and emerge a viable society. . . . Clausewitz, buried in the United States, seems to be alive and prospering in the Soviet Union. . . .
>
> For Soviet generals the decisive influence in the formulation of nuclear doctrine were the lessons of World War 2, with which, for understandable reasons, they are virtually obsessed. This experience they seem to have supplemented with knowledge gained from professional scrutiny of the record of Nazi and Japanese offensive operations, as well as the balance-sheet of British and American strategic-bombing campaigns. More recently, the lessons of the Israeli-Arab wars of 1967 and 1973 in which they indirectly participated seem also to have impressed Soviet strategists, reinforcing previously held convictions. They also follow the Western literature, tending to side with the critics of mutual deterrence. The result of all these diverse influences is a nuclear doctrine which assimilates into the main body of the Soviet military tradition the technical implications of nuclear warfare without surrendering any of the fundamentals of this tradition. The strategic doctrine adopted by the USSR over the past two decades calls for a policy diametrically opposite to that adopted in the United States by the predominant community of civilian strategists: not deterrence but victory, not sufficiency in weapons but superiority, not retaliation but offensive action.

These remarks of Pipes were intended to be frightening, whereas Kennan's remarks were intended to be soothing. And yet, if one looks at the substance of the remarks rather than at the intentions of the writers, there is no incompatibility between them. I have myself little doubt that both Kennan's and Pipes's statements are substantially true. Kennan is describing the state of mind of political leaders who have to deal with the day-to-day problems of managing a large and unwieldy empire. Pipes is describing the state of mind of professional soldiers who have accepted responsibility for defending their country against nuclear-armed enemies. It is perhaps a virtue of the Soviet system that the problems of everyday politics and the problems of preparation for a supreme military crisis are kept apart and are handled by separate groups of specialists. The Soviet military authorities themselves insist vehemently on the necessity of this separation of powers. They know that Stalin's mingling of the two powers in 1941, when for political reasons he forbade his generals to mobilize the army in preparation for Hitler's attack, caused enormous and unnecessary Soviet losses and almost resulted in total defeat. Kennan's picture of the Soviet political power structure is quite consistent with the central conclusion of Pipes's analysis, that Soviet military doctrines are based on the assumption that the war for which the Soviet Union must be prepared is a nuclear version of World War II. We should be relieved rather than frightened when we hear that Soviet generals are still obsessed with World War II. World War II was from the Soviet point of view no lighthearted adventure. One thing of which we can be quite sure is that nobody in the Soviet Union looks forward with enthusiasm to fighting World War II over again, with or without nuclear weapons.

The words with which Pipes intends to scare us, "victory . . . superiority . . . offensive action," are precisely the goals which the Russians achieved, after immense efforts and sacrifices, at the end of World War II. If, as Pipes correctly states, Soviet strategy is still dominated by the lessons learned in World War II, it is difficult to see what other goals than these the Soviet armed forces should be expected to pursue. Pipes makes these goals sound frightening by placing them in a misleading juxtaposition with American strategic concepts taken from a different context: "not deterrence but victory, not sufficiency in weapons but superiority, not retaliation but offensive action." The American strategy of deterrence, sufficiency, and retaliation is a purely nuclear strategy having nothing to do with war as it has been waged in the past. The Soviet strategy of victory, superiority, and offensive action is a continuation of the historical process by which Russia over the centuries repelled invaders from her territoy. Both strategies have advantages and disadvantages. Neither is aggressive in intention. Both are to me equally frightening, because both make the survival of civilization depend on people behaving reasonably.

The central problem for the Soviet military leadership is to preserve the heritage of World War II against oblivion, to transmit that heritage intact to future generations of soldiers who never saw the invader's boot tramping over Russian soil. Soviet strategists know well what nuclear weapons can do. They are familiar with the American style of nuclear strategic calculus, which treats nuclear war as a mathematical exercise with the result depending only on the numbers and capabilities of weapons on each side. Soviet generals can do such calculations as well as we can. But they do not believe the answers. The heritage of World War II tells them that wars are fought by people, not by weapons, that morale is in the end more important than equipment, that it is easy to calculate how a war will begin but impossible to calculate how it will end. The primary concern of all Soviet strategic writing that I have seen is to make sure that the lessons of World War II are well learned and never forgotten by the rising generation of Soviet citizens. These lessons which the agonies of World War II stamped indelibly into Russian minds were confirmed by the late experience of the United States in Vietnam. A Russian acquaintance once asked me how it happened that American nuclear strategists appeared to have learned nothing from the lessons of Vietnam. I had to reply that the reason they learned nothing was probably because they did not fight in Vietnam themselves. If they had fought in Vietnam, they would have learned to distrust any strategic theory which counts only weapons and discounts human courage and tenacity.

Tolstoy's *War and Peace* is the classic statement of the Russian view of war. Tolstoy understood, perhaps more deeply than anyone else, the nature of war as Russia experienced it. He fought with the Russian army at Sevastopol. He spent some of his happiest years as an artillery cadet on garrison duty in the Caucasus. In *War and Peace* he honored the courage and steadfastness of the ordinary

Russian soldiers who defeated Napoleon in spite of the squabbles and blunders of their commanders. He drew from the campaign of 1812 the same lessons which a later generation of soldiers drew from the campaigns of World War II. He saw war as a desperate improvisation, in which nothing goes according to plan and the historical causes of victory and defeat remain incalculable.

Tolstoy's thoughts about war and victory are expressed by his hero Prince Andrei on the eve of the battle of Borodino. Andrei is talking to his friend Pierre.

> "To my mind what is before us to-morrow is this: a hundred thousand Russian and a hundred thousand French troops have met to fight, and the fact is that these two hundred thousand men will fight, and the side that fights most desperately and spares itself least will conquer. And if you like, I'll tell you that whatever happens, and whatever mess they make up yonder, we shall win the battle to-morrow; whatever happens we shall win the victory." "So you think the battle to-morrow will be a victory," said Pierre. "Yes, yes," said Prince Andrei absently. "There's one thing I would do, if I were in power," he began again, "I wouldn't take prisoners. What sense is there in taking prisoners? That's chivalry. The French have destroyed my home and are coming to destroy Moscow; they have outraged and are outraging me at every second. They are my enemies, they are all criminals to my way of thinking. . . . They must be put to death. . . . War is not a polite recreation, but the vilest thing in life, and we ought to understand that and not play at war. We ought to accept it sternly and solemnly as a fearful necessity."

The battle was duly fought, and Prince Andrei was mortally wounded. The Russians lost, according to the generally accepted meaning of the word "lose": half of the Russian army was destroyed; after the battle the Russians retreated and the French advanced. And yet, in the long view, Prince Andrei was right. Russia's defeat at Borodino was a strategic victory. Napoleon's army was so mauled that it had no stomach for another such battle. Napoleon advanced to Moscow, stayed there for five weeks waiting for the Czar to sue for peace, and then fled with his disintegrating army in its disastrous stampede to the West. "Napoleon," concludes Tolstoy, "is represented to us as the leader in all this movement, just as the figurehead in the prow of the ship to the savage seems the force that guides the ship on its course. Napoleon in his activity all this time was like a child, sitting in a carriage, pulling the straps within it, and fancying he is moving it along."

The fundamental divergence between American and Soviet strategic concepts lies in the fact that American strategy demands certainty while Soviet strategy accepts uncertainty as inherent in the nature of war. The American objectives — deterrence, sufficiency, and retaliation — are supposed to be guaranteed by the deployment of a suitable variety of invulnerable weapons. The name of the American nuclear strategy is "assured destruction," with emphasis upon the word "assured." Any hint of doubt concerning the assurance of retaliation creates consternation in the minds of American strategists and even in the minds of ordinary American citizens. This demand for absolute assurance of retaliation is the main driving force on the American side of the nuclear arms race. Soviet strategists, on the other hand, consider the quest for certainty in war to be a childish delusion. The Soviet strategic objectives — victory, superiority, and offensive action — are goals to be striven for, not conditions to be guaranteed. These objectives cannot be assured by any fixed quantity of weapons, and they remain valid even when they are not assured. Soviet strategy sees war as essentially unpredictable, and the objectives as dimly visible through chaos and fog.

WHAT IS IT ABOUT?

The bad news about the bomb can arrive in many different ways. For me, it was an accumulative thing — the result of many encounters with the people who design, build, test, buy, protect, explain, decide where to point, and prepare to deliver nuclear weapons. By "bad news" I don't mean simply the knowledge that these weapons threaten us to an unusual degree. Pretty much everybody has that straight. I mean a belief, an inner conviction, an awareness deep in the primitive center of the brain, that these weapons are really out there, they work, and they will be used if we go on as we are.

It's hard to think of war in peacetime. Americans in particular find the danger difficult to grasp. We live in a heavily militarized country, but we rarely see a military uniform on the street. We missed the worst of the two big wars of the century. We never had to live on turnips, pack our belongings in wheelbarrows and flee an army, huddle in the dark underground while the dust sifted down and the earth shook, be grateful to sisters who earned cigarettes and canned meat from soldiers of an occupying army in the usual way — all routine experiences for Europeans above a certain age. Indeed, some Americans have such difficulty seeing war as anything but a time of excitement that they point to the 20 million deaths suffered by the Soviet Union during the Second World War as evidence that the Russians have been hardened by war, not made cautious by it, and therefore wouldn't shrink from risking another. The Russians I've met (not many — a few dozen) for the most part have been patient, cautious, reasonable, businesslike, and not easily provoked. But the idea that they don't care about all those dead brothers, fathers, and uncles, about the children who starved and froze — that brings color to their faces and passion to their voices. Americans have no such national memory and must depend on what they read — a pallid substitute.

Even defense professionals responsible for the hardware of

modern war tend to forget what their work is leading up to. A civilian analyst who spent four years on Carter's National Security Council once described to me a study he'd done on the use of tactical nuclear weapons in the opening hours of a big war on the Central Front, in Europe. Lots of such studies had been done in the past, but they all killed too many civilians — millions of them; there was no way to limit the war. But one day — it happened to be his daughter's fourth birthday — the analyst got to thinking about Soviet rail lines to the West. How many nukes, he wondered, would it take to isolate Soviet forces at the front? So he got out a lot of military maps and spread them all over the floor. "Whenever you see someone in the analysis business using maps, you can be sure he's a serious person," the analyst said, implying that the rest was just talk. He got out his bomb-effects computer, which looks like a round slide rule, and started drawing circles around rail junctures. Right away it began to look good. He was excited. He really had something. "It's so cheap," he said to himself. Instead of casualties in the millions there might be "only a hundred thousand dead" — far fewer than it would take, presumably, to touch off an all-out nuclear exchange.

After a couple of hours of preliminary work, he left to take his daughter out for a birthday lunch, and it hit him, as they stood in line at McDonald's, what he'd been thinking about all morning: 100,000 dead, *like that*. Images warred in his mind — himself on his knees with his maps and templates, his daughter dead — and he felt ill with the enormity of what he did for a living. Later, of course, he went back to his maps and his plan and wrote a paper on it.

My own sense of the bad news came in fits and starts — for example, at the National Atomic Museum, at Kirtland Air Force Base, near Albuquerque, New Mexico. There you can see bomb casings and missiles for many of the nuclear warheads developed since 1945. The casing for Fat Man — the type of bomb dropped on Nagasaki — looks like a cartoonist's idea of a bomb. It's a gross, bulbous monster with a ridiculous little tailfin. It looks heavy and lethal, but also has a dated, H. G. Wells air about it, as if it belonged to the era of dirigibles and touring cars. It's not frightening. Down the hall, looming up in the dim light like an olive-green whale, is the casing for a Mark 17 — the first American hydrogen, or thermonuclear, bomb that could be dropped by a plane. It's twenty-four feet long and five feet in diameter, and it weighs twenty-one tons, but the numbers don't capture the sense of mass it projects. It truly looks like something that could flatten a whole city.

Later, of course, the warhead designers figured out how to make them smaller. A week after my visit to the National Atomic Museum, I went to Vandenberg Air Force Base, near Santa Barbara, California, where missiles — currently, the MX — are tested, and where a basic course in ballistic missilery is taught to the officers and men who maintain and launch them. There I saw a Mark 12A re-entry vehicle (RV) of the type that carries a W-78 warhead. The Minuteman III carries three such RVs. The MX will carry ten of a similar type, unless the restraints called for by the unratified SALT II treaty are finally abandoned, in which case it could deliver as many as twelve warheads. And the number of warheads on the Russian SS-18 missile could go from ten to twenty-eight. Some American officials think one Russian response to a failure of the Geneva talks, and to deployment of the first Pershing II and cruise missiles in Europe, will be the testing of an SS-18 with more than ten warheads — a sign that all bets are off. Hard as it might be for most people to realize — we can already blow up the world ten times over, can't we? — such a Russian move would cause panic in Washington. But it's precisely discussion of this sort — abstract and detailed — that makes the danger hard to grasp.

The RV that I saw stands about waist-high. It's a slender cone in shape. Its body has a carbon-carbon skin that looks like tightly woven canvas coated with graphite. The nose is polished, round, and about the size of a softball. I don't know what the RV weighs, but three or four would fit comfortably in the back of a station wagon. The yield of the warheads carried by the RV is about a third of a megaton — about twenty-three times the yield of the bomb that destroyed Hiroshima. The Mark 12A does not have an antique air; everything about it says state of the art.

On that same trip I paid a visit to the Arnold Engineering and Development Center (AEDC), a vast complex near Tullahoma, Tennessee, where the military tests airframes, rocket engines, nose cones for re-entry vehicles, and other hardware. A businesslike engineer described the MX development program to me, as well as some of the other projects he'd worked on. One was a study of the shelf life of the Minuteman missile, a matter of some concern to the Air Force. A Minuteman is for the most part a simple device, but nothing lasts forever. Year after year, the Minutemen sit in their silos on the Great Plains, the gyroscopes in their guidance systems spinning away at thousands of revolutions per minute, the tritium for boosting the fission triggers decaying, and the explosive aging. From time to time, the Air Force pulls one of the missiles from its silo, trucks it in secrecy to Vandenberg Air Force Base, replaces the warheads with a lot of sophisticated radio equipment (called telemetry) to monitor the missile's flight, and fires it at Kwajalein Lagoon, in the Marshall Islands. Generally it works. But you can't be too careful, and the Air Force asked the AEDC for a shelf-life study to be doubly sure of the Minuteman. The engineer, a young man in double-knits who looked amazingly like Dick Cavett, described all this in detail, but cautiously. He appeared to have a deep suspicion of journalists. He chose his words with care. They were flat and colorless. Only once did he express anything like passion or a personal point of view. I asked how the study turned out. He said it was conclusive: the Minuteman is a durable piece of hardware; even twenty-year-old missiles are just about 100 percent ready to go. And then he added in a voice of startling intensity: *"You can tell that to the Russians!"*

Recently I've had a good many opportunities to pass on the message, but somehow it has never seemed appropriate. Last May, I spent a week with two dozen Russians at a conference in Minneapolis. In July, I talked at length with another fifteen or twenty during a two-week stay in Moscow. They were all, in their different ways, much concerned by the danger of war between the United States and the Soviet Union. Many things worried them — the motives behind the Reagan Administration's program to build new strategic weapons, such as the MX missile (the "Peacekeeper") and the B-1 bomber, the fearful expense of trying to keep up, the failure of SALT, the apparent impasse of the Euromissile talks in Geneva, the prospect of accurate new American Pershing II missiles in Germany, barely six minutes away from the western suburbs of Moscow. But I certainly never heard anything like doubt that the missiles would work if fired. On this point they required no reassurance.

Russians claim America still has a technological edge, but being behind in the arms race is not what frightens the ones I talked to. They have been behind before. It is war that frightens them — not the chance of losing, but war itself. They have absorbed the bad news. I can only suppose this is a result of the Second World War, in which so many Russians died. Twenty million is, of course, a round number. I have been told that its source was Stalin himself, who wanted to emphasize Russian suffering but did not dare reveal the true figure — said to be even higher — lest it reflect on his leadership. If you ask a Russian whether anyone in his own family was killed during the war, you will generally get a list for an answer.

One of the people I met in Moscow was the physicist M. A. Markov, a leader of the Soviet Academy of Sciences and the chairman of the Soviet Pugwash group, which has been meeting with scientists from the United States and other countries since 1957. Markov is seventy-five and in frail health. When he travels, his daughter, a physician, goes with him. His movements are tremulous and uncertain. He speaks in a wavering voice, but with great passion and urgency. In 1955, he showed up in London, quite unexpectedly, for a conference organized by Bertrand Russell on the danger posed by nuclear weapons. Russell and Albert Einstein had issued a declaration, which became the founding document of the Pugwash movement. Markov quoted from the document as if its language were sacred. "It is the most important declaration that exists in the world today," he said. "It was signed by Communists and non-Communists alike. What kind of wisdom signed this declaration? The danger is for *all* people. The declaration said, 'Remember your humanity, and forget all other things.' It contains the widest possible platform — '*Man, whose continued existence is in doubt . . . !*'" It would be impossible to exaggerate the passion with which Markov spoke. He stressed the gravity of each word: "'*Man, whose continued existence is in doubt.*'" How could you say more than that? Who could remain unmoved by such a danger?

Markov does not share with other Russians the anxiety that American technical abilities will allow the United States to race ahead. "The development of the first bomb shows that if something will be done in the U.S.A., very soon it will be done in our country, too," he said. "As a rule, my point of view is that the arms race is like a piece of iron. If you heat one end of it, very soon the other end will be the same temperature. That's a law of thermodynamics. You may be first, but after a while there will be equality again — but at a very high temperature. It is impossible to violate equality."

Markov is haunted by the possibility of a nuclear war. Sometimes he imagines — he knows the idea is scientifically unfounded — that Mars is a dead planet because its atmosphere was destroyed by a nuclear war. "I do not exclude such a possibility on our planet," he said. He makes no effort to spin scenarios of events that might lead to hostilities. The world is too unpredictable for that. "I once had a long discussion about this with Paul Doty [an American biochemist, also active in Pugwash] in a London restaurant," he said. "I told him the most serious historical events were unpredictable. It was very difficult to predict that in Germany — with such strong Socialist and Communist parties — Hitler could arise. It was hard to predict that his first move would be toward the West, instead of the East. It was not easy to predict that Japan's first move would be toward the U.S., not the USSR. It was hard to predict there would be such a dramatic change in relations between Russia and China."

In this world, things happen. "There is a Russian proverb: Even an unloaded gun will fire sooner or later." Markov told a story to illustrate the point. "When I was very young — about fifteen [in 1923] — I spent my vacation in Siberia with my family. I had a gun to shoot ducks, and one morning I had it with me at breakfast. I was sure my gun was unloaded. My sister sat on one side of me, the samovar was on the table here, and across the table was a cossack. My sister said, 'I know that gun is unloaded, but I don't like to see that dark hole pointed at me.' The cossack said, 'I'm a soldier, I don't mind, you can point it at me.' So I pointed it at the cossack. The gun went off. It had been loaded with solid shot, for wolves, and the bullet passed right through that cossack's hair, right down the middle. At the time I was afraid only of what my father would say. But now it's what almost happened that I feel so strongly."

In Minneapolis last May, the Russian delegation to the conference I attended, which was jointly sponsored by the Institute for Policy Studies and two Russian groups, the Soviet–American Friendship Committee and the Institute of the U.S.A. and Canada, had a firm agenda: they wanted to talk about arms control, the Euromissile problem, and how to get détente going again.

This professionalism on the part of the Russians — illusionless and firm without being overbearing — puzzled many of the Americans. "We know who we think they are," said one of the delegates at a closed meeting of the American group near the end of the conference, "but who do they think we are?" And then, as an afterthought, she added: "We know who we are — we're just a bunch of people." The bunch of people had no official standing of any sort, and limited access to people who had. "The fact they're here talking to us," said another American at the same meeting, "is a sign of just how serious the situation is."

"They" — the ten or a dozen Russians who really counted — clearly felt the same way, but were uniformly polite about it. One of them, Vitaly Kobysh, an official on the staff of the Central Committee in Moscow, told me of a visit to the United States during the 1980 presidential campaign. Even after it was clear that Reagan would win, Kobysh tried to look on the bright side. Perhaps Reagan would turn out to be like Nixon — a hard-liner for the folks at home but a realist abroad, someone with whom the Soviets could do business. In Detroit, Kobysh tried to argue this line with Robert Kaiser, a *Washington Post* reporter who speaks Russian, had spent three years as a correspondent in Moscow, and had written one of the standard books about the Soviet Union. "People told me, 'Wait till he [Reagan] is elected; this is just politics,'" Kobysh said. "Kaiser told me no, this is real. And that affected me. When I returned to Moscow and made my report, I had changed my beliefs, and I told them difficult times were coming." Kobysh felt the chill personally. From Minneapolis he had planned to go on to New York, to discuss with the editors of *Time* the possibility of an interview with Yuri Andropov. But the U.S. State Department refused to extend his visa.

If there was a single dominant theme to Russian remarks at the conference, it was Euromissiles — the Pershing II and cruise missiles that NATO planned to deploy in the absence of a Geneva agreement. "Inevitably there would be a heightened tension," said Vikenty Matve'ev, a columnist for *Izvestia*, the official government paper. "Of course, the sky would not fall, but the ground may shake. We might have to break off the Geneva talks, because these talks sometimes give a false illusion." (Earlier, at lunch, Matve'ev told me, "In this world it's not easy to be an optimist. I have lived long enough, I don't care about myself — but my children . . . ") Another journalist, Fyodor Burlatsky, was even more pessimistic. Deployment would bring "a really dramatic situation in Europe," he said. "It seems to me we are underestimating this situation. I don't want to draw a parallel between then [the Cuban missile crisis, in October of 1962] and now, but . . . "

For the Russians the Euromissiles — the merest handful of new warheads (572), compared with the thousands already deployed on both sides — were nevertheless a direct, almost a pugnacious, threat to the Soviet Union: a symbol of the breakdown of arms-control efforts; even an omen of war. Genrikh Trofimenko, an arms-control expert from the Institute of the U.S.A. and Canada, pointed out that negotiating to *limit* strategic arms, instead of to get rid of them altogether, was an American idea. In the 1950s, the Soviets had argued for general and complete disarmament. "Now the situation is reversed," he said. "The ideologues are in the White House and the pragmatists are in Moscow." Mikhail Milshtein, a retired army general who works for the institute, pressed the same point: "It took almost ten years to reach a second [SALT] agreement, and it takes only one election to repudiate everything. Speaking frankly, my personal opinion — the situation is very gloomy. It seems to me we are moving toward an irreversible stage of the arms race."

So it went. The Russians had come to discuss new weapons. The Americans were first with the bomb, first with a workable thermonuclear weapon, first with the long-range bomber, first with an effective intercontinental-missile fleet, first with hardened missile silos, first with missile-firing submarines, first with multiple warheads that could be independently targeted. Every new system increased the danger. The Soviets had always managed to keep up; they would continue to keep up. In their view there was only one sensible alternative — to parse the problem, isolate each dangerous element, and then hedge, limit, and ultimately reduce the weaponry step by step.

In Washington, in certain intelligence circles, there are analysts who keep close track of the Russians who troop about the world to conferences like this. Of course that's the line, these analysts say, but what they're really trying to do is to lock in their current strategic advantages. Georgi Arbatov [the head of the Institute of the U.S.A. and Canada, who did not attend the conference], Trofimenko, Milshtein — these guys are just salesmen.

These analysts have their arguments. They are technical in nature. The Soviets have their counterarguments. The subleties of parity cannot be settled one, two, three. But in Minneapolis there was no mistaking what was on the Russians' minds. They were plainly worried by and obviously eager to avoid the expensive new round of weaponry symbolized by the Euromissiles.

In the midst of the discussion, one of the American delegates, W. H. Ferry, a consultant to foundations who has been writing about the dangers of the arms race for twenty years, took the floor to make a short statement. I believe I am reporting it whole: "I raise the question here of what this is all about. What issue could possibly warrant the use of nuclear weapons? Are they issues of territory, or human rights? What is it that justifies this confrontation?"

This was followed by a long moment of silence. Perhaps no one could believe Ferry had concluded so soon. No one made any attempt to answer his question. It was never referred to again, by Russians or Americans. It elicited no interest whatsoever.

Michael Howard is a distinguished British military historian and the Regius Professor of Modern History at Oxford University. Many of his articles and scholarly papers have discussed war as a thing, a phenomenon, "a continuing activity within human society," something men *do*. This is a neglected subject. The shelves of libraries groan with the histories of particular wars, battles, and even individual military units. When the authors are writing from personal experience, they sometimes pause to reflect on the deeper meaning of war, the awful gap between the reasons and the thing itself. The reasons are often trivial, the thing itself a matter of fear, pain, and death.

The First World War revealed the awful gap to millions of young men in Europe, including many scores of thousands who had been expensively educated at the great universities of Britain, France, and Germany. Before the war, it had been popularly supposed that Europe was too civilized, too closely intertwined economically, and too sensible ever to fight another general war on the Napoleonic scale. A few writers — notably Sir Norman Angell, in Britain, and the Polish banker Ivan Bliokh — even argued that war was impossible. Modern weaponry was simply too destructive for men to endure. In *The Future of War*, a mammoth six-volume work published in Russian in the 1890s, Bliokh described in detail the terrors of the modern battlefield, swept by machine-gun fire and racked by high-explosive artillery shells. A big war would bring millions of men into the field, he predicted. Rates of fire would force them to dig in. It would be a war of trenches. The advantages of the defense would preclude decisive attacks. A war of attrition would follow — in effect, the siege of whole nations. In the end, deaths in the millions, financial ruin, and famine would settle the matter. The defeated would not lose, in the traditional sense, but collapse. Regimes would be swept away in the revolutions that followed. In *The Fate of the Earth*, published two years ago, Jonathan Schell took an approach similar to Bliokh's. Both simply described the horrors we could expect, given the facts. When Bliokh said war was "impossible" — a term he insisted on with journalists — he meant not that it couldn't happen but that the survival of nations would be at risk if it did. Schell, reflecting the strides of science since, goes a step further and says that now civilization, and perhaps even human life itself, is at risk.

Bliokh's vision was unique in its breadth and prophetic accuracy, but a few military men also got an inkling of what was to come from the bloodletting horrors of the American Civil War and the Prussian use of modern breech-loading artillery in the Franco-Prussian War of 1870–1871 (the subject of one of Michael Howard's books). But the Franco-Prussian War ended too quickly for the bad news to sink in. The Russo-Japanese War of 1904–1905, involving heavy casualties and trench warfare, was too far away. The military observers who saw what happened were mostly of field grade, and the duffers on the general staffs at home did not listen. Thus, only a few prescient military men understood what science, industry, and railroads were doing to the scale of war in the decades before 1914. One of them was Helmuth von Moltke the elder, an architect of the modern German army, who wrote in 1890:

> If the war which has hung over our heads, like the sword of Damocles, for more than ten years past, ever breaks out, its duration and end cannot be foreseen. The greatest powers of Europe, armed as never before, will then stand face to face. No one power can be shattered in one or two campaigns so completely as to confess itself beaten, and conclude peace on hard terms. It may be a Seven Years' war; it may be a Thirty Years' war — woe to him who first sets fire to Europe. . . .

Such premonitions were fully borne out by the horrors of trench warfare on the Western Front between 1914 and 1918. The dead numbered in the millions. Of course men had died in war before, but not like this — blown to bits, buried in collapsing bunkers, drowned in mud, machine-gunned as they tried to make their way through thickets of barbed wire and then left to die of their wounds in no-man's-land. On the first day of the Battle of the Somme, in 1916, the British suffered 60,000 casualties — 20,000 of them deaths. The brief official communiqué called the opening of the Somme a success. It was duly printed in British newspapers, followed by page upon page of the names of the killed and the wounded.

The Somme lasted from July into November. Some 1,300,000 soldiers were killed or wounded on both sides. The advance gained seven miles of shattered ground at its deepest point, but left the German front intact. When the British writer Martin Middlebrook, decades later, interviewed survivors for his book *First Day on the Somme* (published in 1972), he found that many of them still dreamed about what they had been through. Another writer, Paul Fussell, argued, in *The Great War and Modern Memory* (1975), that the First World War permanently darkened the collective mind of Western man, replacing the confidence of the nineteenth century with a foreboding sense of fragility, helplessness, and doom. When enthusiasts of aerial bombing began to write, in the 1920s and 1930s, one of their arguments for strategic attack on cities and factories deep within enemy territory was the chance it offered to avoid another great bloodletting by troops on the ground. The devastation of London, Coventry, Hamburg, Dresden, Berlin, Hiroshima, and Nagasaki duly followed. The significant change at Hiroshima was that one plane, with one bomb, accomplished what it had taken a thousand planes to do before.

The flood of memoirs that followed the First World War broached the awful disparity between the reasons for the war and the war itself. What was it about? How did it start? Why was it allowed to continue? What did it settle? The war bled a generation white, destroyed three of the four dynasties that had ruled in 1914 — the Hapsburgs in Austria-Hungary, the Hohenzollerns in Germany, the Romanovs in Russia — and ended in a vindictive peace, which only set the stage for a new war in 1939. The origins of the war have recently been revived as a subject for scholarly study, for a simple and practical reason: the world of 1914 bears a certain disturbing resemblance to our own. Then, as now, the Great Powers were heavily armed. Two alliances confronted each other. An upstart power — Germany — was demanding an equal role on the world stage. Britain was frightened by Germany's construction of big modern battleships. Why did Berlin need this "luxury fleet," if not to challenge British supremacy on the seas? British Conservatives insisted that new dreadnoughts must be built to deter the Germans, and damn the expense. In 1908 they campaigned for the ships on the slogan "We want eight and we won't wait!" Crises were frequent; demands were routinely backed up by military gestures implying a threat of war. The Great Powers confronted each other in peripheral arenas — the Balkans then, the Middle East now. When Bismarck was asked what he thought would set off the next big European war, he said, "Some damned foolishness in the Balkans." But perhaps the most disturbing contemporary parallel is the confidence that all this long preparation for war meant nothing; there would be no war. For twenty or thirty years the optimists were right. Until 1914, the diplomats always managed to settle things before armies were mobilized and shots were fired.

Why did they fail in 1914? In a recent essay, Michael Howard confessed that he has lately begun to rethink the whole subject of the origins of the First World War. He said that he used to assume that an event so large must have had causes to match — deep undercurrents of social change and irreconcilable differences between nations, pushing events into a kind of inevitable, fatal slide that no mere statesman could hope to brake. But now Howard is not so sure. Maybe it was simple, after all — the result of bungling. Maybe Lloyd George, the British prime minister during the last half of the war, was right when he said "We all muddled into war." We might call this the tinderbox theory of the causes of wars: The problem is not sources of conflict, things nations might be expected to fight *about*, but simply the readiness for war itself. Military strength on one side inevitably arouses fear in the other, which strives to catch up. The first grows alarmed in turn. In such a world it does not take something large to start a war but something small, something unexpected — an assassination in a provincial town like Sarajevo, say — something that might be considered, perhaps for purely tactical reasons, to require a determined response. After that, one thing can lead to another. The armies of Europe did not *have* to mobilize in the summer of 1914. They just did.

You can see the appeal here to a scholar interested in our own day. Clausewitz says that war is the continuation of policy by other means. It is supposed to make sense. But the outbreak of war in

1914 made no sense. Nothing was at stake that could reasonably be said to justify war on a continental scale. Even statesmen at the time admitted as much. But Europe was ready for war. Once the Great Powers began to mobilize, they could not stop. The statesmen of our own day insist that there will be no great war between Russia and the United States so long as war doesn't make sense. Nuclear weapons make it impossible — but impossible, alas, in Bliokh's sense, which is to say, suicidal.

Michael Howard is currently researching a book on attitudes toward war before 1914, but it is slow going. At Oxford, he is besieged with requests for interviews, television appearances, book reviews, advice on military matters. He writes and speaks about strategic questions with an unusual degree of detachment. As a historian, he is naturally inclined to see modern parallels to things in the past, and as a British subject he has a keen interest, but no direct involvement, in what the planners in Washington are up to. It is Americans and Russians who run the world now.

In January of 1980, the London *Times* published a letter from Howard criticizing, but also explaining, the NATO "double decision" of 1979, to negotiate limits on Euromissiles while preparing to deploy Pershing IIs and cruise missiles if the negotiations failed. The English historian E. P. Thompson, a veteran of the British left, read Howard's letter and flew off the handle. He was horrified by the prospect of a nuclear war in Europe, which he felt the "double decision" promised, and he wrote a long, ferocious essay, "Protest and Survive," which loosed a whirlwind antinuclear movement in Britain. Thompson has since apologized to Howard for his hasty assumption that Howard was somehow *for* a nuclear war in Europe, or at least willing to run the risk of one. At the time, Howard the scholar was aghast, he wrote, at finding himself facing "the polemical equivalent of Björn Borg on the Centre Court," but of course he made a return volley. His response pointed out that the threat of nuclear war does not stem from any clearly wrong policy that might be reversed in a trice. This exchange led to a kind of appointment by acclamation of Howard as the establishment's sober critic of European nuclear disarmament, a figure who could be counted on in public forums to damn both

houses, war-fighters and unilateral disarmers alike. This role is far
from being one that Howard chose for himself. He is tired of the
hashing and rehashing of the nuclear question. He would like to
stick to history.

But of course the nuclear question will not let go. Two aspects
of the problem seem to worry Howard. One is a matter of mood.
In a recent review he wrote:

> I am an Englishman whose youth was passed in watching
> the dreadful onset of totalitarianism in Europe, and whose
> young manhood was passed in fighting it. I am a professional
> historian who has spent the last thirty years studying the
> phenomenon of military power. I have noted the appetite of
> powerful states for more power to protect themselves, and the
> edge ideology can give to that appetite. I do not think I have
> any illusions about the Soviet Union. But when I hear some
> of my American friends speak of that country, when I note
> how their eyes glaze over, their voices drop an octave, and they
> grind out the words *the Soviets* in tones of gravelly hatred,
> I become really frightened. . . .

He is also worried, he said in an interview in London last July,
about a kind of over-refinement in the thinking of nuclear-war
planners. "They are pushing precision into an area where it cannot survive," he said. He cited a precept of Aristotle's from the
Nichomachean Ethics: Do not treat any subject with greater precision than is appropriate. Clausewitz's phrase "the fog of war" means
that confusion reigns on the battlefield. There, only the simplest
of plans may be expected to work. The nuclear-war planners, he
feels, have forgotten this elementary point. In 1978, a small group
from the Pentagon went to see Howard at Oxford. They were working on a nuclear-targeting study, which led to Presidential Directive 59, a new U.S. warfighting strategy, two years later. A young
analyst in the group had read many of Howard's books and essays
and admired his work; he hoped that Howard would come up with
some ideas — strategic concepts about what to hit — for beating
Russia in a nuclear war. The group explained what it was up to:
war might come — then what? How could nuclear weapons be
used to weaken and frighten Russia without unleashing the

holocaust? Failing that, what could we strike that would bust up the country so thoroughly that the West could recover first? Some time ago the analyst described to me Howard's reaction to these workaday questions. It was one of the reasons I wanted to see Howard last summer. Howard gave them unshirted hell: Didn't they understand what they were talking about? Nuclear weapons can't be used like that! The devastation would inevitably blur the outlines of any plan. The Russians would have no way of knowing what was coming next. The planners in Washington could forget all their subtleties about escalation dominance. What they would get was apocalyptic horror.

When I asked Howard about this in London, he said he'd been appalled by the discussion of "recovery attacks" — the phrase planners use to describe the final stage of a nuclear war, in which the goal is to cripple the Soviet Union so thoroughly that it will collapse economically and break up politically, undoing in a day what it took the czars centuries to put together piecemeal, by war. "It morally shocked me," Howard said. "Their attitude seemed both sick and mistaken." He said he had quit reading the strategic journals. There was no end to the theory-spinning. It was divorced from reality. In a lecture delivered in 1980, Howard said: "When I read the flood of scenarios in strategic journals about first-strike capabilities, counterforce or countervailing strategies, flexible response, escalation dominance, and the rest of the postulates of nuclear theology, I ask myself in bewilderment: this war they are describing, *what is it about*? The defense of Western Europe? Access to the Gulf? The protection of Japan?"

The study of war is generally neglected for the study of military history, which is concerned with how wars are won, not why they take place. Even a long human life holds room for only one or two big wars. The fact that they are hard to stop, once begun, obscures the fact that they are usually a long time in coming. Before the outbreak of the Peloponnesian War, in the fifth century B.C., the Athenian leader Pericles warned his fellow citizens that in war chance rules, that no one can predict how things will turn out, that even the rosiest prospects may be dashed by unforeseen events. Statesmen understand this point. They thrive as long as war only threatens, and are cautious about war itself, especially big, decisive wars against strong opponents. These are generally slow to develop and are preceded by such extended episodes of quarreling, alliance-making, and tentative skirmishing — all more or less obscured by secrecy — that just untangling the true sequence of events can absorb a historian's whole career. The consequences of such wars can be so vast — possibly including the disappearance of peoples and the eclipse of empires — that the historian's eye is held fast by the awful spectacle immediately before him. The horrors and the relative infrequency of big wars encourage attention to the particular. Thus historians traditionally have been inclined to ask not why we have wars but why we had this one, and then why we had that one. The answers generally stick to the sequence of events, as if there were no such thing as war itself, war as a thing, war as a form of common social behavior, something men in groups habitually and characteristically do.

Perhaps this is inevitable. So much rides on the details. If the First World War had been postponed ten years, a different generation would have died. Rupert Brooke might have spent a long life writing bucolic poetry, and W. H. Auden might have died in his place. The generals of 1914, with their muttonchops and walrus moustaches, would have been mostly in the obscurity of retirement by 1924. The development of aircraft and armored fighting vehicles might have avoided the carnage of static trench warfare. Liberal Western tendencies might have secured a firmer hold in Russia, forestalling the Bolshevik Revolution. Another decade of German submarine-building might have been enough to let Germany starve out Britain when war came. Defeat might have cost the Windsors their throne, and left the Kaiser on his. Who can say? That the potential differences are of such dramatic moment — especially when the war in question is still in the future — tends to narrow the focus of all concerned, leaders and ordinary citizens alike, to the dangers of the day. From the point of view of God it may be immaterial whether war happens now or next year, whether it kills this man or that, whether the side that dictates the peace appears in a gray uniform or a brown. But for men these are the urgent questions, with the result that they study their wars the same way they fight them — one at a time.

This approach begs an important question. Explaining wars by retelling their histories is like trying to explain the phenomenon of divorce by recounting who said what to whom, in every separate instance, through years of quarrelsome marriages. War and the preparation for war are such an integral part of history — the great constant in all times and places — that they may be presumed to constitute one of the great determining characteristics of the human animal. We have a nature; the *tabula* is not quite *rasa*. We live in cities, marry in pairs, and make war against our neighbors. In 1971, J. David Singer, of the University of Michigan, published a study of international wars during the 150 years from 1816 to 1965. He found that there were 6.2 wars in the average decade; that especially intense episodes of violence occurred every twenty years or so; that Europe was the most war-prone part of the world, followed by the Middle East; and that 29 million soldiers had died fighting in the ninety-three wars that took place during the century and a half he studied. Who can mistake a pattern so pronounced? Somewhere in those statistics lurks war as an endemic thing, the sort of war that the British historian Arnold Toynbee once said could be identified as "the proximate cause of the breakdown of every civilization which is known for certain to have broken down."

Toynbee never attempted to say precisely what war is. That would be a tremendous intellectual undertaking, demanding a Darwin, a Marx, or a Freud. But Toynbee's long study of history — he lived to be eighty-six, and wrote till the end — convinced him that the explanation for cataclysmic wars could not be found in the details of who said what to whom and when. He was suffering from chronic dysentery when the First World War began, and so escaped the fate of about half his schoolmates. He was a distinguished sage when Hitler attacked Poland in 1939. He did not watch these wars from lonely academic eminence but was active in establishment circles. He attended the peace conferences in Paris in 1919 and 1946. Twice in his life he was certain there would never again be another big European war — at the beginning of 1914, and at the end of 1918. This confidence could not

survive another great war. The onset of the Cold War convinced
him that the pattern was still incomplete. In 1950 he wrote:

> . . . the most ominous thing about these wars is that they
> were not isolated or unprecedented calamities. They were two
> wars in a series; and, when we envisage the whole series in
> a synoptic view, we discover that this is not only a series but
> a progression. In our recent Western history war has been
> following war in an ascending order of intensity; and to-day
> it is already apparent that the War of 1939-45 was not the
> climax of this crescendo movement.

Toynbee's gloom was not unusual in the late 1940s and early
1950s. There was a wide gap between the observers outside of
government, horrified by the implications of atomic weapons, and
the statesmen inside, who had to reorganize the world. Einstein
might have said that atomic weapons "changed everything," but
statesmen did not agree. The Allies of 1945 were already deeply
suspicious of one another. As early as 1943, an American general
in Sicily remarked to the British bombing expert Solly Zuckerman,
"Zuck, when we've finished with Germany we'll still want you
when we take on the Russians. Don't forget." At war's end, the
United States went on producing fissionable material for nuclear
weapons, and Britain, France, and Russia all raced to catch up.
In 1946, Truman quietly but explicitly threatened to attack Russia
with atomic weapons if it did not withdraw its troops from northern Iran, and Stalin complied. By 1948, talk of war was general.
The speed with which a war-wracked world chose up sides for a
new contest was bewildering. Polemicists on each side leaped forward to explain why the other was to blame, and subsequently
historians — in the West, at least — have filled in the details. In
my own view, a good case can be made that Stalin's absorption
of Eastern Europe, beginning with Poland, virtually guaranteed
enmity with the West, but I doubt that scholarly arguments of
that kind really explain very much. The history helps, but it is like
a medical history that recounts the onset and progress of a disease
without explaining what the disease *is*. These events happened too
quickly, almost automatically, like the exchange of partners in a
dance, as if a Great Power can be expected, by its very nature, to

cast about restlessly for the next-greatest, and then to direct at it questions of a type certain to promote hostility. Why did the United States go on building nuclear weapons? Why didn't Russia disband its army? Why did the United States cut off lend-lease aid to Russia on a moment's notice, in 1945, turning its ships around in mid-ocean? Why did Russia impose client regimes on Eastern Europe? Both sides' official answers to these questions have been patently disingenuous. Both sides were afraid, not of what the other side *did* but because they could do nothing about it — short of war. The essence of the situation, when all the details have been argued to a fare-thee-well, is an elemental fact: in 1945, the United States and the Soviet Union were big, were autonomous, and had a capacity to injure each other. This confrontation had been waiting to happen. Alexis de Tocqueville had foreseen it 110 years earlier in the concluding passage of the first volume of *Democracy in America*:

> There are at the present time two great nations in the world, which started from different points, but seem to tend toward the same end. I allude to the Russians and the Americans. . . . All other nations seem to have nearly reached their natural limits. . . . these alone are proceeding with ease and celerity along a path to which no limit can be perceived. The American struggles against the obstacles that nature opposes to him; the adversaries of the Russian are men. The former combats the wilderness and savage life; the latter, civilization with all its arms. The conquests of the American are therefore gained by the plowshare; those of the Russian by the sword. The Anglo-American relies upon personal interest to accomplish his ends and gives free scope to the unguided strength and common sense of the people; the Russian centers all the authority of society in a single arm. The principal instrument of the former is freedom; of the latter, servitude. Their starting point is different and their courses are not the same; yet each of them seems marked out by the will of Heaven to sway the destinies of half the globe.

Talking about war with Russians in Russia is a curiously unsettling experience. Russians have had a hard life since the expulsion from Eden; history never lets up on them. The miseries suffered by ordinary people in the nineteenth century are well documented. In the First World War, the slaughter was so immense that the soldiers finally threw down their guns, climbed out of the trenches, and set out to walk home. The revolutions of 1917 were followed by a civil war of unparalleled ferocity, in which prisoners, hostages, and ordinary citizens were routinely shot and whole provinces were devastated. Scarcely had the White generals been defeated when Lenin died, Stalin took over, and the ensuing forced collectivization of peasant landholdings resulted in famines, which killed millions. Stalinist terror killed millions more. Hitler killed further millions. Ordinary Russians know all about this terrible history, but the only episode they can talk about freely is the Second World War. This they do. I know of only one other country where everybody seems to have so many horrors to relate — Israel. Doubting the Russians' sincerity when they talk of the pain of war strikes me as willful and perverse.

Unlike Americans, Russians fear that war is really possible. Ordinary citizens encountered by chance in the street invariably bring up the subject. There must never be another war, they say as one. Why can't we be allies again, the way we were in the war against Hitler? They seem genuinely puzzled.

Russian officials take the same line, and back it up with arguments. They cite the numerous public statements of Brezhnev and Andropov calling for peace and arms control, offering to reduce Soviet missiles targeted on Europe to 162 (the number of French and British missiles), pledging "no first use" of nuclear weapons in the event of war, accepting the principle of a freeze, proposing a general European non-aggression pact leading to outright dissolution of the NATO and Warsaw Pact treaties, suggesting a joint U.S.–Soviet study of space-based defense systems and a ban of same, urging serious talks in Vienna on mutual balanced-force reductions, and in general promising a readiness to negotiate an end to the arms race and the Cold War. They insist that Moscow is ready, that this isn't just talk. It is Washington, not Moscow, that has refused to ratify the second SALT treaty, that suspended the talks on a comprehensive nuclear-test ban, that insists on planning to "prevail" in a nuclear war, and that wants to embark on a whole new round of the arms race in space, they say. Soviet diplomats have got their blue suits packed and their briefcases filled with negotiating instructions. You don't believe us? Russian officials say. *Try us.*

Russians differ in dating the turning point in détente. A few say it all began to go wrong in 1974, when Richard Nixon was forced to resign over Watergate and his policies were rejected too. Others say no, it was Gerald Ford's fault for lacking the political courage to go on using the word *détente*, despite the fact that it continued to be official policy. Some Russians say Jimmy Carter began the process when he adopted a "so-called" human-rights policy intended to humiliate the Soviets. Others place the blame on Paul Nitze and the Committee on the Present Danger, which began to campaign actively against the entire SALT process in the late 1970s. But almost all the Russians I talked to appear to agree that things soured drastically after January 20, 1981, when Ronald Reagan became President. The interpretations have one aspect in common: they fail to take any notice whatever of Soviet strategic-arms programs, or Soviet adventures in Angola, Ethiopia, and Afghanistan.

Georgi Arbatov was confronted with a different explanation for the end of détente at a private meeting in Washington last May. Arbatov is probably better known in the West than any other Russian official outside of the Politburo. Since his appointment, in 1968, to head the Institute of the U.S.A. and Canada, he has traveled frequently to the United States and Western Europe, has often appeared on Western television, and has served as an all-purpose spokesman for the Soviet view at conferences and symposia. He speaks fluent idiomatic English, is fully conversant with the nuances of Western opinion, and can hold his own with Western experts on military policy and arms control.

Whether Arbatov counts for anything in Moscow is uncertain, but there is no question that he is taken seriously in Washington. He was granted a visa by the State Department last May on the condition that he not meet openly with the press. At a dinner meeting with a number of journalists, analysts, and government officials, Arbatov presented his view of the recent slide in Soviet–American relations, beginning with the American failure to ratify SALT II after its signing in 1979 by Carter and Brezhnev, and emphasizing the raw hostility in many of Reagan's speeches. He placed the blame for the apparent deadlock at Geneva squarely on the American doorstep.

When Arbatov had concluded, the first question was asked by Edward Luttwak, a well-known author and defense analyst, whose most recent book is *The Grand Strategy of the Soviet Union*. Luttwak's question, after the custom of such meetings, was really a short speech. According to a participant in the meeting, Luttwak's comments went roughly as follows: The Soviet Union often complains that it is ringed with hostile bases. Perhaps the Soviet Union should ask itself why this is so. China has been seeking a working alliance with the West because it is frightened by Soviet military preparations in the Far East. Japan has embarked on a program of re-armament — admittedly, a tentative one so far — for the same reason. Pakistan has been badly frightened by the Soviet invasion of Afghanistan. The rest of the Moslem world is not happy about it either. Both Turkey and Iran have been objects of Soviet ambitions in the past. Why have the Algerians been buying tanks? They have been frightened by Russian arms provided to the Libyans. The nations of Western Europe have no appetite for confrontation, but they reject Soviet claims that the SS-20s represent nothing more than modernization; these missiles are pointed at them, and they don't like it. French and British missiles are pointed at the Soviet Union, just as Moscow claims. But why? Because France and Britain feel threatened. Recent events in Poland were not reassuring to the West. It is not America's doing that Russia is ringed by hostility; the Soviet Union has brought this on itself. Even neutral Sweden, Luttwak said, has been pushed toward hostility. As it happened, a report would be issued the following morning — Luttwak knew this because he had helped to write the report — that would recount in detail the long history of the Soviet Union's deliberate intrusion into Swedish national waters with its submarines. Moscow's bland denials would not stand. Facts were facts. Reagan's hostile remarks could not be blamed for the situation in which the Soviet Union found itself. It was what the

Soviet Union *did* that explained its predicament. According to my informant, Arbatov denied all. His off-hand dismissal of the incidents in Swedish waters eventually leaked to the Swedish press and caused the Soviets much embarrassment.

These are the routines of the Cold War. From year to year they change only in detail. If you ask either side what it wants, it says peace. If you ask either side why there is a conflict, it blames the other. To the obvious questions you get obvious answers. But even so, things seep through — deeper currents of fear and alarm. For American officials, the Russians' most frightening characteristic is their steadiness. Henry Kissinger mentions this in his memoirs. The Russians may not be subtle in their diplomacy, he says, but once they have adopted a policy they stick to it forever. Americans always want to solve everything before the next election. For Russians, the most frightening thing about Americans is our unpredictability. We're all for peace one year, and are beating the drums the next. I heard this charge often in Moscow last summer. For two weeks, I traveled around the city in the company of a chubby young journalist and translator named Alexei, from the Novosti Press Agency. I talked to Arbatov, to a general from the Ministry of Defense, to the head of the Soviet Peace Committee, to M.A. Markov, of the Soviet Pugwash Committee, to a miscellany of Soviet writers, journalists, sociologists, and arms-control experts, and to the editors of *Novy Mir, New Times,* and *Oktyabr.* With the exception of the general, everybody seemed to be operating exclusively on information published in the West. Some of the people I talked to admitted as much. Others, like Arbatov, denied it.

When I asked Arbatov about the submarine incidents in Sweden, he assured me that no such thing had ever happened. The Russian submarine that ran aground in Swedish waters a year ago had merely been lost. The other incidents were all apocryphal. How did he know? He said that he'd had lunch with an official from the Ministry of Defense and had been assured that this was the case. I took that to mean he didn't know but, like everybody else, had merely been given the inevitable line. In Washington, the government officials of one year have returned to teaching, journalism, or think tanks the next year. They move about freely and often keep their security clearances. But in Russia people tend to stay put. Civilian analysts in Arbatov's institute usually remain for life. What the military knows it keeps to itself, while everyone else interested in defense issues must master English and steep himself in the Western literature. As a result, discussion of these issues has a curious hermetic quality.

When I began my discussions in Moscow, Alexei had been twenty days without a cigarette; when I finished, he had been thirty-two days without a cigarette, and no longer had difficulty translating "focus of evil" and "forward-based systems." Like the Russians I spoke with in Minneapolis, the group in Moscow represented much of the class of Soviet officials who have been delegated to explain Russia to the West. On certain points they spoke as if they had all read the same books, but as people they had very different temperaments and histories. Some of them were amazingly well informed. One seemed to have read nothing but *Pravda*. Another was a copper-bottomed old Stalinist *apparatchik*. A third reminded me of myself — a journalist and self-appointed worrier about the bomb. Several struck me as being profoundly decent human beings.

Talking with Russians is a delicate business. They are subject to rigid intellectual discipline. The limits of the permissible are exacting. The Soviets have a long history of presuming upon leftist sympathies and sentimental good will in the West. One wants to be forthcoming, but one remembers the awful gaffes of naive Westerners who have been led down the garden path — for example, Henry Wallace, who visited the notorious slave-labor camps of the Kolyma region of Siberia without ever realizing that the "happy workers" he saw there were political prisoners. But if one wants to talk to Russians one has only two choices — émigrés, with ample reason to be bitter, or official Russians, who have been carefully chosen to present a well-crafted line to the West. I spoke to twenty or thirty of the latter, and they all hewed to the line on the points that mattered.

The principal line went roughly as follows: the Soviet Union desires mutual understanding and better Soviet–American rela-

tions — peace, if you like — through serious negotiations con-
ducted in a businesslike manner on issues of common interest. It
is the United States that is dragging its heels on arms control.
Reagan's attack on the Soviet Union as the "focus of evil" in the
world is not helpful. The Soviet Union has many domestic problems, and no desire for an expensive new round of the arms race.
America has always been first in the field of strategic weapons.
The Soviet Union has been forced to scramble and sacrifice to catch
up. There is now something like strategic parity between the two
sides. The Soviet Union is willing to negotiate reductions in nuclear
arms down to zero, but not unequally. The Soviet Union will never
allow itself to be inferior again. If the Americans go forward with
new strategic programs, the Soviets will tighten their belts and
match us weapon for weapon.

I also heard several secondary lines — on Afghanistan, for
example. Time after time I was told that Moscow would love to
get out of Afghanistan, but can't so long as the Afghan rebellion
continues. Why not? I asked repeatedly. It's their country, let them
settle it. The answer was always the same: the Soviet Union has
a long border with Afghanistan; back in 1979, the United States
was planning a takeover to replace the bases and intelligence
facilities lost in Iran; the rebels were getting arms from China and
the U.S.; the rebels were led by "feudal reactionaries"; and
besides — what can you do when your neighbor says his house
is on fire and begs for help?

This line clearly suggests that the Soviet Union plans to go
on fighting in Afghanistan until it wins — the standard approach
taken by any Great Power, once it has committed its troops and
its prestige. During the Vietnam War, the United States said much
the same sort of thing: happy to go home as soon as the war is
over. That's not the only parallel. We got into these wars for similar
reasons — to back up a faltering client. We seem to have been
responding to the same concerns — what allies would think
abroad, and what hard-liners would say at home. In both cases
inconvenient national leaders in the client states were murdered.
Neither resistance movement could hope to win on the battlefield.
The Soviet military, like the American military before it, appears

to think of the war as a kind of laboratory for new weapons and tactics. Like the U.S. in Vietnam, Russia fervently proclaims its peaceful intent in Afghanistan. One of the few real differences is that the Soviet Union openly supported Hanoi with money and arms in generous measure, whereas the United States trickles arms to the Afghans while officially pretending to be doing nothing of the kind. I mentioned these points during a meeting with the editorial board of *Oktyabr* and asked why I always got the same responses to questions about Afghanistan. When the subject was missilery and the Geneva talks, I was willing to concede faults on my side. Why did I never hear so much as a whisper of doubt on theirs? The American withdrawal from Vietnam required years of painful self-examination and a rupture between citizens and government. Were the Russians afraid to admit that something similar might be demanded of them? How could they reconcile all the talk of peace with a war of conquest in a neighboring country?

Six people were sitting around the table. I paused after each sentence to make sure Alexei translated the whole of it. The editors grew mournful and solemn. Like the other Russians I'd talked to, they hated the Afghanistan question. Even Alexander Prohanov looked ill. He had written a novel about the war, called *A Tree in Kabul*, which I later read. It was a shallow and slavish piece of work, filled with tractors and noble derring-do. When Alexei finished, the chief editor cleared his throat to answer. His voice was heavy with moral seriousness. There were certain points I had to understand: the Soviet Union has a long border with Afghanistan; back in 1979, the U.S. was looking for new bases to take the place of the ones in Iran; the rebels were being armed by China and the U.S.; the rebels were led by feudal reactionaries; and besides — what can you do when a neighbor's house is on fire and he begs for help?

In Russia one hears other secondary lines as well. The Soviet Union doesn't need another "independent peace movement," something that E. P. Thompson, in particular, has stressed in his writings about nuclear war. The Soviet Peace Committee *is* independent. Besides, the Soviets are for peace and disarmament

officially. How can you improve on that? The "so-called" independent peace movement is nothing but a collection of malcontents
and soreheads. E. P. Thompson is a notorious anti-Communist
animated by rabid hatred of the Soviet Union. *Pravda* has never
published one word about him, and never will. As lines go, this
one is pretty irritating, implying as it does that independent peace
movements are required only in the West, where the governments
are all run by imperialists, Russophobes, and stooges of the arms
industry. There was a line on the arms industry, too. In the West
arms mean profits, whereas in Russia no one gets anything out
of preparation for war. However, Western scholars have identified
a Soviet arms industry that operates much like a free market, with
competing design bureaus fighting for contracts to build missiles
and aircraft. The line, of course, admits no such thing. Yet another
line, pushed with unusual vigor, insists that the Soviets' SS-20
missile does not alter the nuclear balance in Europe but represents
nothing more than a modernization of the old SS-4s and -5s —
single-warhead, liquid-fueled, highly vulnerable weapons that have
been pointed at the West since the 1950's. The SS-20 is just a better
weapon — nothing new, no big deal. But, of course, any new,
accurate, solid-fueled (hence quick to fire), MIRVed missile with
three warheads that can hit anything from Russia to the mid-
Atlantic *is* a big deal. I argued this at length with just about
everybody. Was Russia trying to scare the living daylights out of
Europe, as many Western analysts insist, as the first step in a process of "Finlandizing" Europe? Or was the SS-20 a mistake, a fruit
of the restless compulsion to build weapons that has been
characteristic of both sides over the past forty years, something
the Russians had never expected to attract attention? No, no, my
interlocutors insisted; it was just modernization, routine tinker-
ing with the strategic arsenal. Back and forth we went.

Eventually I concluded that the SS-20 had a purpose all right,
but not the one usually ascribed to it. NATO's forward-based
systems had not been included in the first two rounds of SALT,
and the Russians wanted them in. A new weapon threatening
Europe, they figured, would force the agenda of any new talks —
as it has in fact done. I tried out this interpretation on everyone

who might really know what the Politburo had in mind when it decided to build and deploy the SS-20. I didn't expect explicit corroboration, but I hoped the answers might contain at least an echo of the truth. The point, after all, was not immaterial. The controversy over the SS-20 is serious. The weapon has been a driving force behind new strategic-weapons programs on both sides. If the Russians had simply stumbled into this situation, that would suggest that the arms race is truly blind on both sides — the "action-reaction phenomenon" that Robert McNamara cited in a speech back in 1967, when he was secretary of defense. But the Russians all looked blank. There was no "plan" behind the SS-20. The Politburo didn't have anything in mind. It was just modernization.

One day I saw something I'd missed before. I suppose it should have been obvious all along. These people *were* frightened. Unlike American officials, who are willing to entertain more or less any point of view, the Russians are ideologically rigid. As soon as the discussion refined itself to being a question of us against them, they refused to give an inch. Words of concession simply would not come. On Poland, on Afghanistan, on the SS-20, their government held the correct position, and that was that. Perhaps this rigidity helped blind me for a time to a more important difference between Russian and American officials. The Americans are reasonable, well informed, ready to crack a joke or bolster an argument with irony, and moderately forthcoming about the processes and the personalities of government — subjects the Russians never discuss at all. But above all, Americans are confident. Historical optimism is second nature to them: Don't worry, it is going to work out, nothing bad is going to happen.

This is not the characteristic Russian note. When Russians speak of a breakdown at Geneva, it is with genuine alarm. Things have slipped a long way since the détente of the early 1970s. Russians hoped that SALT and Brezhnev's successor would open a new era, one of parity and Great Power cooperation abroad, and economic development at home. But SALT was never ratified, the U.S. refuses to accept parity, the funds for new development must go to arms instead. When Russians speak of hope, they do so in voices heavy and wistful. "You have to have some hopes," said

Stanislav Kondrashov, a journalist at *Izvestia.* "Who said hope is the last thing we bid farewell? How else can we live in this world?" I heard many Russians say they felt it would come to war in the end. I have *never* heard an American say this. I heard many Russians cite Chekhov's famous principle of dramaturgy: If there is a gun on the wall in the first act, it will fire in the third. I have *never* heard an American official or professional defense analyst speak in such fatalistic tones. One man even told me that the American nuclear buildup might force the Russians to launch a pre-emptive attack on the United States. Shocked, I asked Alexei to make sure that the man really meant what he said. At that point, he broke into English and insisted that "pre-emptive attack" was not a mistranslation. "It could happen," he said. "We could be forced to do it." He was a journalist, not a military officer. He did not know the details of Russian strategic planning. Still, even if it indicated only the depth of his own alarm, his statement was frightening.

The Russians I spoke to feel pushed and crowded. The Soviet Union has proven it is a power in the world; why can't America accept this, and deal with it as an equal? Russians frequently cite the American intervention in Russia in 1918 as proof of our long-standing animosity. They draw quick, rough maps of the Eurasian heartland, with bold "X"s marking the vast ring of American military bases surrounding the Soviet Union from Japan to Norway. Most of them insist that current American strategic programs are all aimed at building first-strike capability. Why else would the United States be committed to building the MX — a super-accurate weapon that is vulnerable and must therefore be fired first if it is to be fired at all? they ask. Why is the United States planning to deploy Pershing II missiles in Europe — also super-accurate weapons — only six minutes away from the Soviet missiles and command centers in western Russia? Why is the United States building super-accurate missiles for the new Trident submarines? It is well known that Soviet strategic weapons are mostly land-based, and that they can be threatened by accurate warheads. The Americans write about *limited* nuclear war and *selective* strikes against hard, well-protected military targets. They write about "decapitating" the Soviet Union with nuclear attacks on the institutions that run the country and on the civil-defense shelters where Soviet leaders plan to take refuge. For ten years the Americans have been bleating about the Soviet threat to American Minuteman missiles — a bare quarter of the U.S. strategic force — and citing this threat as proof that the Soviets are patiently preparing for the day when they can rule the world. These "suspicions" reveal what Washington is really thinking. Their own programs will threaten 75 percent of the Soviet strategic force. Are the Soviets to brush all this aside as just talk?

Russians insist that they will maintain parity now that they have finally achieved it. "Don't judge Russian missiles by your TV set," one said after I had told him that the set in my hotel room didn't work. "Some things we *can* do," he said. Some American experts think super-sophisticated new weapons systems may offer a genuine strategic edge; many doubt it. But none doubt that we can build some pretty fancy hardware if we decide to. Russians *say* they can, but with an air of determination, of sheer assertion, that sounded to me, after a while, uncertain. I think they're afraid that the Americans are going to spring a surprise — something so advanced, so magically versatile, so big and expensive, that the Soviet Union will suddenly find itself pushed back to 1950, trying to hide its weakness behind a curtain of secrecy. In Moscow, this self-doubt makes perfect sense. The city is clean and orderly, but decrepit and run-down. Clouds of oil smoke pour from the rattletrap cars, buses, and trucks. In GUM, the big department store on Red Square, the shoppers are crowded twenty deep around the counters. The imported radios and hi-fis sold only in foreign-currency shops cost a fortune. Everything has an archaic air, as if the Soviet Union were still struggling to do 1950 right. Russians see this clumsy backwardness too. Some take a perverse pride in it, as if it reflected a purity of spirit in contrast to the sybaritic materialism of the West. But more of them frankly admire the West. Despite all its sins, the West is *advanced*. So I was not surprised by the note of fear at the prospect of a new round of the arms race in the one field where Russians are weakest. Harold Brown, Carter's secretary of defense, once said, "Our technology is what will save us." The Russians fear that he is right. They fear that we might use a strategic advantage to push them around, or even to attack out of the blue. To an American, these Russian fears are especially unsettling. They are all based on what *we* write and do. I found myself trying to explain these things away as politics and idle theorizing, but the Russians, though polite, did not appear to be convinced.

Imagine, for a moment, that the efforts of the peacemakers have failed and that a third world war has commenced. Imagine, also, that the nuclear arsenals of the Soviet Union and the United States are so evenly balanced that neither side dares to fire its missiles or drop its bombs. Imagine, further, that the main theater of conventional fighting is in central Europe, where the two sides have got most of their tanks and divisions, and that it has become clear the war is going to be a long one — just like the other two big wars of the century. Now take a look at the globe and pick out the probable peripheral theaters of the war. They make a long list, which would include areas of obvious strategic significance, like the Persian Gulf, as well as every country with a substantial Soviet presence. Among them would be Afghanistan, which is already the scene of fighting; China, which has been trumpeting the threat posed by Soviet hegemonists for twenty years; Vietnam, an ally of Moscow and the site of a major Soviet naval base; Cambodia, which is already the scene of fighting; Korea, unless the North elected to side with China; the Middle East, which is already the scene of fighting, including a major war between Iran and Iraq (although neither is currently an ally of the Soviet Union); Yemen; Ethiopia, which has a regime that depends on Soviet support; Angola, which is already the scene of fighting; Cuba; and Nicaragua, which is already the scene of fighting.

There are several things one might say about this list of probable theaters in a third world war that did not end in nuclear holocaust within a week or so. The most obvious is that fighting is already taking place in five of them, albeit at a low level, and that in all but one of them — the Gulf War — a main point of contention is Soviet influence. Another obvious point is that most of these theaters have become arenas of East–West conflict only since 1945. In 1939, the Soviet Union was weak and well hedged about; it was victory in the Second World War that opened the door for the recovery of territories Russia had lost in the First World War, that planted Russia's boots in the anterooms of the West, that left Russia without rival in Europe, and that willy-nilly gave it a role on the world stage. Yet another point, although one subject to endless contention, is that the expansion of Soviet influence is inextricable from the course of the Cold War — that is, the mutual fear that seems to have sprung up in an instant from the ashes of Berlin in 1945. The "ring of bases" of which Russia complains was the result of American fear of a new war. Soviet influence elsewhere in the world is the result of an attempt to leapfrog that ring. The attempt has not been notably successful. How many Cubas and Angolas, after all, would it take to offset the hostility of China? A final point to be made about the scope of a war between Russia and America is that it would be both too vast and too particular in its local details to be settled — if by that we mean settled in the way the question of German power was settled, *once and for all* — on anything but a global scale.

Putting the matter this way suggests that Russia is the problem, and that settling the problem would demand Russia's return to its snow and ice, in Napoleon's phrase. This remains the basic position of the West. But how is the West to force Russia into such a colossal retreat? In Washington, a small but currently influential circle believes that the Soviet Union is an empire of the nineteenth-century variety, the world's last; that its power rests on a frail economic base; and that it may already be in decline. Russia has no allies of importance; its clients in Eastern Europe hate its guts; it can sell nothing but arms and raw materials. No other country shows the slightest interest in Soviet "culture" or imitates Russia in anything whatever except the techniques of domestic coercion. Its scholars do not count for much even in the field of Marxist studies. The noted Soviet analyst Seweryn Bialer has said that if Russia did not possess nuclear weapons it would not even be classed as a major power.

Starting from these premises, some analysts believe that the Soviet Union can be forced into economic collapse, and thence into eclipse, by a combination of expensive arms-building and economic warfare. Reagan's former national security adviser, William Clark, once described the Soviet regime as an "evil and bizarre episode" in human history. The implications of the word *episode* can hardly be taken lightly in Moscow. When I saw Arbatov, he bitterly criticized the American "strategic" approach, as it is sometimes called. Despite its many critics in the United States, the strategic approach is nevertheless "taken seriously here," he said. "These troglodytic sentiments can be found even among the top people in your government. They seem to feel 'Maybe now at last the moment has come when we can do away with them [that is, the Soviets], or undermine them completely.' It explains this attempt to impose on us a much more costly arms race, to try to ruin us economically. Reagan's policy is close to economic warfare. He's trying to undermine our deals, close down our credits. We have to believe it [Reagan's commitment to the strategic approach] is serious. Only in the case if we are not strong enough will it take the form of outright war."

Other Russians addressed this question as well. The strategic approach seemed to baffle and to anger them in equal measure, and their comments all had a similar drift, as if to say, You're trying to destroy us — literally break up our state and change our whole government. You *admit* you're trying to destroy us. And you claim you are committed to peace? If that is peace, what is war?

There is no question that this policy can poison relations, but can it work? Russians insist that they can keep up indefinitely. The CIA recently published a paper claiming that the Soviet Union is less dependent on imports than any other major power, and history suggests that though the defense of empires can wreck economies, this process tends to take a long time, and the final push requires a war, or even a series of wars. Turkey was the "sick man of Europe" for a hundred years, but it held on to a vast empire until the First World War, and would have kept it longer if it had guessed that Britain, not Germany, would be the winner in 1918. The basic weakness of the strategic approach is the obvious one: it is transparently hostile, it precludes accommodation, it encourages arms-building, and the closer it comes to working, the greater the chance of war through fear and desperation.

In the opening pages of *The Peloponnesian War,* Thucydides offered a conventional account of the causes of the war that broke out in 431 B.C. — a typically muddled chain of action and reaction — but added that in his opinion the real cause was much simpler: it was Spartan fear of growing Athenian power. This fear had first been aroused forty-eight years earlier, at the end of the Greek allies' victorious war against the Persians, in 479 B.C., when Athens began to rebuild its city walls and decided to retain its wartime navy, the most powerful military force in Greece. These two facts poisoned the well, and the allies became rivals. Causes do not come much more basic than that.

The three Punic Wars, between Rome and Carthage, had similar roots. After the second Punic war, Cato the Censor, a Roman senator, was sent on a diplomatic mission to Carthage, where he was astonished to find that the city, far from being crippled by the reparations it had paid to Rome, was rapidly regaining its power. From that moment forward Cato added a sentence to the end of every speech he delivered in the Senate, whatever the ostensible subject: *"Delenda est Carthago"* — "Carthage must be destroyed." The history of the Punic Wars is also highly particular, with one "cause" for this one, and another for that. But the real cause of the wars was simpler — the fear aroused in each city by the power of the other. At the end of the third war, in 146 B.C., the Romans tore down the walls of Carthage, sold its citizens into slavery, and sowed the ground with salt.

This is one of the patterns of history: a city or nation rises to power, absorbs or threatens to absorb its neighbors, and finally collapses when it has aroused the fear of more enemies than it can handle. Spain in the sixteenth century, France in the early nineteenth, and Germany in the twentieth are notable examples. All three came close to establishing hegemony over Europe. All three were successfully opposed by Britain, in the last instance with the aid of the United States. Britain's policy had always been the simple one of seeking to prevent the domination of Europe by any single power. But the two wars with Germany destroyed Britain as a world power, and the United States took its place in the defense of Europe. Did Stalin dream of conquering the whole of the Continent? No one can say; Stalin kept his plans to himself. But what he did was enough. He imposed Soviet control over Eastern Europe, redrew its boundaries to his liking, and guaranteed the fact of possession with Russian armies.

The United States and Russia are both Great Powers of the traditional kind. Both have expanded rapidly, over the past two centuries, at the expense of weak neighbors; both are blessed with abundant natural resources; both draw their power from huge populations and economies; both are convinced that the destiny of the world is in their hands; and both are showing signs of the awful financial strain of sustaining a global conflict. For both sides the focus is Europe, where Russian and American armies face each other across the line established by the calamities of the Second World War. There the Americans are far from home but have friendly allies. The Russians are closer to home but keep an eye on hostile clients. The question at the heart of the Cold War — the thing it is most nearly "about" — is which of these two armies will go home first. It is hard to imagine a confrontation with fewer exits.

The problem now is that the closing stages of the traditional pattern always involve great wars, but we — Russia and the West alike — cannot hope to gain from a great war. In the past, when somebody lost, somebody won. Now, nuclear weapons make that unlikely. The side closest to losing retains the power to drag down its rival with it. Many people grasped this point right away in 1945, when atomic weapons destroyed Hiroshima and Nagasaki — but, for the most part, national leaders did not. They thought we were smart enough to conduct a Great Power conflict without sliding into war. They still think so. As a result, we behave as Great Powers have always behaved — raising armies, seeking advantage, and supporting our demands with threats of war when conflict comes to crisis. The only difference now is that we tell ourselves it will never come to war in the end. It will just go on indefinitely.

In one of his essays, E. P. Thompson wrote, "If we ask the partisans on either side what the Cold War is now about, they regard us with the glazed eyes of addicts." I have found this to be true. Over the past year, I have asked perhaps a hundred people — Russians and Americans alike — what it is about. Of course, this is a hard question. I did not expect anyone to sort out the whole matter in an afternoon. But I had in mind a story, possibly apocryphal, I once read about the composer Stravinsky. He had written a new piece with a difficult violin passage. After it had been in rehearsal for several weeks, the solo violinist came to Stravinsky and said he was sorry, he had tried his best, the passage was too difficult, no violinist could play it. Stravinsky said, "I understand that. What I am after is the sound of someone *trying* to play it." I asked my question in that spirit.

But none of the people I approached showed anything more than a polite interest in the question. No one offered the sort of ready answer that suggested he had been thinking about it. No one found it easy to propose the name of someone who *might* have been thinking about it. Their eyes were not exactly glazed, but they were certainly blank. I had figured that the Russians, at least, would be quick to propose a dialectical interpretation. They were not. The few who alluded vaguely to history said all that was behind us now. The responses, after an awkward moment, were pretty much the same: *That's a very interesting question; we ought to concentrate more on that, I agree, yes, but the really pressing matter now is the question of the Euromissiles* — or something else of the kind. It was questions about hardware that interested them, or the details of negotiating positions, or the dangers posed to the fundamentals of deterrence by new weapons technology, or the rights and wrongs of the Soviet use of Cuban proxies in Angola and Ethiopia, or the slippage of Soviet control in Eastern Europe, or the motives behind the counterforce revolution in American military thinking. It is *process* that absorbs the managers and publicists of the Cold War — not words but the Great Game itself, not why we act but what we do. Things can go so terribly wrong tomorrow that it is hard to concentrate on anything but the awful dilemma of what to do today.

Thompson wrote in the essay quoted above, "What is the Cold War now about? It is about itself." I think Thompson is right, with one qualification: the Cold War has *always* been about itself. It's about what happened last week, and what we hope — or fear — will happen next week. The military power of the two sides is in constant flux. Today's allies may falter tomorrow. Each side feels that defeat on its periphery is a threat to its center. Both sides are incapable of explaining why things have to be this way, but act as if fate offered no alternative. When we ask what this great struggle is about we betray our own helplessness. The answers are just words. For nearly forty years we have talked and talked without mitigating the danger that we will fight in the end. No single issue divides us, nothing we can settle through negotiation and compromise. It is only propagandists who insist that the history of the Cold War explains it. The problem at its heart is an elemental one. It is our nature that makes us draw lines in the earth and grimace when anyone approaches in strange garb, not some legalistic litany of rights threatened or violated. The Cold War has a new name, but it follows an old pattern. Among the things we seek or fear from this conflict there is not one on a scale even close to the scale of the war we are preparing to fight with each other. We are trapped in a tightening spiral of fear and hostility. We don't know why we have got into this situation, we don't know how to get out of it, and we have not found the humility to admit we don't know. In desperation, we simply try to manage our enmity from day to day. When Germany fell in 1945, only two Great Powers remained in the world — Russia and the United States. Only Russia has the power to threaten the United States. Only the United States has the power to threaten Russia. We fear each other. We wish each other ill. All the rest is detail.

I have been writing about this subject for the past three years. It is a general rule that if you write about the topics of the day you will be asked to make speeches about them. It comes with the territory. When I'm asked, I always try to say yes. The basic point of my speeches is generally the same: this problem, while simple in essence, is multifaceted, it has deep roots, it is getting worse, and we are a long way down the road to a relationship so poisoned that it can never be set right. At the end of these speeches there are many questions. They range from the weapons themselves —

what they're like, how they work, can they *really* hit a football field from the other side of the globe? (yes), and similar matters — to the inevitable "what about . . ." questions. These come in two types: What about Poland and Afghanistan? What about the Soviet military buildup? What about worldwide Marxist–Leninist revolution? What about the purges, Sakharov, Raoul Wallenberg? The second type focuses on us: What about "massive retaliation?" What about Vietnam and El Salvador? What about the American military buildup? What about the multinationals and the military-industrial complex? What about McCarthyism? What about Lumumba? The full list of questions is monstrous in length. The charges are all serious ones. Any able propagandist can draw up a damning indictment of either side. Ordinary citizens seem to think that the conflict must be about something and that we can solve it provided we can discover who is to blame. My own view is that attempts to fix blame get us nowhere. Many things are at stake in this conflict — indeed, *everything* is at stake — but they are not what it is about. The problem is not evil designs on either side but our complacency in hostility, our willingness to go on as we are, our reliance on threats of annihilation to save us from annihilation. These things are hard to say in two minutes. I answer as I can. Gradually people drift away.

But there is generally one last person with one last question, and I always know what it's going to be. I've been asked this question twenty times. I imagine that gypsy fortune-tellers hear something very similar. Somebody comes in — it's just for fun, he isn't superstitious, he doesn't believe in fortune-telling — and his very first question is: When will I die? The fortune-tellers must see it coming a mile away. I hate the one last question, but somebody always asks it: Are we going to have a war?

How am I to answer? I refuse to give any answer that depends on *if*: if we don't abandon the road we're on, if we don't learn to live with the Russians, if we can't see that the horrors of the Soviet system are *their* problem, if we don't realize that weapons threaten rather than defend, if we go on looking for a military solution, if we trust the managers who say everything is under control, if we refuse to see that it isn't all their fault, if we can't realize that we have got to solve this problem *together*, if men seeking power keep telling themselves there will always be time to set things right after the next election, if we go on clapping one another on the back at the end of each day of armed peace and saying "See? Deterrence works!" . . . The warnings are all old friends by now. We've been repeating them to one another for forty years. They are like a sacred text, promising that it can all be undone. Not one of them shows any sign whatever of being taken to heart by the only men who count — the budget-makers and diplomats who buy the arms and issue the white papers. Sometimes, after these people have returned to private life, they begin to sound worried themselves, and issue the very sort of troubled warnings that they ignored or explained away when they were still in office and might have done something. But perhaps the authority of office is illusory, and the choice was never there. Perhaps a nation in the grip of fear will always choose military power, no matter what. We have chosen power since 1945. We choose power now. I believe we are going to go on as we have done. The implications are clear. It doesn't take a prophet to see the end of a pattern so pronounced. But this last, awful question always comes from someone I've never met before; I'm not sure how he will fare on thin gruel. So I tell him I don't know.

ARCHETYPAL MARS

THE NIGHT SKY (excerpt)

From "Star Myth"

Life is so brief and fragile in the context of the durable and awesome scenery of night, and we have so little contact with the inner sky, that we do not dwell there long in our attentions. One turns away from the stars, fixes a meal, calls a friend. The lesson would be electrifying, refreshing, but we are not in the mood for such lessons. Instead we experience a kind of cosmic loneliness, and we put the stars aside to live our lives. But is this cosmic loneliness a result of the present infinite view of the ruthless stars and galaxies, or are they themselves a symptom of the cosmic loneliness we already feel in a society which has lost spiritual and ecological direction and which already has nothing to offer man for this trip except, as in the beer ad: "You only go around once and you'd better grab for all the gusto you can get!"? No one could seriously believe this as stated; and yet all of us do in some way, and pay a terrible price. The alternative would be to express our own cosmic dimension; yet we have forgotten how, and it is taught almost nowhere.

Astronomers were once our priests, and, whether they know it or not, they still interpret the moral as well as physical structure of the heavens. And they have shown us a universe that would seem to devour without rhyme or reason: stars crushed, galaxies of stars destroyed, stars devouring other stars, black holes devouring everything; they have shown dying suns swallowing their solar systems. Where ancient astronomers found a divine whirlpool, modern ones received the news that the whole of matter was created once in a giant explosion from a space perhaps no bigger than a dime, and they said: there is no moral structure; in fact, there is nothing at all.

After the fact, we can create science fiction stories about passing through black holes into beautiful other universes, but the black holes given in scientific theory are no more habitable than the Sun itself. Man could not pass through them, and certainly consciousness could not. The vast explosions of space dwarf anything imaginable, though on our scale they seem to represent the downfall of vast civilizations, like the fall of the West, the decline of the Roman Empire, or the overthrow of the Aztec Kingdom. Perhaps that is what they are intended to mean, their esoteric nature showing through their material guise. But for now, mankind has been asked to be present at its own funeral, a funeral which took place billions of years in the past and perhaps billions of years in the future. It is an atomic nightmare.

One is uncomfortable thinking about nuclear war; yet the stars are nuclear war writ large — enormous fires whose death throes will destroy planets and whose ultimate compacting (if true as proposed) will mark the end of the material universe. People who carry skulls and dress in death costumes throwing ashes to indicate the consequences of humankind tangling with this energy are enacting, on the one hand, a profound truth about something that has gone wrong in our time (the sloppy use of crude stellar energy in short-term schemes), and, on the other hand, a satire of what is shown in space: death of suns and stars too, death of the universe, which has been offered in place of religion, in place of internal process, and in place of life methodology. Our own age is threatened by a holocaust of man's own making (unless there be accomplice wizards and demons or extraterrestrial intelligences behind man himself), and it is no accident that scientific theology of this age proposes a cataclysm that will obliterate everything and what everything is — things which were ostensibly once brought into being by just such a cataclysm. We have hardly been less arbitrary and cruel to each other.

We have achieved the same proposition that the hermetics espoused for entire opposite reasons: that Heaven and Earth are reflections of each other and the same laws prevail in each. We have made the sky our bedfellow and have put ourselves to sleep in the starry night. It is a coffin, and we no longer look because it is too horrible. The sky is our midwife and our interrer. It is our placenta but also our ashes. Unity is inescapable. The same elements and forces are everywhere. On the one hand, the meaning of the sky is reduced to a human scale, which makes it less mysterious. On the other hand, the scope of the sky and its possible moral structure are put utterly beyond men in a circumstance that is far more terrifying than even the old gods.

Unquestionably, the new sky set men free; the old sky had been a tyrant, ruling men's fortunes, taking away their rights, and setting corrupt priests and kings on their thrones, all in the name of cosmic myth. But it also kept the cosmos sacred and intact. Now we are treated as a speck in a puddle that must be influenced by whatever raindrops, detritus, or lines of force happen here. Coherence has become accidental and random, even if it still exists to hold solar systems and galaxies together, as well as the interior of the atom. We are free men and women, free of the tyrannies of the stars and of those who interpret their will into repressive kingdoms and castes. We are now subject to vast amounts of meaningless information about bigger and bigger things. The sky used to set an example for moral structure. Now it seems merely to permit a moral freedom in line with the principle of shapeless creative hydrogen fire and universal entropy.

Because the sky is so big, it becomes a blank, a zero. Beside it we feel we are innocent and wonder why all this misfortune has befallen us. We feel we are decent people. "Why were we not born in a better place at a better time? Why this planet, this world, this violent history? Why should we be subject to wars, earthquakes, revolutions, famine?" Since we feel we did nothing to cause these things, since they are an interpolation of stellar material into a terrestrial frame, we become isolated and alienated. We connect to nothing.

Isaac Bashevis Singer, the twentieth-century Yiddish novelist, has Asa Heshel wonder about the universe on the eve of Hitler's invasion of Poland. "Meteors shot across the sky, leaving fiery trails behind them. Silent summer lightning quivered in one corner of the heavens, foretelling a hot day. Fireflies shone and were extinguished; frogs croaked; all kinds of winged insects came fluttering into the room and dashed themselves against the walls, the windows, and the bedposts." This is the modern empty universe. John Donne never would have seen it this way. "Asa Heshel thought about Hitler; according to Spinoza, Hitler was a part of the

Godhead, a mode of the Eternal Substance. Every act of his had been predetermined by eternal laws. Even if one rejected Spinoza, one still had to admit that Hitler's body was part of the substance of the sun, from which the earth had originally detached itself. Every murderous act of Hitler's was a functional part of the cosmos."

Passive acceptance of the morally unacceptable is the lot of modern man. From the perspective of ancient man, though, birth in this zone and clime is no accident, and we are not innocent. We are the secret perpetrators, in the mind of matter, of the conditions in which we find ourselves. On some utterly primary level that we no longer experience because it is beyond even the shadows of memory or the old wisdom, we chose and created this. We put ourselves under this sky and sealed its lot upon us. Not only are we destined, but we can view the track of that destiny in the sky, a dark magical mirror of our course.

In ancient stellar culture, a revolution was visible in the changing of the sky. Perhaps this is still true. Today's sky allows that galaxies and stars blow up from their internal forces. No wonder, then, that societies do too. Hitler's ovens are the moral equivalent of a neutron star in a system which once held life. Starvation in Cambodia is the equivalent of a supernova. Why not invade Afghanistan? Comets invade planets; galaxies invade other galaxies, killing a possible billion billion people. Why not put the people out to sea in dinghies? That's what gravity does. That's all that planets are anyway. That's how life was created from the trillions of chemical compounds in the original sea.

In another Singer novel, another character views the starry sky, wondering if there are concentration camps and starvation out there too, or possibly some spark of hope. When he realizes that modern astronomy proclaims the same universal struggle, he is overcome with despair: "A rage against creation, God, nature — whatever this wretchedness was called. I felt that the only way of protesting cosmic violence was to reject life. . . ."

In the last fifty years in particular, we have done away with the remaining vestiges of public morality. The sky stands as a moral lesson only to thugs, looters, and terrorists. It expands ad infinitum;

it explodes without caring for the innocent victims; and it enjoys itself without thought or fear of tomorrow. It has no plan for the future. How strangely like ourselves!

Our own economies expand, and the value of money dissipates with the galaxies of the night sky. Inflation and the expanding universe may be light-years apart in terms of their apparent origins in the modern system, but they share a realm of thought. They indicate equally the inability to set value, the sense that all value is relative. As we find nothing but violence, relativity, and destruction in the sky, we find ourselves surrounded by depravity, rioting, starvation, and advanced weaponry. The "starring of the Earth" is right up to date. Family structure crumbles with the stable Solar System. What is there to live for if the stars no longer care? Why even try to behave decently, with such a ruthless bandit on display every night?

Our knowledge has snowballed, and our means for dealing with nature have put us in an environment mostly of our own making. Yet the basic mysteries are as impenetrable as ever. Our civilization sits beneath the same sky as uncomprehendingly as Stone Age man stood beneath it in his own loneliness. And by the clock of the heavens, a brief second has passed from then till now.

Our ability to transform scientific information has been far outweighed by the amount of that information and its very gloomy implications about our species. Even our local Solar System is disclosed, planet by planet, as a sequence of hellish environments in which our potential survival, if we should suddenly be transported there, would range from a matter of milleseconds to a matter of minutes at the most. The rest is explosions and radiation. The beauty of space is overshadowed by the sense that it is nothing but a noisy brute. It explodes galaxies and worlds in the way that we build and put out campfires. The planets in our vicinity are not neighbors; they are fires, storms of poisonous gases, and dry meteor-pummeled stone. The Martians and Venusians of the 1930s and 1940s, even of five years ago, now seem fantastic wishful follies. Their "remains" are strewn on bouldery plains and around $500°$ carbon dioxide volcanoes. The old mythologies, whether they be of Ice Age man, the mediaeval astrologers, or science fiction writers of the rapidly passing twentieth century, serve a crucial purpose we may only dimly understand. And it is not enough to say that they explain us instead of outer space; it is not enough to reduce them to projections of our own habitation into the uninhabited void.

In the introduction to *Hamlet's Mill*, Giorgio de Santillana and Hertha von Dechend take up this issue from a different perspective. They first acknowledge that the ancient star-wisdom tells us something of cosmogonic beginnings, of "the breaking asunder of a harmony" and the tilting of space. Then they add:

> This is not to suggest that this archaic cosmology will show any great physical discoveries, although it required prodigious feats of concentration and computing. What it did was to mark out the unity of the universe, and of man's mind, reaching out to its farthest limits.

Life attempts to express its own innermost truths, and these, if they are not expressed, will lodge more deeply in unconsciousness to make themselves known in other ways. If we ignore the stars, we ultimately feel the loneliness and mortality even more deeply, for the sky is a fact. The stars are there, like them or not, and though we can hang out in a covered city all night and greet the Sun as a kind of electric light in the morning, we must ultimately come to terms with who we are and the nature of the scenery here.

Just because we are no longer archaic does not mean we no longer require a cosmogony or that we have solved the problems of the ancient priests. Our position is more tenuous than we realize. De Santillana and von Dechend continue:

> Einstein said: "What is inconceivable about the universe is that it should be at all conceivable." Man is not giving up. When he discovers remote galaxies by the million and then those quasi-stellar radio sources billions of light-years away which confound his speculation, he is happy that he can reach out to those depths. But he pays a terrible price for his achieve-ment. The science of astrophysics reaches out on a grander and grander scale without losing its footing. Man as man can-not do this. In the depths of space he loses himself and all notion of his significance. He is unable to fit himself into the

concepts of today's astrophysics short of schizophrenia. Modern
man is facing the nonconceivable. Archaic man, however, kept
a firm grip on the conceivable by framing within his cosmos
an order of time as an eschatology that made sense for him
and reserved a fate for his soul.

It is not a case of primitive wishfulness or lack of apprecia-
tion of the harshness of the cosmos. Archaic cosmology was just
as fierce and merciless as our 250-miles-per-hour Jovian clouds and
black holes swallowing light itself. The Hindu gods retain some
of the original clarity of the mythic universe. Shiva is the sentinel
of both love and death, the devourer of life and the source of life.
As Shiva dances, the whole cosmos shimmers as his reflection. His
throat is blue from a poison that he drank in order to save mankind.
And then there is black Kali, goddess of disease, murder, evil,
wisdom, revelation. "It was a prodigiously vast theory," according
to de Santillana and von Dechend, "with no concessions to merely
human sentiments. It, too, dilated the mind beyond the bearable,
although without destroying man's role in the cosmos. It was a
ruthless metaphysics."

Anu fulfills his promise to scorned Ishtar by flinging a Bull
of Heaven onto the Earth, a bull whose every snort eradicates
hundreds of warriors. Enkidu rips the right thigh out of the animal
and hurls it back in Ishtar's face. Disease itself is sent to punish
this brazen despoiler. The body of Osiris is shredded through the
cosmos. Triton blows back the flood with his radiant conch shell.
Marduk shoots the Hyades into the squadron of cosmic monsters,
dispersing them into the heavens. Isis flees Typhon, sprinkling the
ground with ears of wheat. Odin sends a storm through the Milky
Way. Samson pulls the house of the Philistines down on himself.
Surt bursts from the divided heavens with a sword of fire. Phaëton
drops the reins of the Sun's chariot at the sight of the Scorpion,
and the zodiac is shattered, the forests scorched; the body of the
usurper lies in the Eridanus. King David sings to bring the waters
up from the Abyss. Quetzalcoatl disappears into the great sea. The
ancient Shah Kai Khushrau fades from the mountaintop into the
sunless sky while the five paladins sleep. He is the last of his kind.
"Farewell for ever!"

It is no accident, in a mythical view of things, that an aroused Islam tries to drive the Western World out of the Near East, i.e., out of the sacred sky of ancestry and myth. Revolutionary Islam, in Iran, old Persia, virtual homeland of astrology and the Kings of the Sky, now attempts to break through the meaningless marketplace static and peg things again to a holy event. Public beheadings are acceptable, but eroticism and hallucinogens are not. If the Ayatollah Khomeini seems utterly rigid and unyielding, it is because he imitates that old sacred political way of doing things. His rules make no sense for human beings as we conceive them in the modern world, but they make total sense for planets and stars which must guard absolute orbits. In exile in Paris, he had no power to take over Iran, but Iran chose him as a figure for itself. The people, the Revolution, chose him, not apparently because he was eloquent on their concerns or educated on the type of society they wanted, but because he represented the old gods and the strength of ancient times. He brought back the unyieldingness of cosmology that preceded this modern tumult of races and values and marketplace politics. From the point of view of Islamic revolution, Big Bang Theory and pornography and crime are sworn accomplices in the Western World. The ostensible neutrality of astrophysics and international law merely obscures that.

It is not simply a matter of spiritual development and personal meaning. If we were more star conscious, we would be ecologically more astute and politically and economically more cross-cultural and wise. The false boundaries and passing meanings of decades and ways of life would be guided by something more central and enduring. It would help our energy crisis if we thought more clearly and profoundly about how energy itself originates in the stars and finds itself located on the planets.

People don't conceptualize energy resources in any realistic long-term sense. Michael Collins, the astronaut who stayed in the capsule during that 1969 lunar visit, understood as he watched the Earth from space. We are like ants, digging up everything under the surface, oil and coal, as if it were limitless and as if this behavior were enlightened, or even sane. The only future that man can have at this rate must be set imaginarily in future worlds of outer space. In terms of the Earth, man has failed to grasp in any economically or politically viable way that it is a planet, a single planet. There are no others; to imagine them does not create them. And what have we made or left for our children, our children's children, and their children? They certainly will know and understand when time has thrown it into shocking focus.

Meanwhile, science has given us another sky with the seeds of a new ecological morality. The fossil fuels are solar energy, altered by photosynthesis and aeonic chemical activity. The winds are also solar, or gravitational, in their origin. The tides are lunar gravitational energy. Life is stellar chemistry. All the rivers flow into all the seas, and all the clouds arise from the whole and stand against it atmospherically. The lightning and the radiation of the ionosphere are aspects of a single field. It is one boundaryless chemical droplet, stemming from its seas and lapping up into ice, with clouds strung through the invisible winds. "Brown-red is the color," wrote the poet Charles Olson, "of the brilliance of earth."

This was the first gift of Whole Earth consciousness. We were allowed to see a unity directly, and it was a unity expressed throughout mankind: in other ways in the writings of the alchemists and Taoists, in Zuni creation myths and the *I Ching*. Nature is a one, a harmony of diverse elements, and it acts as a one: the clouds, the Arctic ice, the open seas, the Sun penetrating the whole thing, making its radiance in the guts and giving it a blue aura that separates it from the surrounding space as a fine engraving is different from the unmarked jade around it. If it were not for our fearful greed and fatal existential doubt, we could almost come home in this century.

The same night sky poses unlimited energy to an energy-starved world. Or how is it energy-starved when photosynthesis, winds, and global tides are its daily gift from its immediate cosmic neighbors? The two must go together: death by too much energy, panic from too little energy — panic and starvation.

We may not wish to take the Shiite path ourselves, but we can see where contemporary science and morality have taken us. It is not even certain that any of us, or any living thing on this planet, can survive them, despite the billions of years that were put into getting us here. We live now with the knowledge that our civilization will be buried even more deeply than the temples of Rome, and that we will be showered by more than just the dust of winds and human forgetfulness and ignorance. Our heavenly city must be covered with the debris of an exploding Sun and the electric dust of a dissolving universe. We can no longer pretend to be making unlimited progress, so we war and murder in the cosmic void. No hope and no place to go; such is our disappointment and rage. Denis Diderot became deeply troubled by a forerunner of this notion in 1765; what got into his brain like a tiny insect that he could not dislodge until it threatened to topple his entire encyclopedia was the possibility that an unnamed comet, tearing out of the random blankness of the cosmos, might destroy the Earth in a cataclysmic collision. It did not relieve him to think that it was not likely to happen, certainly not in his lifetime. It bothered him that he could not put away the worry and that he could come up with no simple solution to such a pedestrian and almost light notion. In its sheer simplicity, it must mask something terribly profound.

It did. What was a whisper to Diderot would become a gong in the center of another city only two centuries later. It was no idle thought; it was the forerunner of a madness, an obsession in which man would become trapped.

Diderot feared that knowledge of this comet would take away all mankind's reason for noble activity and self-development. "No more ambition, no more monuments, poets, historians, perhaps no more warriors or wars. Everyone would cultivate his garden and plant his cabbages."

He got the details wrong, but he certainly captured the mood. When the implication of universal Darwinism became clear to George Bernard Shaw, he wrote: "If it could be proved that the whole universe had been produced by such Selection, only fools and rascals could bear to live." And such is the case, though we do not think of ourselves as fools and rascals; instead we are the mutants and accidents of directionless turmoil.

Without initially being aware of it, man severed one thread

that held him to the sky, and then followed the other into the future; by now it has expanded to replace the original cosmos with new blueprints from the heart of matter. Since we are born and die within this technological nexus, and since we could not survive without it, many of us may laugh at the idea that the old magical sky held anything true or important in it. But we are biased, being the very interested partisans of the present order and not having lived any other way.

It is not simply that we have moved into spiritual darkness. By learning natural laws and creating a technological society based on them, we have become more humane and gentle in many ways. We have broken the tyranny of some of the cruelest of the old gods. Persian and Incan societies may have been in touch with the heavens in ways we are not, but those paths led to star-justified wars, slaughters, slavery, and sacrifice. In any case, even the last of the old human magi emphasize that this was the path that man was meant to travel, and he could no more evade the current transition, the initiation into the conscious knowledge of matter, than he could evade being incarnated in the first place. The dream is still that we can keep the best of the new order, and, through long painful discipline and meditation, reexperience the basis of the ancient wisdom — not recover it from texts and magical lineages, though these will always be clues and guides along the way, but create it anew in terms of the actual condition of the present Earth in the cosmos. This means that the next hermeticism and astrology will have in them aspects of astrophysics and microbiology. And they will not be initiated in pop images of black holes and extraterrestrial intelligences. These may come into play in totally unexpected ways, or they may wither into period pieces of our troubled times.

We have reached a turning point. It is a priority of the new consciousness — the society emergent in the occultism, radical politics, and Whole Earth philosophy of the sixties — that only a breakdown of the current technocracy, with its laws of time and space, will lead to a greening of America and a new heavenly city on Earth. It will be a nonnuclear city, a city derived from Zen, telepathy, perhaps the vital power in pyramids, and old-fashioned solar energy (it will be Città del Sole). It may even get energy from black holes and quantum physics. It will be a science fiction city which may speak to other intelligences, though not necessarily by radio telescopes. It will restore the botanical and healing power of the Earth. It may be all of these things, some of these things, or none of these things, but these alone as images stand for the new heavenly city, the new order. It cannot happen any longer as pure astral magic and with disregard for the laws of the universe we now know from physics and biology. But these sciences must give birth to occultism and religion anew, borrowing something from a past golden age of which most has been lost and most had already been lost by the time of Plato, presiding over the birth of a new star-wisdom, a new music both arcane and modern, so that the fields of flowers and grains and the body of man and woman can once again be a primordial reflection of the starry firmament. In these fields, greening and starring can be the same thing.

Will Baker

THREE MONKEYS, I AM FATHER

Tsitsi, the Faithful

The first two came quick as squirrels,
tails questioning, their faces small
and old as time. Carlos and Cuñado hissed,
threshed a branch, teased until they
skittered here, there, through leaves
and crisscross of vines.

Now they are just above. Cuñado nocks an arrow,
draws, and with a sudden sigh it slides
through air, through the little body.
It excites her. Her legs jerk and anxious
fingers fondle the hard shaft,
an awkward pendant she drags
this way and that.

Frantically he scurries up, down,
squeaks, plucks at her shoulder:
Come! Come! We must away!

Cuñado's eyes and teeth glisten.
Again he nocks, draws, releases.
The arrow rises rapid as a swallow,
slows through flesh, halts, halfway
red. He pinwheels from branch
to branch, forgetting her now
as she has forgotten him, and the hunters
hoot at this slapstick agony,
this silly tale of fidelity.

Finally Cuñado climbs to throw
them from the tree and down
to Carlos, who presses a thumb
through matchstick ribs. Brow
and sideburns of frost, the walnut
skulls turn, mouths open,
as they shudder into death.

I fold them in a broad leaf
together, a last embrace,
tails flagged out.

Oshtéro, the spider

She was all afternoon squatted on
Cuñado's back, the vine rope under
her long black arms, knees lashed
to elbows. She seemed to nod,
and gaped at me with a stupid lip
drooling blood. Alive she was
an angular, sloping shadow
through green caverns. In death
she did not curl but came down
like syrup through the trees.

Once the vines gave way at a joint
so Cuñado did a new knot hiking
an arm high in farewell gesture.
She preserved it so until sundown'
when we lay them all on a mat
by the fire. There she seemed to gaze
straight up to heaven and raise
that hand to the next evolutionary rung.

Carlos' wife puts water to boil.
A child brings a candle from the hut.
The blade goes brisk back and forth
across a flat rock. By arm and leg
the carcass is upended, head down
in the steaming pot, then out;
from dark fur the wife begins to peel
an ivory doll's skull. Next pathetic
shoulders, a sunken chest. By trick
of fire and candlelight she seems to duck,
embarrassed, before she goes ass up
into the kettle again.

By the men's fire I am joshed,
offered a tiny forearm already crisp.
They have noted the heavy pelt
on my chest, the fuzz at my cuffs,
the shadow on my chin. Here is your son,
your daughter, they say, running
a brown hand over my wrist.
Their faces are smooth as river stones.
Their eyes are deep and full of light.
His son! they say. It is his son!
Then they only eat and laugh,
with nothing in between.

EMBRYOGENESIS (excerpt)

From "Self and Desire"

We live in a world where the slaughter of innocents has reached epidemic levels and members of our species treat other species as objects, statistics, or mere industrial machinery. Animals are hunted and tortured for pleasure, butchered for food we do not need, and maimed in useless experiments. Guinea pigs are injected with carcinogens, cats are lobotomized, and monkeys are made to run on treadmills until they drop from exhaustion, but the treadmill never stops. There is no one to intercede for their lives. They are true political prisoners. Behind the masks of self-important scientists and so-called objective experiments sits merely another legally protected pornographer. Of course, the experimenter imagines his tests are important in the context of the academic bureaucracy he serves; he loses planetary perspective: the animals are defined as different from us in a way that justifies his going as far as he wants without doubt or remorse. Does he not see that their bare liver and nerve sheaths are his liver and nerve sheaths, that they shed the same blood and weep the same tears? At least those "savages" who tortured and maimed their captives did so in a ceremony that recognized the courage and honor of the victim, and then put their own lives on the line in the same battle.

Finally we cannot interrupt the animals because we cannot address them. We can only enrage them, distract them, torture them, bore them, or trick them (and ourselves) into believing we are not there. They will keep their dignity forever. The experimental scientist towers over the bee in generations of intelligence but is puny against the fixed time of its species. Most experiments are arrogant and useless, they do not even have to occur. We cannot hide our brutality behind statistics and careerist papers. We are far too old for that; we have been through the executions of the tribal elders and the sacrifice of children, women, and other sentient beings to the dark spirits behind the Sun.

The mayhem of our species comes not only from misogyny, not only from the traumas of brutalized childhoods; it is also what we inherit from not being human (though not necessarily from being animal). It all happened so long ago; even the old men of the Australian Aborigine tell us it was at the dawn of time, or before time itself. The mythologized account of the crime echoes through the generations: "The men of the Dreaming committed adultery, betrayed and killed each other, were greedy, stole and committed the very wrongs committed by those now alive."

In the summer of 1983, Will Baker was invited on a hunting trip in the Peruvian Amazon by two Asháninka Indians, Carlos and Cuñado. Soon after they begin tracking, a monkey couple ("their faces small and old as time," Baker writes) comes through the trees to look at them. Cuñado nocks his arrow, draws, and fires. The female starts as the shaft enters her small body; her fingers fondle its hardness, and she drags herself back and forth, uncomprehending. The unsuspecting male runs up to her and pulls at her shoulder, trying to hurry her away. Cuñado's next arrow pierces him, and he bolts from her aid and pinwheels through the branches. The hunters "hoot at this slapstick agony, this silly tale of fidelity." The question is not: why do we kill for food? Not yet anyway. The question is: why are we laughing? How long can we remain in the jungle in darkness in a night of faraway stars?

Even Freud must have realized, in the remorse of his later years, that the primal act goes far beyond the genital symbolism in which it masks itself. It is a transformation rite happening neither here nor elsewhere, neither in time nor outside of time, and involving events indecipherable as such but fundamental to the crisis of human life:

"I saw the soul of a man. It came like an eaglehawk. It had wings, but also a penis like a man. With the penis as a hook it pulled my soul out by the hair. My soul hung down from the eagle's penis and we flew first toward the east. It was sunrise and the eaglehawk man made a great fire. In this he roasted my soul. My penis became quite hot and he pulled the skin off. Then he took me out of the fire and brought me into the camp. Many sorcerers were there but they were only bones like the spikes of a porcupine.

"Then we went to the west and the eaglehawk man opened me. He took out my lungs and liver and only left my heart. We went further to the west and saw a small child. It was a demon. I saw the child and wanted to throw the *nankara* (magical) stones at it. But my testicles hung down and instead of the stones a man came out of the testicles and his soul stood behind my back. He had very long *kalu katiti* (skin hanging down on both sides of the subincised penis) with which he killed the demon child. He gave it to me and I ate it."

There is no longer any name for this. There is no tribunal, no judge. There isn't even a convenient psychosis. The death camps appear on the face of history like raindrops splattered on the glass. In the Australian version it isn't malevolent; it is just a shadow masked by a nightmare itself masked by the rudiments of a ceremony. And if we hope to find the evidence or explanation for it in the embryology described elsewhere in these pages, we will be as sorry as those who look to the documents and (now) the videotapes of history in an effort to escape it. We are not likely to find our way out by the animal or the aboriginal shaman either.

In 1761 Georg Wilhelm Steller described an instance of loyalty on the battlefield among sea cows attacked with harpoons by Russian sailors:

"When an animal caught with the hook began to move about somewhat violently, those nearest in the herd began to stir also and feel the urge to bring succour. To this end some of them tried to upset the boat with their backs, while others pressed down the rope and endeavoured to break it, or strove to remove the hook from the wound in the back by blows of their tail, in which they actually succeeded several times. It is most remarkable proof of their conjugal affection that the male, after having tried with all his might, although in vain, to free the female caught by the hook, and in spite of the beating we gave him, nevertheless followed her to the store, and that several times, even after she was dead, he shot unexpectedly up to her like a speeding arrow. Early the next morning, when we came to cut up the meat and bring it to the dugout, we found the male again standing by the female, and . . . once more on the third day when I went there by myself for the sole purpose of examining the intestines."

The expedition slaughtered so many of these animals that they were extinct within 27 years of their discovery. To many scientists this is the only crime — but that is too much grief for us, too little for Steller's sea cow. If animals have rights, if they exist (like us) to experience and explore the universe and to feel the ancient wonders of their tissues and psyches, then they have rights as individuals, not just as members of endangered species. But there seems little chance of remedy in the next century or even the next millennium, if we ourselves survive. Justice for animals is a cause we are still approaching at great distance.

Instead, we have in the present the acrimonious debate between those who uphold the right of the woman to abortion and those who uphold the right of the foetus to life. The battlelines are, as usual, drawn in the wrong place. To put such weight on the lives of the unborn is sanctimonious unless the plea is a general plea of compassion for all sentient beings (or at least all human beings). To make accusations of murder against women who abort unwanted embryos without opposing slaughter and oppression in general is not charity; it is moral duplicity. What about the millions of children and animals who die so that other creatures can maintain a higher standard of living and consume them and their goods? What about the murders of children and adults in the undeveloped world, either directly through the armies and police of the nuclear-scientific hegemonies and their client states, or indirectly through policies of economic imbalance and resource exploitation? Do the anti-abortionists oppose killing in war? Do they oppose the mass production of implements of torture and murder to be sold to the highest bidder or provided to our surrogate enforcers?

This nation exists through the theft of land from its previous occupants, the systematic murder of aborigines, embryos and all. But, unfortunately, conquest has been the rule rather than the exception. Some tribes kill their own young to keep families small; surely they would destroy other tribes for a spring, a valley, or hunting ground. Infanticide and genocide form a cycle over millennial time.

But to say that the embryo is not alive, or not human — not yet sentient and thus not murderable — is another form of self-deceit. We have come to value the spoken word so much that we mistake journalism for reality. The marketplace and work force replace our inner voices, our somatic wisdom, replace even desire. "Pro-choice" means nothing if it does not include the unarticulated choice of the living soul of the embryo. Its hunger for life is as strong as ours — its desire for unfoldment — even before it has words in which to express a personality. A court may rule that the embryo has no rights, but the cells and gathering consciousness of the creature are real and seek manifestation. We should not diminish the mystery we are by pretending that all experiences can be institutionalized. Courts of law cannot redress the seeming biological injustice making women alone the carriers of the zygote. Progressive technology with its massive bureaucratic governments does not understand who we are, so we should not put our identity in its hands. The role of the woman as the bearer of life is ancient beyond words; it is not just an unfair allotment or a capitalist exploitation; it is an unsolved mystery and an opportunity, as life itself is. The embryo is alive within days of its conception; it is an individual. That does not preclude an abortion if it is out of phase with the conscious individuation of its mother, but it is equally impossible to abort the foetus without killing the person incarnating there.

No act can be without consequence. Even the death of a fly requires atonement, although we may push it out of mind a thousand times, as we crush the body, before we notice. The makers of weapons operate under the same anaesthetic until they are awake.

As we approach the millennial turning point of Western civilization, we are obviously trapped in a number of highly polarized ideological battles. The Biblical fundamentalists are at war with the pure scientific materialists as to what religion will be imposed on the next generation (which will make its own decisions anyway). Neither side perceives that its entrenchment represents a character neurosis more than a commitment to the truth. People do not see that their rigidities transcend ideology and are a symptom of their inability to mix freely in the life and energy of their times.

The nuclear activists rightly blame the military establishment for arming the Earth beyond any strategic rationality and thereby jeopardizing all life forms. War is not just glorious revolution or "politics by other means"; it is an addiction to a "power high": the war chiefs have always enjoyed the rush of the battle, whether they ride mounted with their troops or sit before the glitter of three-dimensional video units. War is also an indulgence of machismo fantasies, a denial of the "weakness" (the *tao*) and universal feminine within. This last-ditch resistance to our humanity is disguised as heroism.

But destructive activities cannot be ended by decree, and they certainly cannot be convinced to end by the demonstrations against them. In serving to expose the collective disease, formal protests are healing to all, even the targeted enemies, but in rhetoricizing and oversimplifying the causes of violence, indignation also becomes self-aggrandizing and falsely absolving of the protesters. The architects of weaponry and makers of war operate ever under the mystery of the undiagnosed causes of war. The lessons of Napoleon are submerged in Tolstoy; the texts of Tolstoy are further deconstructed by the living scripture Hitler and the Third Reich engraved into the spine of Europe. The black magic of human warfare recedes back through Machiavelli, Philip of Spain, Theodoric and the Vandals, Alexander of Macedonia to the Egyptians and Stone Age conquistadors. Hitler's unintentional warning echoes like the meditation gong through "Apocalypse Now" in Vietnam and Cambodia, the Red Guard furies, and the tribal genocide of modern Africa. Until we as a species experience the true mystery of war and peace, or until enough of us meet its old warrior gods individually to change human consciousness, it will not be possible to disarm. The current stalemate represents how far we have come and how far we have not come from unquestioned violence and the compulsion of the battle. The weapons and the generals are not themselves the causes of war; they are the symptoms of our latency and incubation; they cannot be eliminated without being replaced from within.

We embody the collective shadow as well as the psyche. The horror of the nuclear weapon is that it existed in our fantasy so long — and not just in the fantasy of the warlord and tyrant — in *all* our fantasies, as a projection of both power and fear, and the ultimate horror/allure of a sleeping dragon within raw dust. The "death rays" of Zeus and Saturn are also the death rays of the Martians and the high-frontier space chiefs. They are the struggle of mind over matter, of frustrated idealism and unachieved self-knowledge let loose in the charmed cave of the shaman and the workshop of the alchemist. The wound is self-inflicted, though we still suspect a malefic force. Witness Robert Ardrey's lyrical version of a twentieth-century credo:

"Our history reveals the development and contest of superior weapons as *Homo sapiens'* single, universal cultural preoccupation. Peoples may perish, nations dwindle, empires fall; one civilization may surrender its memories to another civilization's sands. But mankind as a whole, with an instinct as true as a meadowlark's song, has never in a single instance allowed local failure to impede the progress of the weapon, its most significant cultural endowment.

"Must the city of man therefore perish in a blinding moment of universal annihilation? Was the sudden union of the predatory way and the enlarged brain so ill-starred that a guarantee of sudden and magnificent disaster was written into our species' conception? Are we so far from being nature's most glorious triumph that we are in fact evolution's most tragic error, doomed to bring extinction not just to ourselves but to all life on our planet?"

The message of the twentieth century is that we can no longer evade anything (instinct or not). The nuclear bomb has even turned the Third World War into an excruciating dialogue we must maintain with daily attention despite all distractions, or it will begin. Behind closed doors the enemy diplomats continue to speak to each other because they are trapped in the same ancestral language, the same pathology, the same polar fantasies of golden cities and of ashes and toxic air, the same guilt. There is always the chance that, despite their opposed interests, the words themselves, the armored feelings will force them to acknowledge each other's realities. But what then?

Despite proposals for nuclear freezes and mutual destruction of weapons I suspect we may have to talk until the end of time, simply to survive. Or we had better plan for this long a dialogue, just as we must plan for the radioactive matter and other poisons we have created. We are also the species that spoke so long ago of turning swords into plowshares. If it were simple we would have done it, assuredly. And even though it is difficult — in fact, impossible — we have no other choice but to bear this hope through time along with the bombs and the holocausts. 'Pure deterrence,' just as Henry Kissinger and the military existentialists would have it — a deadly game of unenacted battles and unwritten treaties and their partial violations until the end of time.

We now approach Mars in all our nakedness. We stand alone in the heart of the battle with only the Word. Olive branch in one hand, grenade in the other (as usual) — we stand always for revolution, for justice, for truth; inevitably we stand for the Earth. And the terms of our survival till now remain a mystery.

Those who oppose exploitative pornography and sadomasochistic sex insightfully draw attention to the (mostly male) association between violence and sexual pleasure. Pornography is not innocent titillation or harmless erotic fantasy: in the context of epidemic psychopathology in the culture of the West it provides images of disease for those who are already sick. The full expression of eros will be healing and medicinal only in the context of social and economic justice, in a world where men and women live comfortably with each other in the truth of their own biological natures.

Pornographers represent unknown hungers as the irresistible and deadly things they are. We are now enslaved by ghosts masquerading as eros, lusts that threaten to trivialize our actual capacity for sexuality. Our sadomasochism is a pathetic exaggeration of our true suffering. This hunger goes hand-in-hand with our general materialism — a desperate rush to get everything, in an illusion that by getting everything in the most explicit way we will not be shortchanged or denied. The strip shows, snuff films, and public empathies of bondage and sodomy inflame this illusion, displace it, and numb us to the subtlety of our actual drives.

Pornography is a symptom of our bribery and trivialization of gods and goddesses whose power is much greater than ours. They retaliate not to harm us but to express their existence, which is a law of nature. "Attempts to commercialize the gods," writes the psychologist Edward Whitmont, "merely make them more demonic."

Despite our haste we are never quick enough to be superficial, and our unattended bruises become traumas. For instance, rapists often smugly claim that their victims also seek the primal sex act. When women protest similar kinds of propositions from their boyfriends, they intuit that the aboriginal event cannot be recovered or even sexualized satisfactorily. They prefer to experience their individual eros through their own personalities, rather than through some shadow of primordial lust. We cannot solve the ancient mystery, so we come to value our dignity and individual expression far more than the muck of collective eros. Our bodies may respond to animal darkness, but we are in the process of differentiation, and when murder becomes eros we are truly lost. Even if rape may sometimes be orgastic in the victim, it is not pleasurable, and it is surely traumatic.*

When young children are kidnapped and sodomized or mutilated by adults, otherwise merciful men and women propose the most brutal vengeance. And so the pornographic current spreads through the rage and revulsion it inspires: at the core of

---

*"I'm not sure if a 'rape victim's pleasure' is 'pathological,'" writes Jeannine Parvati in response to this passage. "Perhaps if we are watching a Greek tragedy, yes. Here's another view — I was raped once, hitch-hiking as a trusting teen. Scoping out my options, I chose pleasure. It wasn't terribly traumatic — though once when I reminisced about all my previous lovers, I left him out. Eventually, imaginally, I've even embraced that repulsive rapist as a lover. Pleasure as healer. Is this *pathos*?"

this disgust must lie some attraction to the acts, or they would not compel such spontaneous need for revenge and suppression. If it is realized in some of us it is nascent in all of us. Most people haven't the slightest predisposition toward pornographic and abusive deeds, but these exist on the edge of their "normal" sexual behavior, in fantasy spheres and unbidden nightmares. The desire for vengeance is always partly a self-loathing, a reaction against the failure to suppress entirely the pornography within. So the warlike aspect of our shadow self goes to war against war, or is thrilled to be a warrior, either in reality or imagination. The death penalty is meant to obliterate not only the hated murderer who expressed the atrocity but every aspect of sympathetic imagination of it in us. When we participate in the second murder, the punitive one, we give new energy to the original crime. The event cannot be resolved or concluded in any way. The murderer is never a total alien; he must always be one of us.

Aboriginal justice once sought to heal the wound by obliterating time. In some native societies a murderer is asked to replace the victim in the victim's family. Having deprived that family of one of its offspring he must become the thing he has taken away. Some murderers actually adopt the clothes, the wife, the children, and the parents of the one they have killed. In very small tribes the familiarity between members makes the group a large family. The act of homicide is dealt with not as the atrocity of an outsider but from within the understanding of the clan. Since the murderer will be reborn into the tribe again and again, he must be diagnosed and cured; he must return to humanity. The family dispels the darkness by taking in what is left of the human being in the murderer. They accept the ultimate collectivity of the species and may, even unconsciously, consent that the bond of murder is still a bond, however agonizing and degrading. The victim likewise will return in subsequent generations, so the crime must be expiated in all aspects before his soul seeks blind revenge. Among animals in general, and visibly among packs of mammals, this replacement is axiomatic; the individual is the species.

"I have seen it done with my own eyes, and have not recovered from my astonishment," wrote Fabre of the mantises.

Robert De Ropp answers him in the words of the Marquis de Sade:

"Oh, rest assured, no crime in the world is capable of drawing the wrath of Nature upon us; all crimes serve her purpose, all are useful to her, and when she inspires us do not doubt but that she has need of them."

When Idi Amin served a former minister's head at the dinner table, Frank Terpil, the CIA renegade, did not balk. "How could you go on working for him?" the reporter asked.

"I don't make the rules. This is what the world is."

The universe doesn't recognize me. I must start over from the beginning.

Someday, says Dostoyevsky's Inquisitor, "the beast will crawl to us and lick our feet and spatter them with tears of blood. And we shall sit upon the beast and raise the cup, and on it will be written, 'Mystery.' But then, and only then, the reign of peace and happiness will come for men."

Ivan protests, in the name of Dostoyevsky and, in fact, for all of us: "Not justice in some remote infinite time and space, but here on earth, and that I could see myself. . . . If I am dead by then, let me rise again, for if it all happens without me, it will be too unfair. . . . I want to see with my own eyes the hind lie down with the lion and the victim rise up and embrace his murderer. I want to be there when every one suddenly understands what it has all been for."

The horrors are finally integrated because there is nothing else to do with them. The mantis has its young, and they too mate, breed, and devour. The wars end, and the dead are buried. Years later the identities of those in the cemeteries fade as the whole generation passes like some forgotten Dakotan tribe — even the memory of their existence blurred with all other existences.

As an emerging current of conscious desire, our faint incipient ego encounters the unexperienced desires of the cells, their hunger for substance, their unceasing differentiation which consumes old cells in the birth of new ones. Computers notwithstanding, we cannot create mind from a sterile liquor, and we cannot reform nature by a rational attack upon its perversions. Our task is more difficult. We can reclaim the darkness only by conducting its radiance through our lives.

And there is no rule of thumb: one person can nurse the sick in Bangladesh while another person irrigates a small farm in pre-Columbian Arizona. Some dispel evil through kung-fu or aikido, while others spread discord through the same arts. No one is totally diabolical; every person enacts some quantum of photosynthesis — but likewise, a portion of the darkness sticks to any life.

The Sioux Indian prays for his game and lures it to come to him by the beauty and integrity of his chant, the clarity of his attention. Animals may have the power to call to other animals to become their food, or they may collaborate across species in remorse and understanding at the moment of the kill. An unexamined telepathy could join the hunted and hunters throughout the planet, but, as the first shamans intuited — only when the hunt obeys the great ceremony, not when slaughter goes beyond scrupulous attention. The closeness of our cells to each other, animal to animal, assures a sympathy of some sort — a sympathy expressed in eros, a force of love not necessarily separate from the required cannibalism of species within nature. All thoughts are already universal on some level, even without planetary telepathy.

It is perhaps the eros of the hunt that rapists and sadomasochistic pornographers abuse. To portray human bodies with guns and knives around erotic organs is to proclaim the alienation of not only desire but power itself — is to proclaim the loss of the ceremony in which all of these lusts and aberrations are transformed and sated without degradation or wasteful violence.

Even the great healer, Paul Tillich, kept pictures and accounts of women beaten and crucified. "Nature, society, and soul are subject to the same principle of disintegration," he wrote. "They all are possessed by demons, or, as we should say, by psychic forces of destruction."

But his wife, upon discovering these artifacts after his death, added: "I was tempted to place between the sacred pages of his highly esteemed lifework these obscene signs of the real life that he had transformed into the gold of abstraction."

The evidence appears in the congenital dysfunction of our race. We are joined through the animal kingdom to some original strand, call it sexuality or virus, foreshadow it in parasitic worms or sharks. The clergy sheds no light at all, wanting only proof of their apocalyptic myths. It was bloody from the beginning, but that does not mean it will stay that way forever. We don't in fact know.

We cannot be carnivores without being killers too. From the point of view of plants we are just another mutant that has lost the ability to feed directly out of Sun. What if this ability were regained and transmitted through the cells? This would be remarkable considering the thousands of years of predation our metabolism embodies. Our apologia for the whole animal kingdom is based on the circumstantial evidence that there is no other path to knowledge. Yogis still promise we can someday materialize the right chords to draw our sustenance out of vibrations of air, without killing even plant life, to draw from the Sun and the psychic field around us, but if that's where we're headed, we obviously have a long way to go.

We have a dilemma with consciousness itself. We can extend our sympathy, even disingenuously, to famine victims in Africa or boat people in Vietnam, but what about whole civilizations destroyed on other planets, individuals in pain on worlds around other suns? If we were to accomplish a lasting peace on our world, would we then have to worry about other planets that perhaps do not even exist? But if they do, they are part of the universe, part of consciousness; and, ultimately our sympathy must be extended through eternity to those victims too, creatures we could never know. Not because it does any good but because it forces us to view the crisis in its actual bigness while at the same time reminding us that we do not know who and where we are and thus what powers we have. If we could bring peace to this planet, we could probably bring peace to the universe.

We do not know. But that is not the problem. The problem is that we pretend to know, or think we should pretend. We think we know what we are and what the world should be. But nothing about cell life or DNA or the self-assembly of tissue suggests we have any idea of whence we come into being. Our whole culture and technology might be an evasion of our natural condition, our true dormant power. We could be avoiding our own natures, missing the solutions to our crises; worlds without end more fulfilling than this one might be within our grasp. But these lie in the margins of an unconscious inner life we presently flee in all our ideologies and institutions. It would seem now to have to begin in silence again: we must drop all our expectations and see just how quiet and observant we can be — keeping our eye perfectly on each thing as it arises. We have created so much noise; yet the thing we are is so soundless and perfect it might simply become.

James Hillman

WARS, RAMS, ARMS, WARS

On the Love of War

You will recall, if you saw the film *Patton*, the scene in which the American General, who commanded the Third Army in the 1944–45 drive across France into Germany, walks the field after a battle: churned earth, burnt tanks, dead men. The General takes up a dying officer, kisses him, surveys the havoc, and says: "I love it. God help me I do love it so. I love it more than my life."

This scene gives focus to my theme — the love of war, the love in war and for war that is more than 'my' life, a love that calls up a God, that is helped by a God and on a battlefield, a devastated piece of earth that is made sacred by that devastation.

I believe we can never speak sensibly of peace or disarmament unless we enter into this love of war. Unless we enter into the martial state of soul, we cannot comprehend its pull. This special state must be ritualistically entered. We must be 'inducted', and war must be 'declared' — as one is declared insane, declared married or bankrupt. So we shall try now to 'go to war' and this because it is a principle of psychological method that any phenomenon to be understood must be empathetically imagined. To know war we must enter its love. No psychic phenomenon can be truly dislodged from its fixity unless we first move the imagination into its heart.

War is a psychological task, which Freud recognized and ad-

First delivered at the Conference, "Facing Apocalypse", Salve Regina College, Newport, R.I., June 1983. To be published in completed form in the collected papers and discussions of that conference by Spring Publications, Dallas (participants in "Facing Apocalypse" were: Danilo Dolci, Norman O. Brown, Robert J. Lifton, Denise Levertov, David L. Miller, Mary Watkins, Wolfgang Giegerich, Robert Bosnak, James Hersh).

dressed in several papers. It is especially a psychological task because philosophy and theology have failed its over-riding importance. War has been set aside as history, where it then becomes a sub-chapter called military history. Or, war has been placed outside the mainstream of thought into think-tanks. So we need to lift this general repression, attempting to bring to war an imagination that respects its primordial significance.

My method of heading-right it, of penetrating rather than circumambulating or reflecting, is itself martial. So we shall be invoking the God of the topic by this approach to the topic.

*

During the five thousand, six hundred years of written history, there have been at least fourteen-thousand, six-hundred recorded wars. Two or three wars each year of human history. Since Edward Creasy's *Fifteen Decisive Battles* (1851), we have been taught that the turning points of Western civilization occur in battles such as Salamis and Marathon, Carthage, Tours, Lepanto, Constantinople, Waterloo, Midway, Stalingrad . . . The ultimate determination of historical fate, we have been taught, depends upon battle, whose outcome in turn upon an invisible genius in a leader or hero through whom a transcendent spirit is manifested. The battle and its personified epitome become salvational representations in secular history. The statues in our parks, the names of our grand avenues, and the holidays we celebrate commemorate the salvational aspect of battle.

Neglected in Creasy's decisive battles are the thousands of indecisive ones, fought with equal heroism, yet which ended inconclusively or yielded no victory for the ultimate victor of the war; nor did these battles produce commemorative epic, statue or celebration. Unsung heroes; died in vain; lost cause. The ferocity of battle may have little to do with its outcome, the outcome little to do with the outcome of the war. Verdun in the Great War of 1914–18 is such an example: a million casualties and nothing decisive. The significance of a battle is not given by the war, but by the battle itself.

Besides the actual battles and their monuments, the

monumental epics that lie in the roots of our Western languages are to a large proportion 'war books': the *Mahabarata* and its *Bhagavad Gita*, the *Iliad*, the *Aenead*, the Celtic *Lebor Gabala*, and the Norse *Edda*. Our *Bible* is a long account of battles, of wars and captains of wars. Jahweh presents himself in the speeches of a War God* and his prophets and kings are his warriors. Even the *New Testament* is so arranged that its final culminating chapter, *Revelations*, functions as its recapitulative coda in which the Great Armageddon of the Apocalypse is its crisis.

In our most elevated works of thought — Hindu and Platonic philosophy — a warrior class is imagined as necessary to the well-being of humankind. This class finds its counterpart within human nature, in the heart, as virtues of courage, nobility, honor, loyalty, steadfastness of principle, comradely love, so that war is given location not only in a class of persons but in a level of human personality organically necessary to the justice of the whole.

Have I carried my first point that battles and the martial are not merely irrational relapses into archaic pre-civilization? The martial cannot be derived merely from the territorial imperative of our animal inheritance: "this is my realm, my feeding and breeding space; get out or I'll kill you." Nor do wars arise simply from industrial capitalism and its economic distress, the mystiques of tribes and nationalism, the just preservation of a state, masculine machoism, sociological indoctrinations or psychological paranoia and aggression. (Paranoia and aggression, if explanatory principles, themselves require explanations.) No, wars are not only man-made; they bear witness also to something essentially human that transcends the human, invoking powers more than the human can fully grasp. Not only do Gods battle among themselves and against other foreign Gods, they sanctify human wars, and they participate in those wars by divine intervention, as when soldiers hear divine voices and see divine visions in the midst of battle.

Because of this transcendent infiltration, wars are so difficult to control and understand. What takes place in battle is always

* Cf. Millard C. Lind, *Yahweh is a Warrior*, Scottdale, Pa.: Herald Press, 1980.

to some degree mysterious, and therefore unpredictable, never altogether in human hands. Wars "break out". Once commanders sought signs in the heavens, from birds. Today, we fantasy the origin of war in a computer accident. *Fortuna* — despite meticulous battle plans and rehearsals, the battle experience is a melee of surprises.

We therefore require an account of war that allows for its transcendent moment, an account that roots itself in *archai* — the Greek word for first principle — *archē*, not merely as archaic, a term of historical explanation, but as archetypal, evoking the trans-historical background, that divine epiphanic moment in war.*

This archetypal approach holds that ever-recurring, ubiquitous, highly ritualized and passionate events are governed by fundamental psychic patterning factors. These factors are given with the world as modes of its psychological nature, much as patterns of atomic behavior are given with the physical nature of the world and patterns of instinctual behavior are given with the world's biological nature.

*

I want now for us to enter more closely into the epiphany of this archetypal principle, this God, Mars. Here is a reading from Ernst Junger's diary, recording the start of the last German offensive in 1918:

> "The great moment had come. The curtain of fire lifted from the front trenches. We stood up — we moved in step, irresistibly toward the enemy lines. I was boiling with a mad rage, which had taken hold of me and all others in an incomprehensible fashion. The overwhelming wish to kill gave wings to my feet. The monstrous desire for annihilation, which hovered over the battlefield, thickened the brains of the men

---

* Compare Patton (*The Secret of Victory*, 1926): ". . . despite the impossibility of physically detecting the soul, its existence is proven by its tangible reflection in acts and thoughts. So with war, beyond its physical aspect of armed hosts there hovers an impalpable something which dominates the material. . . . to understand this 'something' we should seek it in a manner analogous to our search for the soul."

in a red fog. We called each other in sobs and stammered disconnected sentences. A neutral observer might perhaps have believed we were seized by an excess of happiness."

The scholar of Japanese culture, Donald Keene, has collected *tanka* and hundreds of other writings expressing the feelings of major Japanese authors (including liberals, leftists and Christians) during the 1941–45 war. I shall quote only passages referring to Pearl Harbor. Nagayo Yoshio, author of *The Bronze Christ*, on hearing of the declaration of war with the United States, wrote: "I never thought that in this lifetime I should ever know such a happy, thrilling, auspicious experience." The novelist and critic, Ito Sei, on the same occasion said: "I felt as if in one stroke I had become a new man, from the depths of my being." Honda Akira, scholar of English literature, wrote: "I have felt the sense of a clearing. Now the word 'holy war' is obvious . . . a new courage has welled up and everything has become easier to do."

Glenn Gray, in his book, *The Warriors* — the most sensitive account of war experience that I know — writes:

> "...veterans who are honest with themselves will admit the experience in battle has been a high point in their lives. Despite the horror, the weariness, the grime, and the hatred, participation with others in the chances of battle had its unforgettable side. For anyone who has not experienced it himself, the feeling is hard to comprehend and for the participant hard to explain to anyone else — that curious combination of earnestness and lightheartedness so often noted of men in battle."

These positive experiences are puzzling. It is the positive experience that we must reckon with because the savagery and confusion, the exhaustion and desertion correspond with what is objectively taking place. Those responses do not need explanations. But how mystifying the lightheartedness in killing, the joy of going into battle, and that infantrymen with bayonets fixed, snipers in ambush, torpedomen in destroyers report no particular hatred, little heroic ambition, unconcern for victory, or even passion for their cause for which they stand exposed and may even volunteer to die. Instead, they sometimes report altered states of perception, intensified vitality, a new awareness of the earth's beauty and nearness of divinity — their little plot, their meagre, grimy life suddenly transcendently sweet. "It is well that war is so terrible," said Robert E. Lee, "we would grow too fond of it."

And, beyond all else, is the group-bonding to the platoon, the crew, a buddy.* Love in war. Thomas Aquinas notes that comrades in arms display a specific form of friendship. This battle-love is complex, gentle, altruistic and fierce. It cannot be reduced merely to modern psychologisms: boosting masculinity with macho codes of honor, peer-pressure that successfully represses cowardice, the discovery and release under the duress of battle of repressed homosexual emotion. Moreover, so strong and so transcending the aims of war itself is this love that a soldier, in fidelity to his buddies, may more easily shoot down his own officer than an enemy in the opposite trench.

To illustrate this love in war, I shall condense from S.L.A. Marshall† an incident from his account of the desperate American retreat from the Yalu after the failed invasion of North Korea. There was a tight ravine under enemy fire through which funnel the only escape route lay. "From end to end this sanctuary was already filled with bodies, the living and the dead, wounded men who could no longer move, the exhausted . . . the able-bodied driven to earth by fire. It was a sump pit of all who had become detached from their vehicles and abandoned to each other . . . 200 men in the ditch so that their bodies overlapped. Americans, Turks, ROK's. . . . Yet there was cooperative motion and human response.

---

* Careful sociological research into the motivation of the American soldier (in World War II) shows that the factors which helped the combatman most "when the going was tough" (as the quotation was phrased) were *not* hatred for the enemy or thoughts of home or the cause for which they were fighting. The emotions that did appear under battle duress — that is, when Mars was acutely constellated — were prayer and group fidelity. Piety and the love of fellows are what the God brings. (Samuel A. Stouffer *et al.*, *The American Soldier: Combat and its Aftermath*, Princeton Univ. Press, 1949, II: 165–86.)

† S.L.A. Marshall, *The River and the Gauntlet*, N.Y.: Morrow, 1953, pp. 300–01.

Men who were still partly mobile crawled forward along the chain of bodies . . . As they moved, those who were down and hurt cried: "Water! Water!" . . . Long since, nearly all canteens were dry. But the able-bodied checked long enough to do what bandaging they could . . . some stripped to the waist in the bitter cold and tore up their undershirts for dressings. Others stopped their crawl long enough to give their last drop of water . . . the wounded who were bound to the ditch tried to assist the able-bodied seeking to get out. Witnesses saw more of the decency of men than ever had been expected."

Love and war have traditionally been coupled in the figures of Venus and Mars, Aphrodite and Ares. This usual allegory is expressed in usual slogans — make love not war, all's fair in love and war — and in usual oscillating behaviors — rest, recreation and rehabilitation in the whorehouse behind the lines, then return to the all-male barracks. Instead of these couplings which actually separate Mars and Venus into alternatives, there is a Venusian experience within Mars itself. It occurs in the sensate love of life in the midst of battle, in the care for concrete details built into all martial regulations, in the sprucing, prancing and dandying of the cavaliers (now called "boys") on leave. Are they sons of Mars or of Venus?

In fact, we need to look again at the aesthetic aspect of Mars. Also there a love lies hidden. From the civilian sidelines, military rites and rhetoric seem kitsch and pomposity. But look instead at this language, these procedures as the sensitization by ritual of the physical imagination. Consider how many different kinds of blades, edges, points, metals and temperings are fashioned on the variety of knives, swords, spears, sabers, battle-axes, rapiers, daggers, lances, pikes, halberds that have been lovingly honed with the idea of killing. Look at the rewards for killing: Iron Cross, Victoria Cross, Medal of Honor, Croix de Guerre; the accoutrements: bamboo baton, swagger stick, epaulets, decorated sleeves, ivory-handled pistols. The music: reveille and taps, drums and pipes, fifes and drums, trumpets, bugles, the marching songs and marching bands, brass, braid, stripes. The military tailors; Wellington boots, Eisenhower jackets, Sam Brown belts, green berets, red coats, "whites".* Forms, ranks, promotions. Flags, banners, trooping to the colors. The military mess — its postures, toasts. The manners: salutes, drills, commands. Martial rituals of the feet — turns, steps, paces, warriors' dances. Of the eyes — eyes front! Of the hands, the neck, the voice, ramrod backbone, abdomen — "Suck in that gut, soldier." The names: Hussars, Dragoons, Rangers, Lancers, Coldstream Guards, and nicknames, bluejacket, leatherneck, doughboy. The great walls and bastions of severe beauty built by Brunelleschi, da Vinci, Michelangelo, Buontalenti. The decorated horse, notches in the rifle stock, the painted emblems on metal equipment, letters from the front, poems. Spit and polish and pent emotion. Neatsfoot oil, gunsmith, swordsmith; the Shield of Achilles on which is engraved the whole world.

*

Our American consciousness has extreme difficulty with Mars.† Our founding documents and legends portray the inherent non-martial bias of our civilian democracy. You can see this in the second, third and fourth constitutional amendments which severely restrict military power in the civilian domain. You can see this in the stories of the Massachusetts Minutemen versus European mercenaries and redcoats, and in the Green Mountain boys and the soldiers of the Swamp Fox — civilians all. And you can see it in the casual individualistic Texans at San Jacinto versus the Mexican officers trained in the European mold.

Compared with our background in Europe, Americans are idealistic: war has no place. It should not be. War is not glorious, triumphal, creative as to a warrior class in Europe from Rome and the Normans through the Crusades even to the Battle of Britain.

---

* "Tomorrow I shall have my new battle jacket. If I'm to fight I like to be well dressed." (Attributed to General Patton, C. M. Province, *The Unknown Patton*, N.Y.: Hippocrene, 1983, p. 180.)

† Cf. Thomas J. Pressley, "Civil-Military Relations in the United States Civil War" in *War*, L. L. Farrar, ed., Santa Barbara: Clio, 1978, pp. 117-22; Otis A. Pease, "The American Experience with War," *op. cit*, pp. 197-203.

We may be a violent people but not a warlike people — and our hatred of war makes us use violence against even war itself. Wanting to put a stop to it was a major cause of the Los Alamos project and Truman's decision to bomb Hiroshima *and* Nagasaki, a bomb to "save lives", a bomb to end bombs, like the idea of a war to end all wars. "The object of war", it says on General Sherman's statue in Washington, "is a more perfect peace." Our so-called double-speak about armaments as "peacekeepers" reflects truly how we think. War is bad, exterminate war and keep peace violently: punitive expeditions, pre-emptive strikes, send in the Marines. More fire-power means surer peace. We enact the blind God's blindness (Mars *Caecus* as the Romans called him, and Mars *insanus, furibundus, omnipotens*), like General Grant in the Wilderness, like the bombing of Dresden, overkill as a way to end war.

Gun control is a further case in point. It raises profound perplexities in a civilian society. The right to bear arms is constitutional, and our nation and its territorial history (for better or for worse) have depended on a citizen-militia's familiarity with weapons. But that was when the rifle and the *Bible* (together with wife and dog) went alone into the wilderness. The gun was backed by a God; when it stood in the corner of the household, pointing upward like the Roman spear that *was* Mars, the remembrance of the God was there, and the awe and even some ceremony. With the neglect of Mars, we are left only the ego and the guns that we try to control with civilian secular laws.

If in the arms is the God, then arms control requires at least partly, if not ultimately, a religious approach. The statement by the Catholic Bishops is a harbinger of that recognition. We worry about nuclear accident, but what we call "accident" is the autonomy of the inhuman which in the case of arms, as any instrument of death, are sacred objects that remind mortals that we are not *athnetos*, immortal. The fact that arms control negotiations take on more and more ritualistic postures rather than negotiating positions also indicates the transcendent power of the arms over those who would bring them under control. Military expenditures of course "overrun" and handguns "get out of hand". I do not believe arms control can come about until the essential nature of arms is first recognized.

Our immigrant dream of escape from conscription into the deadly games of Mars on the European battlefields cannot fit Mars into the American utopia. Hence that paradox for Americans of a peacetime draft and the violence that conscription can occasion. This clash of archetypal perspectives — civil and military — appears sharply in Sicily in 1943 when General Patton slapped two conscripted soldiers who were in hospital for anxiety states.* To the appalled General (a son of Mars), they were malingerers, cowards without love for their fellows. To the appalled American nation of civilians, Patton was the coward, slapping the defenseless sick, without love of his fellows.

By the way, our customary language betrays a bias in favor of the civil — simply by calling it civil. Were we speaking from the military perspective, "civil" would be called "merchant" for these were the traditional class terms in many societies, including India, Japan, and in the Platonic division where the merchants were lower than the warriors (*Phaedrus* 248d) who were not permitted property (*Republic* IV). Traditionally, the warrior class favors the son; the merchant class, the daughter. By slapping his soldiers, Patton was treating them as sons; the civilian (i.e., merchant) reaction experiences them as mistreated daughters.

Although the office of President does combine civil and military, head-of-state and commander-in-chief, and though that office has been held by notable generals — Washington, Jackson, Grant and Eisenhower — and men with military careers, it has been the habit in recent years for the presidency to founder upon this double role: I think of Truman and Korea, Kennedy and the Bay of Pigs, Johnson and Viet Nam, Carter and Iran, and now perhaps Reagan and Central America. Unlike the Roman Republic where Jupiter and Mars could rule together, our republic pretends to have no God of War, not even a department of war. This repression of Mars rather than ritualization of Mars leaves us exposed

*On the slapping incident, see: Brenton G. Wallace, *Patton and his Third Army*, Westport CT: Greenwood, 1946, pp. 207-09; Ch. M. Province, *The Unknown Patton*, N.Y.: Hippocrene, 1983, pp. 191-92, 71-86; H. Essame, *Patton: A Study in Command*, N.Y.: Scribner's, 1974, pp. 103-17.

to the return of the repressed, as rude eruptive violence, as anxiety about armaments and military expenditures, as rigid reaction formations disguised as peace negotiations, and as paranoid defenses against delusional enemies.

*

So far I have been stressing the distinction between the military and nuclear imaginations. I have considered each to be moved by its own archetypal power, powers that do not easily accommodate in a secular monotheistic consciousness, because that consciousness identifies with a single point of view, forcing others into opponents. Oppositional thinking and true believing are makers of this consciousness.

Now, let me make a second distinction: between the military and nuclear imaginations: the martial is not necessarily nuclear nor is the nuclear necessarily martial. The civilian rejection of Mars, however, has so pushed the martial over into the nuclear that we can't think of war without thinking of nuclear war. Mr. Reagan, in fact, calls war "the unthinkable", a mystic's notion of a God beyond thought, beyond image. War is not unthinkable, and not to think it, not to imagine it, only favors the mystical appeal of apocalyptic nuclearism. Remember Hannah Arendt's call to thinking? Not to think, not to imagine is the behavior of Eichmann, said Hannah Arendt. So let us go on thinking all we can about Mars, now in distinction with the nuclear.

Mars in the Roman Republic where he was most developed as a distinct figure was placed in a Champs du Mars, a field, a terrain. He was so earthbound that many scholars trace the origins of the Mars cult to agriculture. This helps my point: Mars did not belong to the city. Not until Julius Caesar and caesarism were troops allowed in the city. The focus of martial activity has usually been less the conquest of cities than of terrain and the destruction of armies occupying terrain. Even the naval war in the Pacific (1941-45) followed this classical intention of gaining area.

The martial commander must sense the lay of the land. He is a geographer. The horse (an animal of Mars) was so essential for martial peoples because horses could realize the strategy of winning terrain. Martial strategy is archetypally geo-political.

The nuclear imagination, in contrast, calculates in terms of cities, and its destructive fantasies necessarily includes civilians. The city (and thus the civilization, whether taken out by ICBM's or kept as intact prizes by the neutron weapon) is the main focus of the nuclear imagination. The land between Kiev and Pittsburgh (hence Europe) is relatively irrelevant.

A second contrast between the martial and the nuclear: Mars moves in close, hand-to-hand, Mars *propior* and *propinquus.* Bellona is a fury, the blood-dimmed tide, the red fog of intense immediacy. No distance. Acquired skills become instantaneous as in the martial arts. The nuclear imagination, in contrast, invents at ever greater distance — intercontinental, the bottom of the sea, outer space. Because of the time delay caused by distance, the computer becomes *the* essential nuclear weapon. The computer is the only way to regain the instantaneity given archetypally with Mars. The computer controls nuclear weapons, is their governor. Whereas the martial is contained less by fail-safe devices and rational computation than by military ritual of disciplined hier-archy, practised skill, repetition, code, and inspection. And by the concrete obstacles of geography: commissary trains, hedgerows, bad weather, *impedimenta.*

Our civilian republic has not become fully conscious of the distinction I am laboring. The civilian soldier rebels against military rituals as senseless. He does not grasp that they serve to contain the God of War and so must be obeyed — as Patton insisted — religiously, as if the military were a religious order.

So, too, our civilian republic is not enough aware of the distinc-tion between military and nuclear, thereby entrusting the control of nuclear explosions to the military in the person of General Grove. Considering the volatile commixture of the God of War with the spiritual, apocalyptic appeal of nuclearism, it is miraculous that we have had only test blasts.

A further difference between martial and nuclear is in their visions of transcendence. They show two elemental imaginations of fire: war and the fire of earth; apocalypse and the fire of ether or air. And two different animals: the ram of territory and head-on collision; the eagle of piercing surprise and the uplifting rapture of nuclearism.

The nuclear imagination, further, is without ancestry. Nothing to look back on and draw upon. History provides no precedents. There is a broken connection, to use Lifton's phrase, between sudden, hideous and collective extinction and deaths modelled by the ancesters. The martial imagination is steeped in memorials. Past battles and military biographies are the ongoing texts. We tramp the battlefields, ponder the cemeteries. There are Swiss depictions of battles, for instance, showing skeletons in the ranks: here are the ancestors fighting in our midst.

The rhetoric of Mars in war-journals, poems and recollections speaks of attachment to specific earthly places, comrades, things. The transcendent is in the concrete particular. Hemingway writes that after World War I: "abstract words such as glory, honor, courage . . . were obscene beside the concrete names of villages, the numbers of roads, the names of rivers, the regiments and dates." How rare for anyone to know the date of Alamogordo (or even where it is), the date of Hiroshima, of the first hydrogen bomb explosion, or the names of people or places or units engaged. Gone in abstraction. Glenn Gray writes: "Any fighting unit must have a limited and specific objective. A physical goal — a piece of earth to defend, a machine gun nest to destroy, a strong point to annihilate — more likely evokes a sense of comradeship."*

Martial psychology turns events into images: physical, bounded, named. Hurtgen Forest, Vimy Ridge, Iwo Jima. A beach, a bridge, a railroad crossing: battle places become iconic and sacred, physical images claiming the utmost human love, worth more than my life.

Quite different is the transcendent experience of the nuclear fireball. The emotion is stupefaction at destruction itself rather than a heightened regard for the destroyed. Nuclear devastation is not merely a deafening cannonade or fire-bombing carried to a further degree. It is different in kind; archetypally different. It evokes the apocalyptic transformation of the world into fire, earth

---

*J. Glenn Gray, *The Warriors*, N.Y.: Harper Colophon 1970, (condensed).

ascending in a pillar of cloud, an epiphanic fire revealing the inmost spirit of all things, as in the Buddha's fire sermon:

> "All things, O priests, are on fire . . . the mind is on fire, ideas are on fire . . . mind consciousness is on fire."

Or like that passage from the *Bhagavad Gita* which came to Oppenheimer when he saw the atomic blast:

> "If the radiance of a thousand suns
> Were burst at once into the sky
> That would be like the splendour of the Mighty One."

The nuclear imagination leaves the human behind for the worst sin of all: fascination by the spirit. *Superbia.* The soul goes up in fire. If the epiphany in battle unveils love of this place and that man and values more than my life yet bound with this world and its life, the nuclear epiphany unveils the apocalyptic God, a God of extinction, the God-is-dead God, an epiphany of Nihilism.

Apocalypse is not necessary to war. Let me make this very clear: Apocalypse is not part of the myths of Mars. Mars asks for battle, not wipeout, not even victory. (*Nike* belongs to Athene, not Ares.) Patton supposedly said: "I like making things happen. That's my share in Deity." Apocalypse is inherent not in the Martial deity, but in the Christian deity. Fascination with a transcendent Christ may be more the threat to the Christian civilization than the War God himself. Are not civilizations saved by their Gods also led to destruction by those same, their own, Gods?

There is one more distinction, one that may be of the most therapeutic significance. If nuclearism produces "psychic numbing", stupefaction, stupidity, Mars works precisely to the contrary. He intensifies the senses and heightens fellow-feeling in action, that energized vivification the Romans called "Mars Nerio" and "Mars Moles", molar, massive, making things happen. Mobilization. Mars gives answer to the hopelessness and drifting powerlessness we feel in the face of nuclear weapons by awakening fear, Phobos, his Greek companion or son, and rage, *ira*, wrath. Mars is the instigator, the primordial activist. To put the contrast in eschatological terms, Mars is the God of Beginnings, the sign of the Ram. March is his month, and April, Mars Apertus, opening, making things happen. Apocalypse may lift veils, but it closes down into the truly final solution, after which there is no re-opening, no *recorso*. Broken the wheel.

*

I seem to have been making a case for the lesser of two evils, and to have so favored Mars that you may have heard me as a war-monger. But so would be to hear me only literally. Rather than warmonger, see me as ram-monger, Mars-lover. Take my talk as a devotional ritual of imagination to constellate his awakening power. In this way we may call him up and yet deliteralize him at the same time.

It was an ancient custom and is still a modern psychological technique to turn for aid to the very same principle that causes an affliction. The cure of the Mars we fear is the God himself. One must approximate his affects in order to differentiate them. *The Homeric Hymn to Mars* (Ares), in Charles Boer's translation, makes this clear:

> "Hear me
> helper of mankind,
> beam down from up there
> your gentle light
> on our lives
> and your martial power
> so that I can shake off
> cruel cowardice
> from my head
> and diminish that deceptive rush
> of my spirit, and restrain
> that shrill voice in my heart
> that provokes me
> to enter the chilling din of battle.
> You, happy God
> give me courage
> to linger in the safe laws of peace
> and thus escape
> from battles with enemies
> and the fate of violent death."

It seems that the more we can love Mars, as in this hymn, the more we can discriminate (to use its words): the deceptive rush of the spirit, the shrill voice that provokes into battle, and at the same time shakes off cruel cowardice from my head.

This imaginative devotion to Mars provides a mode of deliteralizing beyond interpretation of the meaning of the God, beyond a mental act of seeing-through. Here, by deliteralizing I mean: to be fundamentally penetrated by an archetypal power, to participate in its style of love so that its compulsion gives way to its imagination, its angelic, message-giving intelligence. Then the God is experienced in the event as its image, the event no longer requiring my psychologizing for the image to be revealed.

Just this is my aim now, right now as I am speaking: not to explore war or apocalypse in the service of prevention, but to experience war and apocalypse so that their imaginations become fully realized, real. *We* cannot prevent; only images can help us; only images provide *providentia*, protection, prevention. That has always been the function of images: the magic of sacred protection.

We do not know much nowadays about imagining divinities. We have lost the angelic imagination and its angelic protection. It has fallen from all curricula — theological, philosophical, aesthetic. That loss may be more of a danger than either war or apocalypse because that loss results in literalism, the cause of both. As Lifton says, "The task now is to imagine the real." However, like so much of our imagination of the archetypal themes in human nature, the wars we now imagine are severely limited by modern positivistic consciousness. We imagine wars utterly without soul or spirit or Gods, just as we imagine biological and psychological life, social intercourse and politics, the organization of nature — all without soul, spirit or Gods. Things without images.

Wars show this decline of ritual and increase of positivism, beginning with Napoleon and the War between the States (1861-65). The Great War of 1914-18 was stubborn, massive, unimaginative; the dark Satanic mill relocated in Flanders, sixty thousand British casualities in one single day on the Somme, and the same battle repeated and repeated like a positivist experiment or a positivist

logical argument. The repetition of senselessness. Our wars become
senseless when they have no myths. Guadalcanal, Inchon, May
Lai — battles, casualities, graves (at best); statistics of firepower
and body-count — but no myths. The reign of quantity, utterly
literal.

Lacking a mythical perspective that pays homage to the God
in war, we run the dangers of both war 'breaking out' and 'loving
war too much' — and a third one: not being able to bring a war
to a proper close. The Allies' demand for "unconditional surrender"
only prolonged the Second World War, giving "justification" for
the atomic bomb. Polybius and Talleyrand knew better: masters
of war know how and where and when to ease out the God's fury.
The very idea of an unconditional surrender evokes the blind rage
of Mars *caecus, insanus*, the last-ditch suicidal effort. Surrender
requires ritual, a *rite de sortie* that honors the God and allows his
warriors to separate themselves from his dominion.

*

My thoughts have been intended to regain the mythical
perspective. My thoughts have not been aimed at finding another
literal answer to either war or nuclearism. We each know the literal
answer: freeze, defuse, dismantle, disarm. Disarm the positivism
but rearm the God; return arms and their control to the mythical
realities that are their ultimate governances. Above all: wake up.
To wake up, we need Mars, the God of Awakenings. Allow him
to instigate our consciousness so that we may "escape the fate of
violent death", and live the martial peace of activism.

A Frenchwoman after the Second World War tells Glenn Gray:
"Anything is better than to have nothing at all happen day after
day. You know I do not love war or want it to return. But at least
it made me feel alive, as I have not felt before or since."

Imagine! Is she not saying that war results not from the
absence of the God but from his presence? For, we long for pur-
poseful action, hand-to-hand engagements, life lived in terms of
death, seriousness and lightheartedness together, a clearing. The
Frenchwoman's "nothing at all . . . day after day" is the nihilism
of the nuclear age. Nuclear doom occurs not only in the literal

future out there when the bomb goes off. Doom is already there
in our numbed skulls, day-after-day, nothing-at-all. Mars can
awaken us out of this nihilism, and its realization in an Apocalypse, with his *phobos*, fear. It may be our most precious emotion. We have everything to fear, except fear itself.

I have tied our numbing with a blocked imagination and the
blocked imagination with the repression of Mars and his kind of
love. But fifty minutes, as we know from psychotherapy, isn't
going to lift very much repression. I hope, however, that I have
been able to evoke enough of Mars for you to feel him stir in your
anger and your fear, and in the outward extension of imagination
that will probe such questions as:

How lay out the proper field of action for Mars? In what ways
can martial love of killing and dying and martial fellowship serve
a civilian society? How can we break apart the fusion of the
martial and the nuclear? What modes are there for moving the
martial away from direct violence toward indirect ritual? Can we
bring the questions themselves into the post-modern consciousness
of imaginal psychology, deconstruction and catastrophe theory?
Can we deconstruct the positivism and literalism — epitomized
by the ridiculous *counting* of warheads — that inform current
policies before those policies literally and positively deconstruct
our life, our history and our world?

Let us invoke Mars. At least once before in our century he
pointed the way. During the years he reigned — 1914-1918 — he
destroyed the nineteenth-century mind and brought forth modern
consciousness. Could a turn to him now do something similar?

Yet Mars wants more than reflection. The ram does not pull
back to consider and iron takes no polish in which it can see
itself. Mars demands penetration toward essence, pushing forward
ever further into the tangle of danger, and danger now lies in the
unthought thicket of our numbed minds. Swords must be *beaten*
into plowshares, hammered, twisted, wrought.

Strangely enough, I think this deconstruction is already going
on, so banally that we miss it. Is the translation of war from
physical battlefield to TV screen and space fiction, this translation of literal war into media, mediated war, and the fantasy

language of wargames, staging areas, theatres of war and theatre commanders, worstcase scenarios, rehearsals, and the Commander-in-Chief, and actor — is all this possibly pointing to a new mode of ritualizing war by imagining it?

If so, then the TV war of Viet Nam was not lost. The victims died not only for their cause (if there was one) or their country (if it cared). They were rather the sacrificial actors in a ritual that may deconstruct war wholly into an imaginal operation. Carl Sandburg's phrase: "Someday they'll give a war and no one will come" may have already begun. No one need come because the services for Mars are performed nightly at home on the tube. In a media society, will not capitalist war-profiteering shift its base from a military-industrial complex to a military-communications/information complex, the full symbolization of war?

If war could be contained in imagination, why not as well the nuclear bomb? A translation of the bomb into imagination keeps it safe from both military Martialism and civilian Christianism. The first would welcome it for an arm, the second for an Apocalypse. Imagination seems anyway to be the only safe place to keep the bomb: there is no literal positive place on earth where they can be held, as we cannot locate our MX missiles anywhere except as images on a drawing board or dump the wastes from manufacturing them anywhere safe.

However — to hold the bomb as image in the mind requires an extraordinary extension, and extraordinary daring, in our imagining powers, a revolution of imagination itself, enthroning it as the main, the greatest reality, because the bomb, which imagination shall contain, is the most powerful image of our age. Brighter than a thousand suns, it is our omnipotent God-term (as Wolfgang Giegerich has expounded), our mystery that requires constant imaginative propitiation. The translation of bomb into the imagination is a transubstantiation of God to *imago dei*, deliteralizing the ultimate God term from positivism to negative theology, a God that is all images. And, no more than any other God term can it be controlled by reason or taken fully literally without hideous consequences. The task of nuclear psychology is a ritual-like devotion to the bomb as image, never letting it slip from its pillar of cloud in the heaven of imagination to rain ruin on the cities of the plain.

The Damocles sword of nuclear catastrophe that hangs upon our minds is already producing utterly new patterns of thought about catastrophe itself, a new theology, a new science, a new psychology, not only burdening the mind with doom but forcing it into post-modern consciousness, displacing, deconstructing and trashing every fixed surety. Trashing is the symptom, and it indicates a psychic necessity of this age. To trash the end of the century of its coagulated notions calls for the disciplined ruthlessness and courage of Mars. Deconstructing the blocked mind, opening the way in faith with our rage and fear, stimulating the anaesthetized senses: this is psychic activism of the most intense sort.

Then — rather than obliterate the future with a bomb, we would deconstruct our notion of 'future', take apart Western Futurism, that safe repository of our noble visions. Care, foresight, renewal, the Kingdom — these have been postponed forever into the future. Rather than blast the material earth with a bomb, we would deconstruct our entombment in materialism with its justification and salvation by economics. We would bomb the bottom line back to the stone age to find again values that are sensate and alive. Rather than bring time to a close with a bomb, we would deconstruct the positivistic imagination of time that has separated it from eternity.

In other words: explode the notions; let them go up in a spirited fire. Explode worldliness, not this world; explode final judgments; explode salvation and redemption and the comings and goings of Messiahs — is not the continual presence of here and now enough for you? Put hope back into the jar of evils and let go your addiction to hopeful fixes. Explode endings and fresh starts and the wish to be born again out of continuity. Release continuity from history: remember the animals and the archaic peoples who have continuity without history. (Must the animals and the archaic peoples go up in flames because of our sacred writ?) Then timelessness could go right on being revealed without Revelation, the veils of literalism pierced by intelligence, parting and falling to the mind that imagines and so welcomes the veiling. No sudden rending, no apocalyptic ending; timelessness as the on-going, the extraordinarily loving, lovable and terrifying continuity of life.

Charles Poncé

A NOTE ON THE LOVE OF WAR
for Jabir

> I think they will not go on lying thus even for a little, much
> though they are in love, I think they will have no wish for sleep-
> ing, but then my fastening and my snare will contain them
> until her father pays back in full all my gifts of courtship I
> paid out into his hand for the sake of his bitch-eyed daughter.
> The girl is beautiful indeed, but she is intemperate."
>
> *Odyssey*, Book VIII, 315–20

i.

Athene was known as one "who signifies practical understanding . . . thinking through . . . and mastery over the moment."[1]
She is imaged as moving through battlefields bringing courage to
one warrior, strength to another and to all a tacit demand that
the warrior always act justly. She might aptly be thought of as
the personification of "the civilized art of war, so intimately connected with progress in culture . . ."[2] It is she who caused the entire issue of war to become a conscious, deliberate, civilized matter of manners. One might think of her as a *pharmakos*, a medicine
that will stay the brutal hand, a justice of reason and insight that
brings the madness of war under control. Ares, as we shall see,
is the personification of all that is cowardly, unreasonable, trai-
torous and brutish in war. Athene as the war goddess was the
first representation of war as a reasonable way of going about the
difficulties spawned by certain types of social reality. We first find
these exigencies clearly discussed in the dialogues of Plato.

The initial model in the creation of the perfect or ideal city
in Plato's *Republic* is an agricultural community. Socrates states
that a city's first and chief need is the provision of food for existence and life, the second and third being housing and raiment.[3]
But its citizens then need to be wary of "not begetting offspring
beyond their means lest they fall into poverty or war."[4] The message

is simple: overpopulation leads to war. Glaucon then asks what difficulties would arise should Socrates plan a city that included meat-eaters, and Socrates simply revises his earlier model:

> The territory . . . that was then sufficient to feed the then population, from being adequate will become too small . . . Then we shall have to cut out a cantle of our neighbor's land if we are to have enough for pasture and plowing, and they in turn of ours if they too abandon themselves to the unlimited acquisition of wealth . . . We shall go to war as the next step, Glaucon.[5]

Whereas an agricultural society needs merely attend to the standing numbers of its citizens, a meat-eating society must also regulate the life-cycles of animals, a task at which it inevitably fails, leading to the attempt to expand tribal boundaries.

Warfare, in turn, prescribes how a community or city should design its institutions. In answer as to why the laws of Crete went so far as to prescribe common eating times for all of its citizens, the Cretan Clinias answers that because "the peace of which most men talk . . . is no more than a name; [and because] in . . . fact, the normal attitude of a city to all other cities is one of undeclared warfare," the Cretan legislators "constructed the universal scheme of all our institutions, public and private, with a view to war."[6] Thus an army's need to mass together while eating as a defensive measure becomes the culinary style of a city. This idolization of war with the ritualization of eating suggests that the instinct hunger played a major role in ancient warfare. The Hindu Sankaracarya comments upon a passage in one of the *Upanishads:*

> By what sort of Death was the universe covered? . . . By *Hunger,* or the desire to eat, which is a characteristic of death . . . He who desires to eat kills animals immediately after. There 'hunger' refers to death . . . 'Death' here means Hiranyagarbha as identified with the intellect, because hunger is an attribute of that which is so identified . . . That death of whom we are talking . . . *created the inner organ called mind, characterized by deliberation, etc. and possessing the power to reflect on those effects."*[7]

In other words, the instinct that leads to death also gives rise to a reflective moment. Hillman informs us that it is Athene that lies behind a type of institutional consciousness that mothers "non-religious, secular brotherhoods . . . conventions of like-minded men, the nomothetic standards of science, business, trade, professions, and government and their unavoidable norms of inclusion and exclusion."[8] Athene is the personification of the deliberation Sankaracarya spoke of and which in time becomes a social standard or collective consciousness that defines a specific department of a culture. Her "style of psychopathology is most vividly imaged in her function of protectress of the 'city,' where the preparedness of her *pronoia* is also the military defensiveness of paranoia . . . the defensive postures that are archetypally necessary to civilized normality."[9]

This civilized normality was reflected in the midsummer Panathenaia held in yearly celebration of Athene's birthday, and the subsequent institution of the Great Panathenaia which took place every fourth year. This latter festival (ca. 566/5 B.C.) was allied with a program of athletic contests comparable to the Olympic games established in the eighth century B.C. Its procession displayed its dominant military aspect, the logo for the entire event being that of an "armoured Athena brandishing her spear,"[10] in commemoration, of course, of her warlike aspect. The high point of both festivals was a free meat meal for a considerable portion of the Attic and Athenian community, enacted through the distribution of meat in quota to each *deme*, or district, in "accordance with its participation in the ritual."[11] As far as can be estimated, a little over 100 cows were part of the sacrificial ritual. A financial document outlining the expenses and procedures for these festivals reads as follows:

> When they have led the procession they are to sacrifice to the goddess all the cows on the great altar of Athena, except for one on the altar of Victory having chosen it in advance from the best quality cows. When they have sacrificed to Athena the City Goddess and Athena Victory out of all the cows . . . they are to distribute the meat to the people of Athens."[12]

Aside from the burnt offerings to the goddess, the meat had to be transported off of the Acropolis for distribution. That is, no ritual feast was allowed in the sanctuary in contrast to other such ritual settings on other occasions.

The Panathenaia served to ritualize the state of undeclared warfare that exists within every community or city, its natural paranoia regarding the infringement of its property. The Festival sacrifice satiated the paranoia by providing the community with a yearly token feast. The message was simple: you need not fear for your livelihood, nor need you resort to arms against our neighboring cities. The Goddess has fought the war for you, and now provides for you.

Foucault has pointed out that in classical thought madness was understood as simply the empirical form of an "underlying realm of unreason which threatens man and envelops . . . all the forms of his natural existence."[13] Pushing up against the edge of every soul, and therefore every community or city or nation of souls, is the specter of unreason, "*an area of unforseeable freedom* where frenzy is unchained."[14] This freedom and frenzy and the terror they instill are figured in the Titan Ares, "the maniac who knows no justice,"[15] and in his sons Fear and Terror. But they have their origins in the emotional experience imaged through the god of panic, the goat-god Pan, the God of Nature. The very existence of such a god indicates that the Greeks were well aware that all of humanity is present and subject to the unreason of Nature and to the fear of that without limit.

ii.

Hermes is the god of the boundary and the marketplace. In cultures evolving from unstable villages to established city-centers, the boundaries of villages become a neutral ground where trade and commerce may occur between normally hostile factions. In such a manner the concept of the marketplace originated, its existence dependent upon a mutually wagered truce, albeit one charged with suspicion and distrust. Hermes' role as guardian of the crossroad may have its origin here. It is within this context that we must view the athletic contest — essentially as an "occasion for trade. . . . In historical times a market was held in connection with the Panhellenic games . . . the merchant being protected by the 'sacred truce' proclaimed on these occasions."[16] The establishment of the athletic games in the Great Panathenaia therefore reveals yet another move by Athenian consciousness to ward off war, ritualizing even strife as the inevitable result of colonial expansion. This archetype, a reflective quality of soul growing out of an attempt to modify an instinctual response to reality in the image of the goddess Athene, thereby came to incorporate the instinct imaged by the figure of Hermes and all that he stands for. As the god of the boundary, Hermes represents the wealth that may be attained by stepping over the boundary either through commercial venture and exploration or theft; he is also the god of thieves.

Hermes, in his role of god of flocks and shepherds, is not a deity of cattle but begins his life as a cattle-thief: on the day of his birth, he steals the cattle of his brother Apollo. It is a simple act but one that punctuates what classical and primitive cultures repeatedly inform us is the cause of war — the desire or need to gain food or property. Thus, in Sanskrit the term for war, *goshu gantum*, translates into "to go to war for cows." The Quamranites' song of victory displays the same idea:

> Arise, O Valiant One!
> Lead away Thy captives, O glorious Man!
> Do Thy plundering, O valourous One!
> Set Thy hand upon the neck of Thine enemies
> And Thy foot upon the heap of the slain!
> Strike the nations Thy enemies
> And let Thy sword devour guilty flesh!
> Fill the land with glory
> And Thine inheritance with blessing
> A multitude of cattle in Thy pastures . . . "[17]

Similar *Old Testament* instances are too numerous to cite here, but a passage from *Joshua*, XI:14, 23, is typical:

And all the spoil of these cities and the cattle, the people of

Israel took for their booty; but every man they smote with the edge of their sword, until they had destroyed them, and they did not leave any that breathed . . . So Joshua took the whole land . . . [and] gave it for an inheritance to Israel according to their tribal allotments. And the land had rest from war.

Clearly, early warfare grew out of practical concerns. If you couldn't grow your food, you stole it; and if you couldn't steal it, you took it by force.

Hermes' theft of his brother's cattle sprang from his sudden longing to taste flesh. He thereby became the first (amongst gods and mortals) to both hunt or steal and kill animals for food. The sacredness of this imagined first-moment in the minds of the Greeks — the sacredness of the guarantee that husbandry and hunting assured — is revealed in their "choosing" Hermes as the inventor of sacrifice. From that time forward, in their minds, the gods were to be so petitioned (by sacrifice) at the outset or successful completion of any enterprise of significant communal or personal value — be it fertility, war, gain, or death. In the *Homeric Hymn*, however, Hermes' initial longing for meat is quickly followed by his rejection of it after he gets it.

Athene's call for and rejection of meat during her festival communicates the Hermetic desire for the accumulation of another's wealth through theft or war, but Lopez-Pedraza points out that the pathology of those who reject meat "reveals a distortion in or a lacking of relationship to . . . the flexibility and versatility of this archetype."[18] The versatility referred to here lies in the fact that in the soul Hermes represents that in the soul which allows us not only to establish and recognize boundaries, but to cross over them — the soul's ability to foray into what is seemingly foreign and hostile to the mind. This is the drive element behind search and research, curiosity and exploration, invention and the destructive force that exists Shiva-like at the heart of creativity. It is to be contrasted with meat phobias which present "a pathological picture: a fantasy of purity and cleanliness, a rigidity, a feeling of superiority, and an unconsciousness of any cruelty or destructiveness in themselves . . . The image of Hermes' need to eat meat suggests that when the archetypal images which can connect us with an instinctual eating are missing, then eating becomes a system, paranoiac if you want."[19]

Every instinct bears its pathology and its own salvation. The paranoia at the edge of eating gives rise to the Grace we acknowledge either before or after meals. Somehow, we fear, the very stuff of our existence could be denied us on a daily basis. We give thanks to a transpersonal reality we assume has in some manner determined us fit for our daily bread.

The value of Hermes to Athene, and of Athene to Hermes, lies in how the one meets or echoes the other's needs. Athene, the armed goddess of the center and the immoveable finds value in the Hermetic boundary-line because by it centrality is firmly established. Hermes, the mercurial god of gain and loss, of movement and crossings, finds value in the expansive colonialism of the Athenian mind, discovering therein a safe harbor for his gifts of barter and trade, of shrewdness and cunning. Their pathologies on the other hand come to the fore when one becomes identified or identifies itself with the other's essence. The limitless possibilities of Hermetic reflection dissipate the fixidity of the center that Athens defines, as does the cautionary and contemplative Athenian reflection hinder the quick sleight-of-hand element in Hermetic curiosity.

iii.

Each sub-group or clan of the Maring, a tribe of the mountains of New Guinea, hold competitive pig festivals approximately every twelve years. There are three stages to these festivals. The first is the *kaiko*, during which time the pigs grown over the twelve-year period are slaughtered. Allies are invited to the feast, each clan attending receiving a quota of pig-meat to distribute among their group. This distribution of meat consolidates alliances. Much the same principle is operative in the Panathenaia festival described above. The only difference is that in the Greek festival the distribution of a free meat-meal serves as symbolic deterrent to war, whereas in New Guinea the feast signals the beginning of war. The Maring meal leads directly to ritual martial preparations and then a period of warfare between enemy clans, the end of which is signalled unconciously by the total depletion of the pigs by each warring faction, accompanied by the loss or gain of territory. This is followed by the planting of rumbins, or sacred trees, a truce signal. After another twelve years or so, the rumbins are uprooted and the entire cycle begins again.

> Every part of this cycle is integrated within a complex, self-regulating ecosystem, that effectively adjusts the size and distribution of . . . human and animal population to conform to available resources and production opportunities.[20]

It is a small jump from the causes of warfare among the Maring to those of the Athenians. The similarities between these two meat festivals suggest that the Greek city states developed out of a response to primal socio-economic needs not too dissimilar to those the Maring still face. It is simply, again, the issue of population control and food supply. The manner by which a community solves this problem — warfare being but one solution — is to all appearances determined by the ability of that community to divert the natural and instinctual drives that Hermes and Ares represent into the ritual expressions of an Athenian archetype. In short, the natural fear and paranoia a community has in regard to encroachment — what Hillman above called a paranoia "archetypally necessary to civilized normality" — must in some manner be limited and defined by both Hermetic and Athenian factors if Ares is not to have his way. At least, in the past this seemed to be sufficient.

In 451 B.C. the city of Athens passed a law stating that citizenship would be restricted to those whose parents were themselves citizens.[21] Population control was taken under the state, nature thereby somewhat circumvented. The Athenians had (if only on one level) passed beyond the necessity of primitive warfare as "one of the cutoff mechanisms that help to keep human populations in a state of ecological equilibrium with respect to their habitats."[22] In Maring culture, the planting of the sacred rumbin trees and their care fell to the war magician. Their uprooting brought strife and the disturbance of each clan's living

space. Athene's claim to the Acropolis was also arboreal, origi-
nating with the olive. In Athens, the olive-tree came to be known
as the "Athens-tree" and the "Citizen Olive;" the olives were
thought of as the citizens themselves.

> Tradition had it that the dozen olive trees that grew from the
> sacred olive trees that grew in the garden of Academos had
> been propagated from the sacred olive on the Acropolis.
> These trees also seemed intimately related to the city itself,
> for their name, the *moriai*, is derived from *moros* or *moira*,
> 'fate.' The olive was the life-tree of Athens, in short, and upon
> its fate the city depended."[23]

The destruction of the original olive tree, or the *moriai*, was
believed to signal the destruction of the city, undoubtedly by war.
It is of interest to note, therefore, that the destruction of rumbin
trees always leads to just that.

The establishment of a city, a *polis*, is an attempt to stabilize
the "natural" panic that must have existed among pre-agricul-
tural tribes continually forced to migrate and invade new territories. When we discover that practically every day in Athens, in
honor of one deity or another, major animal sacrifices were performed, we must ask if these sacrifices didn't at some level com-
pensate for and divert the nomadic impetus of a more primitive
culture within. Here the sacrificial aspect of Hermes is full-
blown. His lust for meat is our lust for provision and its guarantee. It is an instinct, and as with most rituals that have grown out
of instinctual responses, we have forgotten its source and the
manner in which we once had to satisfy its need. We no longer
need war. We no longer need to uproot the rumbin tree.

iv.

Aristotle informs us that "natural passing-away and coming-
to-be take place in equal periods of time. Therefore the periods,
that is the lives, of each kind of living thing have a number and
are thereby distinguished for there is an order for everything, and
every life span is measured by a period, that this is not the same
for all but some are measured by a smaller and some by a greater

period."[24] In other words, the background of the cosmos is a fixed order against which the flow of being extends itself, measured and defined by what the Greeks personified in the figure of the *Moiraia*, or fates. One might at first think death by war unnatural and an exception, but Plato tells us that war is natural in that it is brought about by the body's "loves and fears and all sorts of fancies and a great deal of nonsense."[25] Thus, it is the body's desires that give rise to war, for "all wars are undertaken for the acquisition of wealth, and the reason why we have to acquire wealth is the body, because we are slaves in its service,"[26] a service he adds that contaminates the soul.[27] The *New Testament* James, in so many words, repeats the message:

"What causes wars, and what causes fighting among you? Is it not your passions that are at war in your members? You desire and do not have; so you kill. And you covet and cannot obtain; so you fight and wage war."[28]

Plato speaks of the art of medicine as a defense system to be compared with war.[29] One would think that, if war is a contaminate of the soul, a medicine should be applied. However, Plato also warns us that,

> . . . diseases unless they are very dangerous should not be irritated by medicines, since every form of disease is in a manner akin to the living being, whose complex frame has an appointed term of life. For not the whole race only, but each individual — barring inevitable accidents — comes into the world having a fixed span . . . beyond which no man can prolong his life. And this holds also of the constitution of diseases; if anyone regardless of the appointed time tries to subdue them by medicine, he only aggravates and multiplies them . . . provoking a disagreeable enemy by medicines.[30]

"Unless they are very dangerous" is the key phrase here, for obviously the Athene who became manifest in the genesis of Western civilization was an applied and necessary elixir at the time. Without her we would find ourselves still in the position of the Marings. The social and political machinery that lies at the root of our present culture could not have come into being without the reflective stance Athene symbolizes. This type of "medicine" permits a necessary cultural leap. But what worked then may no longer be applicable to conditions as they exist at this new global threshold. The technological advances that civilization has achieved have turned the entire earth into a community of villages. But the community at large has at its disposal the ability not only to stave off — if not eradicate — the ancient cause of panic, but to destroy itself if it fails to make yet another leap. Marvin Harris warns:

> I am saying that warfare is an ecologically adaptive lifestyle among primitive peoples, *not* that modern wars are ecologically adaptive. With nuclear weapons, war can now be escalated to the point of total mutual annihilation. So we have arrived at a phase in the evolution of our species when the next great adaptive advance must either be the elimination of nuclear weapons or the elimination of warfare itself.[31]

Mere reflection, along with the type of bargaining that it gives rise to in the modern world, can no longer bring an end to war. It instead rationalizes war, transforming it through a gaming type of consciousness, the war-manners resulting in such civilized demands as the Geneva Convention's World War II ruling that paratroopers not be fired upon until they touched ground. If we are going to depend upon Greek mythology at all, then we must bring to it the power of reflection and criticism that it taught us to use; we must learn to read with archetypal eyes, to in-sight the depth, the patina of history that mythic language has generated through the many-faceted permutations of its original insight over time. We can no longer read the words at the surface of the page; we must go beneath them, for the words themselves have brought us to an underplace in ourselves.

In the *Phaedo* we find Socrates stating that the soul can get a clear view of things only when it activates its ability to reflect. But he adds that this can come to pass only when the soul can "ignore the body and becomes as far as possible independent."[32] Whereas in our earlier quotes we found Socrates informing us that the cause of war is the body's demand for pleasure, here it is implied that war could be done away with if only reflection could gain the upper hand, if only the natural desire of being could somehow be circumvented. Athenian reflection at the outset, applied in proper measure during a human developmental period when it was fresh and had not reached its expiration date, was indeed medicinal and needed; but its continued application at this time cuts us off from nature itself. It is too heady, too legalistic, too removed from the immediacy of life. To be cut off from body — from our bodies and the body of the world — to the extent that Socrates suggested, is no longer tenable. As in any educative process extreme methods and attention are needed at the outset. Once learned, such methods make of the thing learned a single-mindedness that leads to the exclusion of other and newer methods. It is at this point that the pathological paranoia necessary to defend ourselves from Unreason becomes the power hunger of the paranoid and the anorexic. The sacrifice of the animal in Classical times becomes the sacrifice of our own animality in modern times. What flesh we set on fire in the past on the altars of the Acropolis, we now set on the altar of the world for one final nuclear holocaust. The fiery spiritualism of the anorexic, the Socratic ideal finally realized, is upon us. Palazzoli, referring to the spiritualism of the anorexic, quotes Romano Guardini's observations regarding the psychological climate of the disease:

> Material worries and irritations drop away. The confines of reality and yes and no, the horizon of the possible grows ever wider . . . The spirit becomes more sensitive; more far-seeing and more acute, the conscience more quick and lively. The sensitivity to spiritual choices increases . . . The inner life is, as it were, laid bare . . . The awareness of spiritual power is increased and with it *the danger of losing sight of what is assigned to each one of us, of the limits of our finite existence, of our dignity and our abilities.* Hence the dangers of pride, magic and spiritual intoxication.[33]

It is a well-known fact that the greater portion of anorexics are adolescent girls from reasonably comfortable middle and upper class families. We Americans are ourselves a young and comfortable culture when compared to our world neighbors. The ideal body-image of our culture is an adolescent thinness, and our concern with diet borders on the pathological. We have lost contact with Hermes and have become isolationists. We trust Athene in her most extreme form. Our religious connection to Being has become more of a concern with non-being: ten-thousand schools of spiritual attainment that with cool, hip, spaced-out detachment promise to make us spiritual elitists, week-end Messiahs. Our final koan is "Make love not war"; we speak of karma, but ignore the lessons of history which is karma.

> With very few, if any, exceptions, the conspicuous figure in the home of anorexic girls is the mother; . . . they evince open or secret disgust with the flesh, with sex, with excrement and with physical lust.[34]

Here we see reflection itself pathologized: the extreme form of Athene, the virgin goddess who was known as *Meter*, mother. But this is not the mother of the body, it is the mother of the apron-string as worry-bead, the rationalizing, paranoid, overly-protective mother become an institution of legalities that tells us what we can do with our bodies (the abortion issue) and our minds (here include all those areas of mental health that scientifically label modes of being, and then perform physical, social, and philosophical lobotomies on the basis of their invented personality profiles), and that finally informs other nations how they should be.

The *Moirai* with which we opened this section were three in number: *Lachesis* (Measurer), *Klotho* (Spinner), and *Atropos* (Unbendable). Athene, as the goddess of spinning and weaving, takes on certain characteristics of the *Moirai*. She was at times represented holding spinning-spindles, and called *Athene Moria*, Athene the Fateful.[35] In this representation we see the power of the city and the state usurping the power of fate. To a certain degree such grounding of transpersonal animistic religious ideas is a necessary adjunct to the development of consciousness: the more extensive the latter becomes "the more differences it will perceive, and the more it will emancipate itself from collective rules, for the empirical freedom of the will grows in proportion to the extension of consciousness."[36] By the same token however the emancipation from one collective set of rules — animistic theologies, in this instance — does not in itself guarantee either the extension or development of consciousness. It might simply reflect a shift in perspective, pro or con of the issue at hand. When we are speaking of a collective perspective, whether it be ancient or modern, we are still presented with the danger of the fact that once we arrive at a uniformity of consciousness, or more properly a uniformity of consensus, we might simply have fallen back into an unconscious condition. "The more unconscious a man is, the more he will conform to the general canon of psychic behavior."[37]

Athenian consciousness, given birth to by an assiduous application of the instinct to reflect — that instinct which can be seen in a cat contemplating the distance of a leap it intends to perform — can also go too far. It can justify its leap on the animistic supposition that it has eight more lives to live — or that at least twenty percent of the world's population will survive a nuclear war, or that one need simply keep up first-strike capabilities in order to maintain peace. We push Athene too far. We have become identified with her, and have become the warring-mother in her zeal to care for and protect.

In the not too distant past, war was a matter of hand-to-hand combat, physical and immediate. When you killed a man, you felt his skull collapse beneath the blunt end of your club. His death vibrated through your body. No less a felt experience was the initial resistance and sudden yielding of muscle, sinew, and bone to lance, sword, knife, and dagger. Such were the sensations that the warrior carried about in his memory, dreamt of, sometimes had overtake him at dinner. Death to the other was neither coincidental nor accidental as it is with modern weaponry; it was connected to you as its genatrix. As the other died, you were the personification of death to him, of his meeting with Thanatos whom several classical sources identified with Ares.[38]

Neither Hades nor Thanatos were agents of death as powers in their own right. To the Greek death was simply an inversion of life, never an enemy, simply part of the fabric of natural occurrence.[39] Matters have changed.

v.

Ares' birth was a retaliatory event. His mother, Hera, went through three parthenogenetic attempts to create a son who would be "glorious amongst the gods,"[40] in answer to Zeus' androgenetic creation of Athene. The first attempt, Hesiod informs us,[41] yielded the dwarf-smith Hephaestus, "the least of us all," whose turned-back feet caused him to walk with the rolling gait that brought derisive laughter to the gods.[42] With the aid of the Great Mother, Gaia, in her second attempt she bore the monstrous serpent Typhon. "Bringing one evil thing to another," she left this creature in the charge of the dragoness of Delphi. Her third and final attempt yielded the war god Ares. Hera would herself in time come to despise this son's barbarity, asking Zeus on one occasion if he would be angered if she were "to smite Ares with painful strokes and drive him out of fighting?" Zeus immediately gave her permission to "Go to it then, and set against him the spoiler Athene who beyond all others is the one to visit harsh pains upon him."[44] Shortly thereafter we find the wounded Ares complaining to Zeus, whose retort reveals the Greek attitude towards the god of War:

> Do not sit beside me and whine, you double-faced liar. To me you are the most hateful of all gods who hold Olympus. Forever quarreling is dear to your heart, wars, and battles. Truly the anger of Hera your mother is grown out of all hand nor gives ground.[45]

We are indeed in the presence of "a backward god of most limited function, inspiring little real devotion and no affection, associated with no morality or social institution."[46] Of all the deities he was loved by only one — Aphrodite, goddess of love.

Simply put, Aphrodite is the compulsive aspect of the soul.[47] She is self-love, not other-love, in need of constant attention. She is the drive element in war, the love of war, the hunger of the body that forces us over the boundaries of reflective sensibility. As Socrates said, all wars occur because of the body's passions, or because of the desire to guarantee that one's needs will be continually fulfilled. These needs, should they go beyond the boundary of reflection, attempt to make of a periphery yet another center, becoming Titanic in their drive. Love of country becomes justified love of war. That the god of war was born *after* Athene might give a clue to Hera's message — that reflection and reason alone cannot stave the desire for invading or taking what another person or country has. When reflection fails, Aphrodite must return, Ares trailing behind her.

FOOTNOTES

1. Walter F. Otto, *The Homeric Gods* (Beacon Press: Boston, 1964), pp. 52, 55.
2. Lewis Richard Farnell, *The Cults of the Greek City States* (Caratzas Brothers: New York, 1977 reprint of 1909 edition), Vol. V, p. 407.
3. Plato, *Republic* II, 369c, d.
4. *Ibid.*, II, 372c.
5. *Ibid.*, II, 373d, e.
6. Plato, *Laws* I, 626 ff.
7. Swami Madhavananda, trans., *The Brhadaranyaka Upanishad* (Advaita Ashrama: Calcutta, 1965), pp. 25–6, my italics.
8. James Hillman, "On the Necessity of Abnormal Psychology: Ananke and Athene," in *Facing the Gods* (Spring Publications, Inc.: Texas, 1980), p. 28.
9. *Ibid.*, pp. 30–31.
10. H. W. Parke, *Festivals of the Athenians* (Cornell University Press: New York, 1979), p. 34.
11. *Ibid.*, p. 49.
12. *Ibid.*, p. 48.
13. Michel Foucault, *Madness & Civilization* (Vintage Books: New York, 1973), p. 83.
14. *Ibid.*, p. 76
15. Homer, *The Illiad*, Bk. V, 755.
16. Norman O. Brown, *Hermes The Thief*, (Vintage Books: New York, 1969), p. 44.
17. Quoted in Marvin Harris, *Cows, Pigs, Wars and Witches* (Vintage Books: New York, 1978), p. 157.
18. Rafael Lopez-Pedraza, *Hermes and His Children* (Spring Publications: Zurich, 1977), p. 29.
19. *Ibid.*, p. 30.
20. Harris, *op. cit.*, pp. 40–41. All references to the Maring are from this work.
21. Raphael Sealey, *A History of the Greek City States* (University of California Press: Berkeley, 1976), p. 299.

22. Harris, *op. cit.*, p. 56.
23. *Ibid.*, p. 149.
24. Aristotle, *De Generatione et Corruptione*, 336b: 10 ff.
25. Plato, *Phaedo* 66c.
26. *Ibid.*
27. *Ibid.*, 66b.
28. *The Letter of James*, 4:1, 2.
29. Plato, *Epinomis*, 976a.
30. Plato, *Timaeus*, 89b–c.
31. Harris, *op. cit.*, p. 57.
32. Plato, *Phaedo*, 65c.
33. Mara Selvini Palazzoli, *Self-Starvation* (Aronson: New York, 1978), p. 75.
34. *Ibid.*, p. 39.
35. Luyster, *op. cit.*, p. 149.
36. C. G. Jung, "The Spirit of Psychology," in *Spirit and Nature: Papers From the Eranos Yearbooks* (Pantheon Books: New York, 1954), Vol. 1, p. 372.
37. *Ibid.*
38. Joseph Fontenrose, *Python: A Study of Delphic Myth and Its Origins* (University of California Press: Berkeley, 1980), p. 329.
39. Emily Vermeule, *Aspects of Death in Early Greek Art and Poetry* (University of California Press: Berkeley, 1979), p. 37.
40. Carl Kerenyi, The Gods of the Greeks (Thames and Hudson: London, 1974), p. 151.
41. Hesiod, *Theogony*, 1, 929 ff.
42. Homer, *The Illiad I*, 599.
43. "To Pythian Apollo," *Homeric Hymns*, 1. 350 ff.
44. Homer, *The Illiad*, Bk. V, 762 ff.
45. *Ibid.*, 889 ff.
46. Farnell, *op. cit.*, p. 407.
47. For a further discussion of this, see my *Papers Toward a Radical Metaphysics* (North Atlantic Books: Berkeley, 1983), p. 47 ff.

THE SPIRITUAL WARRIOR

WARRIORS OF THE INNER WORLD

There are many warriors of the inner world, but the main warriors are simplicity, sincerity, purity, aspiration, dedication and surrender. These divine warriors help the seekers discover God. Together they fight against bondage-night and ignorance-day. Their supreme commander is faith.

Simplicity shortens the road that leads to God-discovery. Sincerity expedites the journey. Purity feeds the seeker and the journey together. Aspiration loves the journey. Dedication enjoys the journey. And surrender completes the journey.

Simplicity is a very simple word, but it embodies tremendous power. When we enter into the spiritual life, we value this most significant achievement. We have countless desires. But from our list, if we can take out one desire, then to that extent our life becomes simple. When it becomes simple, an iota of peace dawns in our mental firmament. Each time we become simple, simpler, simplest, our desire-life becomes short, shorter, shortest. Then we enjoy peace of mind; we enjoy Light and Delight.

Sincerity is our peerless achievement. If we can become sincere, then we can run the fastest in our spiritual life. When we make friends with insincerity, at every moment we have to justify our insincere life. Once we tell a lie, we have to tell twenty more lies in order to justify that particular lie. And each time we tell a lie, we add a heavy burden to our shoulders. How can we run the fastest when there is a heavy load on our shoulders? But when we are sincere, we accelerate our progress; we run the fastest like a deer.

Purity is of paramount importance in the spiritual life. Purity means the power of receptivity. When our heart is inundated with purity, we feel that our inner receptacle has become large, larger, largest. Peace, Light and Bliss enter into that vessel from above. And inside the vessel we see our divine qualities sporting, dancing and fulfilling their reality's Light and Delight. Purity is receptivity's capacity. When we are pure, immediately our self-expansion, our divine reality, looms large.

Aspiration, dedication and surrender. Aspiration is our journey's start. Aspiration is the flow of our journey, the continuous, endless journey itself. Aspiration is an inner cry. This cry liberates us from the meshes of ignorance. This cry eventually makes us one with the Eternal, the Infinite and the Immortal. When we aspire, we feel that deep within us there is a higher reality which we unfortunately right now cannot claim as our very own. But there comes a time when, on the strength of our own aspiration, we can claim this reality — our own reality, our highest, supernal reality — as our own, very own. Each time we aspire, we bring to the fore our own hidden, divine, immortal reality.

Dedication. When we dedicate ourselves to a cause, we expand our own reality existence. This dedication is not done under any compulsion. Responsibility has not been thrust upon us. It is we who want to expand our reality, so we adopt the right approach and try to expand ourselves through dedication. One becomes many; again, many become one. As an individual, when we dedicate ourselves devotedly, soulfully and unconditionally, we grow into the many. And when we do this as a collective body, we become one. So it is through dedication that we become many and that we become one. When we become one, we fulfill God as Infinity's Silence, birthless and deathless Silence. When we become many, we fulfill God as the eternal, infinite sound, birthless and deathless sound. Finally, we fulfill God as the soundless Sound.

Surrender. Surrender completes the journey. This surrender is our conscious awareness of our highest reality. It is not the surrender of a slave; it is the surrender of the finite in us to the Infinite in us. The unlit, obscure, impure existence of ours is making surrender to the illumined, pure and perfect existence of our own reality-height. We are not surrendering to a second or third person. We are surrendering to the divine within us, to the Infinite within us, to the Immortal within us. Surrender here is our conscious and constant expansion, illumination, liberation and perfection. Each time we surrender our earth-bound existence to our Heaven free life, we enjoy Nectar, divine Bliss.

When a seeker establishes his body's reality-oneness with the Will of the Supreme, he becomes the simplicity-warrior. When a seeker establishes his mind's reality-oneness with the Will of the Supreme, he becomes the sincerity-warrior. When the seeker establishes his vital's reality-oneness with the Will of the Supreme, he becomes the purity-warrior. When the seeker establishes his heart's reality-oneness with the Will of the Supreme, he becomes the aspiration warrior. The same seeker, in the course of time, when he establishes his life's reality oneness with the Will of the Supreme, becomes the dedication-warrior. Finally, when the seeker consciously, devotedly, untiringly, unreservedly and unconditionally establishes his soul's oneness-reality with the Will of the Absolute Supreme, he becomes the surrender-warrior.

As there are many divine warriors of the inner world, even so there are many undivine warriors of the inner world. The main undivine warriors are insecurity, fear, doubt, lethargy, disobedience and indulgence.

Insecurity starts in the mind, but the mind is not aware of insecurity at the beginning. From the mind it enters into the vital and finally it comes to the physical consciousness. At that time we are fully aware of the presence of insecurity. Insecurity is a poisonous disease. If we do not get rid of it, this poison spreads and destroys the whole system eventually.

Fear is worse. Fear of the unknown, not to speak of fear of the unknowable, is a fatal disease within the seeker's life. The seeker is afraid of everything that is not in his domain, of anything of which he is not aware. He fears others, he fears the unknown, he fears the Vast; finally he becomes afraid of himself. He has a knife. When he looks at his knife, fear enters into his mind. He feels that at any moment this knife can cause an accident in his life. He enters into the kitchen. There is a stove, and he uses it at his sweet will. But even when the stove is not on, he is afraid it may catch fire. At every moment he is afraid of his own possessions, not to speak of others' achievements or realities. When he is afraid of himself, he loses badly, miserably, in the battlefield of life. Fear is a fatal disease.

Then comes doubt. When the seeker treasures doubt with a view to judging others, he digs his own grave. Each time he doubts someone, he digs his grave. If we judge others with our unlit human mind, with the intellectual mind, with the sophisticated mind, the persons whom we judge do not lose an iota of their achievement, of their reality. But we lose. How do we lose: When we start doubting others, we offer something of our own existence to the outer world; something of our own reality goes and eventually we become very weak.

Doubt is the almost incurable disease in us. When we doubt others, we feel that we are now sitting on a high pedestal and, at the same time, we are on a safe footing. But this is a deplorable mistake. We cannot judge others. We do not know their heights; we do not know their depths. We do not know what is actually happening in others. It is the cosmic Will that is operating in and through each and every individual. So we are in no position to judge others. Each one is guided, moulded, shaped and prepared by the Will of the unseen Hand.

First we doubt someone and immediately afterwards we try to see whether we are correct in doubting that person. Then we begin to judge and doubt ourselves. When we doubt ourselves, we lose everything. So we should follow the path of faith. Faith is the commander in us. Faith tells us of the existence of Reality and Truth in us, for us. Then faith tells us that we not only embody the Truth, eternal Truth, infinite Truth, but we as a matter of fact *are* this transcendental Truth, this universal Truth ourselves. But right now we are not aware of it precisely because we have made friends with ignorance.

Then comes lethargy. When the Hour of God strikes, if we do not respond, then we cannot start our journey. The road is long, very long. When the Hour strikes, owing to lethargy, if we do not respond to the call of the Hour, we unconsciously lengthen our road. The mind becomes totally immersed in ignorance and feels the road is longer than the longest. When the Hour strikes, if we do not respond, then the road is bound to become longer than it was before. So those who wallow in the pleasure of lethargy will have to walk along the road that never ends.

Disobedience is the worst weakness in the seeker's life. A seeker may listen to the inner dictates quite often. But if one day he disobeys the inner command, then he is bound to notice a hole in the life-boat which is destined to take him to the Golden shore of the Beyond. His life-boat has sprung a leak. Gradually the hole will become large, larger, largest, and his spiritual boat will capsize and sink. But if he is obedient, then his life-boat will sail fast, faster, fastest towards the destined Goal, the Goal of the highest every-transcending Beyond.

The last undivine force or warrior is indulgence. When we enter into the world of indulgence, we run backward. We enter into the animal kingdom. We believe in evolution. From the stone world we came to the plant world. From the plant world we came to the animal world. From the animal world we came to the human world. Now we have to go to the divine world. But if we enter into the world of indulgence, then instead of running forward we run backward. And each time we run backward, we again make friends with our old friend doubt.

A spiritual seeker has to be aware of these undivine forces: insecurity, fear, doubt, lethargy, disobedience and indulgence. The divine warriors have only one thing to tell us: accept light and reject night. Acceptance of light is the only thing that is needed. Night is the ignorance within us. Ignorance-night binds our body, blinds our eyes, stabs our heart. Ignorance-night represents the undivine warriors of insecurity, fear, doubt, lethargy, disobedience and indulgence. When we are attacked by these undivine warriors, the divine warriors come to our rescue and offer us perfection-light. As the representative of the Supreme, this perfection-light first liberates us, then illumines us and grants us vision. It grants vision to our eyes and then immortalises our heart. This is what perfection-light does for us.

There are divine warriors of the outer world as well as the inner world. The outer warriors are our divine personality and divine individuality, which say, "I am of God and I am for God." The inner warriors do not fight outwardly. They become one with God's Will and in this way feel that they are establishing God the eternal Truth and Light in the inner world. The outer warriors feel that they have to fight. The hero-warriors fight for God's victory on earth at every moment in the outer world.

The outer hero-warriors want to establish the Kingdom of Heaven on earth. They want to see the Infinite in the finite. But the inner hero-warriors see that Infinity is already there in the finite. They see that the finite does not have the eye to see the Infinite, whereas the Infinite can envision its own presence in the finite itself. The inner warriors are aware of what they eternally are, whereas the outer warriors are not aware of what they eternally are. Therefore, they do something in order to become. By doing something, the outer warriors want to become. The inner warriors feel that they don't have to become: they already are.

But there comes a time when the inner and outer warriors become one, inseparably one. The inner warriors bring to the outer warriors the message of realisation: realisation of the infinite Truth, eternal Light and immortal Delight. And the outer warriors try to manifest the divine realities, the divine treasures that are offered to them by the inner warriors. The inner warriors bring these realities to the earth-arena. The outer warriors manifest these realities in the earth-arena. This way both the inner warriors and the outer warriors complete the cosmic Lila, the divine Game.

University of Ottawa
21 February 1976

YOU DO NOT KNOW
WHAT A SINGLE THING IS

MASTER DA FREE JOHN: Consider this ashtray. This very ashtray itself is the object that I have used for some time now to demonstrate and consider this necessary philosophy, or "love of wisdom," relative to Divine Ignorance. This is the object I have used. And I have said to you on occasion, and it remains true even to this day, that, from a practical point of view, from a chemical point of view, from an aesthetic point of view, from the point of view of any ordinary discipline of knowing, you may know all kinds of things about this ashtray and its origin and its content. But no matter what you may know about it, before and after and while you know anything about it, you do not know what it is. I mean what it is . . . is . . . you have not the slightest knowledge of what it is. And none of your experience increases your awareness of what it is.

This same logic pertains to everything. No matter what you may come to realize by experience about anything, you still do not know what it is. All of us belong to this realm of ambiguity. None of us knows what any other human being is. We just simply do not know it. In our practical involvement with one another, we know about one another — but we do not know what we are. Knowledge, in other words, does not penetrate to this degree. It never has.

This failure of our conventional knowledge is not just a reflection of the silliness or stupidity of ancient beings. It is also fundamentally a reflection upon our own existence, and also, therefore, upon the existence of all other beings who have ever lived. The atoms that are in this ashtray have existed for perhaps twenty billions of years — far beyond the mere five billion of the Earth. They come out of the manifest cosmos, from the center of the explosion that manifested everything.

We know very little about anything, ultimately. And we do

not know what it is in fact. Thus, our mind itself, even our own existence, is totally, unqualifiedly, inevitably, irrevocably, and irreducibly Ignorant. No one, regardless of his or her sophistication or experience, no one, not even myself, knows what a single thing is. Not what anything is, you see. This presumption of Divine Ignorance could have been made at any time in the past, and it can be made at any time in the future. No matter how much experience intervenes, no matter how sophisticated men and women become, no matter how much we may know about anything through experience, we still do not and will not know what it is. What it is.

What is a shape? What is a place? Where is it? We do not know. That is not what we know. We presume something that is like knowledge, but in fact we do not know. All that may be said about our consideration, our understanding, our belief, our experience is this: Not only now, but not at any time in the past, in any civilization, even the most magnificent beyond belief, nor in the future on this Earth in any great moment, nor in any other occasion, any planet, any place, in all of the manifestation of existence, does any individual know what anything is.

Ignorance is the Principle of existence. This is absolutely true. We do not know what anything is. We are totally mindless, and totally beyond consolation or fulfillment, because there is no way to know what anything is. The only thing you can know about anything is still about it. But you do not know what it is . . . is . . . is . . . or why it happens to be. You have not the slightest knowledge of what it is. And no one has ever had it. Not anyone. Not Jesus, not Moses, not Mohammed, not Gautama, not Krishna, not Tukaram, not Da Free John, no one has ever known what a single thing is. Not the most minute, ridiculous particle of anything. No one has ever known it, and no one will ever know it, because we are not knowing. We do not know what anything is. The summarization of our existence is Mystery, absolute, unqualified confrontation with what we cannot know. And no matter how sophisticated we become by experience, this will always be true of us.

This Teaching, then, will never be transcended. Upon this

absolute Truth we must build our lives, and I must build my Community of devotees. This Truth is summary, unqualified, irredeemable, irreducible, and absolute. It can never be changed. No matter what sophisticated time may appear, no matter when, in the paradox of all of the slices and planes of time, any moment may appear in which beings sit together as we do, oblivious to Infinity, no matter what time may appear in which men and women consider the moment, no one will ever know what anything is. That is the Truth.

Becoming submitted to that Truth is spiritual life. It leads you to the transformation of all other occasions. All the possibilities of your experience are transformed by this disposition. Obviously, then, it is very important to Realize this Ignorance, because it is the only digit at Infinity that can transform your existence. Everything else only modifies your existence and amounts to a contraction in your consciousness, a summation upon a point.

We exist in the moment of Infinity. Look — everyone who ever looked like us has died. Every one of us will die. In the meantime, we are capable, in the form of our structure, to experience all kinds of things, to be associated with all kinds of influences. But if we abandon this Truth, this understanding, this intuition of the Nature of our experience, all experience will accumulate upon us. We will, therefore, adapt to experience in itself, and we will become the reflections of it.

We are awakened at Infinity only if we can realize that the fundamental point of our existence is not knowledge at all. There are no answers. This is the whole point. We do not know at all. We do not know where we are, we do not know who we are, we do not know what the past is. We are trying to look good — but we do not know. We are trying through the force of experience to achieve a summation that glamorizes us, but we do not know what anything is. That is the point.

This Realization does not move us to go within at all. It moves us, shattered, into the present pattern of relations at Infinity. No matter what arises in the configuration of our experience, we still do not know what anything is. All the accumulations of our experience move us into moods, attitudes, presumptions, but we still do not know at all. Where is this place? Where is it? Where is it? Where is it, exactly? I mean, really? We haven't the slightest idea. Nobody has any idea. No matter who may claim your worship, nobody knows. Some people may look better than others, but still, nobody knows.

DEVOTEE: Master, this description of our existence implies extreme vulnerability.

MASTER DA FREE JOHN: On the basis of this logic, whereby we do not know what anything is, whereby we are not in control, it is clear that we are not even created by anything Objective and Absolute. We are in a Condition of absolute, unqualified Mystery. That Condition obliges us in our attention and our feeling. That is what it is to be a man or a woman: to be rested upon Infinity without any consolations whatsoever.

There is no Truth within. There is no Truth in the past, and there is no Truth in the future. Having no consolations, we exist in this moment, floating in space, wherever that is, totally sublimed, beyond consolation or belief, without the slightest fraction of abstract verbal consideration to console us, without the slightest fleshy prominence standing out against Infinity to make us happy. That is our Condition, you see. That is the Truth of It. That is It. That is all there is to It. And It is not an answer. There are no answers in It. All your struggling for information, for answers, is just more of the same old foolishness. It is open-ended. You go to your death without knowledge. Thus, you also go to your life without knowing.

Nevertheless, there is an obvious Law: Everything does change, everything prominent passes, everything that appears is temporary. And, therefore, the Law of the universe is change itself, the sacrifice of everything present. Having realized that there is no knowledge, having seen that everything changes, how shall we live?

The ultimate pleasure to which we may sacrifice ourselves is at best someone else's pleasure. What if you were to sit down to dinner and eat a lobster? You might enjoy yourself, but it would be dead. And if it had been able during its lifetime to conceive of this meal as the ultimate moment toward which it was progressing through sacrifice, even so, the moment of being eaten is totally unavailable to its consciousness. Thus, there is no moment <u>toward</u> which you move by sacrifice. Sacrifice is simply the Law, the disposition of love.

Sacrifice is inherently happy, inherently free. It has no answers. That is all I can tell you. It is not that I can tell you concretely that something will happen. Yes, things will happen, but they will also pass. Yes, you will survive your death, I can guarantee you that. But you will survive it in another form that also dies. Everything will change. Thus, it is not in time that we have the Eternal Vision. It is in our disposition, in our love, in our sacrifice. By throwing everything away and being totally willing to be dead you are not only free in this moment, but you are also profoundly happy, and ridiculous.

No one is here to give you any answers. There is no Creator Deity in charge of you, like a parent. There is no such Person, no God like that, nor any Spiritual Master like that. I am here to instigate this love, or sacrifice, in you, and there is no answer, no result. The act itself is the Happiness. If you can begin to become fully sympathetic to this Argument that I bring to you, then you will simply be Happy and completely bereft of answers. In your ordinary life it is simply a matter of whether you are Happy or not. Are you Happy? Will you give it up? Will you be mad? Will you be without information, without answers? Will you be faced on Infinity? Just as you are right now? It is completely mad, you see.[1]

DEVOTEE: But there is a sense . . .

MASTER DA FREE JOHN: The sense that you are happy is your self-possession. In Divine Ignorance there is not even that. There

---

[1] The universe, so carefully constructed into a "cosmos" by the human mind, is in reality a wholly paradoxical, chaotic process. Therefore, to the mind which expects to see order everywhere, it must appear as mad. In Enlightenment, which is equivalent to one's becoming identical with the infinite Chaos of existence, is preceded by the experience of ego-death—the "loss of one's mind". Hence the ultimate disposition of continuous God-Realization is often referred to as the state of Divine Madness.

is simply this mysterious affair that is always Happy, without cause. That is it, not all your presumptions that you are happy, that you are giving it up, that you are in love. It is all the same old absolute Magnificence. It is not the same as a moment of déjà vu, as if it had already happened. It has never happened, and it always has happened, this moment. Select any moment, and I am still telling you this. What a ridiculous matter! What a plan!

Consider the configuration of our relations. We sit here relatively happy. But consider all of the other billions upon billions upon billions of beings. Not just the other billions of human beings on Earth — consider the billions of beings in this room. Every time you take a breath — are you all breathing while I am talking to you? — you suck in and snuff out billions of beings, tiny, organized, self-conscious, knowledgeless, stupid, defenseless, incarnate entities. In your breathing, in your ingestion, in your thinking and talking, in your loving and your lovemaking, in everything that you do, you are responsible for the murder of billions of beings every day. And you are no more important than they in the scheme of Infinity. It seems to you that you take a little while longer in life than the amoeba on your eyebrow, but what do you amount to? You are eaten, snuffed out, murdered, pulverized, shaken in your snuffing, and there is no opportunity for happiness except through the Intuition of the Real. If the Real manufactures all this devastating insanity, that is Its business. Our business is to be happy, to Realize the logic that is at the core of God and remain happy.

Without that Intuition, there is no way to be happy in the face of mere experience. Somebody recently told me he saw a construction worker who suffered a terrible accident. Demolition workers were smashing a building, using one of those incredible, giant lead balls to crush a wall. I don't know how it happened, but the lead ball hit the man in the head as he stood on a scaffold. He survived, but with only about one-third of a face. The rest of it was a concave, smashed, disgusting mass. Such a possibility is also yours.

It does not make any difference how much you love, how much insight you enjoy — you could be snuffed out. You may even continue to live in that kind of wretched form. I read a story some weeks ago about a soldier in the Vietnam war. The man in front of him stepped on a bomb or a mine and a fragment of shell hit the soldier above the eyebrow and leaped through his brain. Now half his brain is missing — they had to amputate half his brain! You can experience that.

The possibilities for life are not just magnificent, they are disgusting. If you are committed to the "Great Plan," you must admit that you can suffer far more than you can enjoy. Now that you have appeared in a form, there is far more to suffer than there is to enjoy.

You must give it all up — all of it! The enjoyments and the torments. And then you will enjoy the Vision of Eternal Life and move through the paradox of changes in God. I do not know why that is, you see. I do not know why that Vision is the only possibility for happiness — but it certainly is the only possibility for happiness.

Whether there is a future beyond death or not is for you to discover. All the dead are heroes, but nobody knows about them. Nobody knows where they are, or what it is. What a life! What a moment!

All of us are dying. All of these shapes get snuffed out with trembling stupidity and insanity. When the body dies, the brain becomes active for a moment and begins to show you lighted shapes and to dissolve you beyond the elements. First you get fleshy, and then you get watery, then you get fiery, then you get airy, then you start screaming and nobody can hear you, and the body shakes all over the place, and then you are dead. I certainly wish you could acknowledge the Vision of Eternal Life while you are alive. If you can, you will love somebody, and if you cannot, you will not.

And let us not pretend that we exist in a Disney world of beauty. This life is many-sided, and we do not know what it is. Our happiness depends on the total inspection of this life. Let us recognize the situation in which we find ourselves and become manly on the basis of this observation, so that we may be lovers and friends. Let us acknowledge this terrible circumstance and be happy, and stop placing stupid obligations on one another. We exist in a place that is open-ended, an edge to Infinity, and we are dying. The only way we can comprehend this complication is by sacrificing it and becoming lovers and friends. Nothing else that you may project in your lifetime can change the fact that you are still a fleshy, homely being that can be crushed by circumstance.

You all, however, are still organized around your experience and your possibility. You have not gone mad yet. You have not yet become disorganized in God. You are still profoundly oriented, in your desiring and the mechanics of your motivation, toward ordinary things. Some of those things make you look good and some of those things do not make you look good. That is the summation of your life. But spiritual life is about Truth, not about a cure. It is about the inspection and recognition of this torment in which we live. Having penetrated it, you may realize the Sublimity that transcends this life, but you will not realize <u>something</u> <u>else</u>. You will just enjoy the capacity to be free while alive, so that this life may pass away. It must pass in any case.

Da Free John is not listening to voices, you see. Da Free John does not have any visions. I have <u>had</u> visions, I have <u>heard</u> voices. I have done everything that you yet look forward to, enclosed as you are in the first three stages of life. You think, "Oh, beyond here it is all so beautiful." I can just hear it. Nonsense! All of it is a torment. All of it is stupid. All of it is terrible, until you penetrate it and become free, objectless, diffuse, and absolutely unqualified Happiness. Then everything will fall away from you, and you may be restored to the lightspeed of Existence even while alive and also at your death, and far less of the paradoxical eternity of manifestation may be your destiny. But in life itself I cannot promise you any more.

Sooner or later you must come to this point of absolute despair in which you will be awakened to absolute Happiness. And when you have become awakened to absolute Happiness, life will fall away. In the meantime, you will be a lover, you will be happy, you will generate the force of Infinity to your friends, but you will die, and so will they. There are no answers in this lifetime. And that is it.